ISBN 978-1-330-34143-8
PIBN 10033631

1 MONTH OF
FREE
READING

at

www.ForgottenBooks.com

By purchasing this book you are eligible for one month membership to ForgottenBooks.com, giving you unlimited access to our entire collection of over 700,000 titles via our web site and mobile apps.

To claim your free month visit: www.forgottenbooks.com/free33631

PHYSICAL, INTELLECTUAL, MORAL, AND SPIRITUAL.

A Course of Lectures

BY

JAMES FREEMAN CLARKE.

"Life is short, art long, opportunity fleeting, experiment uncertain, and judgment difficult."
FIRST WORDS OF THE APHORISMS OF HIPPOCRATES.

THIRD EDITION.

BOSTON:
JAMES R. OSGOOD AND COMPANY.
1880.

CONTENTS.

INTRODUCTORY CHAPTER.

SELF-CULTURE.

INTRODUCTORY CHAPTER.

The Beginnings of Culture, in Childhood. — Natural and Artificial Methods in the Education of Children.

EDUCATION is made up of three grand divisions. First, INSTRUCTION, or knowledge communicated to the intellect; second, TRAINING, or exercise of the faculties; third, DEVELOPMENT, or education in its special meaning, — the unfolding of the whole nature of man. These three constitute Education in its largest sense.

Of all this Education, the school and college contributes a part, but a much larger part comes from other sources. Nature educates, life educates, society educates. Outward circumstances, inward experiences, and social influences, make up a large part of human culture. But at present, let us see what schools ought to do, what they actually do, and what they might do.

A boy begins to go to school, say at seven years of age; and he leaves college, say at twenty-one years. He has then spent fourteen years in study;

and the object of nearly all his study has been to store his mind with knowledge. What, then, does he know?

After fourteen years' study he ought to know a good deal. First, to speak, read, and write his own language well, and to be acquainted with its principal authors. Secondly, as so much time is given to Latin and Greek, he ought to be able to read easily a Latin or Greek work, at sight. Next, he should know the main facts of Geography and Universal History, and the chief dates of political events, — also such facts in the history of Greece, Rome, France, Italy, England, Spain, Germany, and the United States. He should read easily two or three modern languages. Then, in science, he should know the present condition of Geology, Chemistry, Natural Philosophy, Astronomy, Botany. He should understand the condition and progress of the useful arts and the fine arts, and some elements of Theology, Medicine, and Law. He ought to know something of Social Science, including Politics and Political Economy. Finally, he ought to know something about his own body and soul, his faculties and powers, the laws of thought and of physical culture. In fourteen years ought there not to be learned at least as much as this?

Now, what is the fact in the majority of cases? Usually that when he leaves college, he knows enough Latin to translate Virgil and Cicero without a dictionary; enough Greek to translate the

Iliad *with one*. He has a smattering of French and possibly of one or two modern languages. He is pretty well acquainted with Algebra and Geometry, — and he has nearly forgotten what he learned in school of Geography and History.

Does not this show that our methods of education, as yet, have not reached the point at which they aim? They do not constitute an art. For what is an art? An art is a method, based on science, of doing anything thoroughly and effectually. If the thing to be done is a useful thing, it is a useful art; if a beautiful thing, it is a fine art. For example, the making of a shoe is an art. It does not come by nature or inspiration; it has to be taught; but any one can learn to do it, so that with moderate capacity and attention, he is sure to be able to make a real shoe, when he has learned the art. Now education will become an art when a person of average capacity shall be able to teach all scholars of average capacity, so that at the end of their course they shall really *know* the thing taught in that course. At present, such is not the case. If the teacher is a man of genius, an enthusiast capable of inspiring enthusiasm; and if the scholar has the power of being quickened into a like enthusiasm, then the scholar really learns, but not otherwise Agassiz could inspire such an interest in *Gasteropods* and *Echinoderms* that a large part of his class should graduate with an intimate personal knowledge of those little people. That is the result

of genius, however, not of art. What we need is
to have the art of education so perfected, that a
teacher of average intelligence shall be able to inspire a similar ardor in each study. How can this
be done? I answer, by *following. the method of
nature* in teaching.

How does Mother Nature teach? She takes on
herself the most difficult part of all the course, and
she does her work thoroughly. Hers is the real
Primary School. She says, "I will take the little
child who knows nothing, and I will teach him to
know the use of his own body, the nature of the
world about him, and the articulate language of
his country." And she does it. The little thing
learns to see, hear, touch, taste, walk; to jump, run,
climb, hold objects, know what is hard and soft,
heavy and light, round and square; to know wood,
stone, earth, water, air; to distinguish between
things near and distant, sounds remote and close by.
Finally, she teaches him to speak a language; he
having no other language to learn it by. When I
learn Latin, I do it by finding the equivalent in Latin
of some English word which I already know. But
the little child learning his own language has no
words to learn by. It is one of the most marvellous
things; if it were not so common we should see it;
a little child learning to speak. The difficulties he
surmounts are far greater than we should encounter
in learning Chinese or Sanskrit. And, observe, he
does not acquire a smattering of language, but he

learns it thoroughly, so as to be able to use it for all practical purposes.

Now, how does the dear mother do all this? What is her method?

FIRST, — She mixes nine parts of pleasure and one of pain, nine of hope and one of fear, in her system. We do just about the opposite, in ours. We imagine the child is not studying if it is having a good time. In Nature's school it is only studying *when* it is happy, it only works when it is at play. See the little child at play, or perhaps at what its mother calls mischief, — it is trying to make its shoe swim in a basin of water. Stop, mamma! don't scold, it is learning a lesson in Hydrostatics. What! it has broken the window with its ball, and stands absorbed at that mystery of broken glass? Well, it was becoming acquainted with the nature of an elastic body, and by accident has learned what is cohesive and what frangible. It is digging in the mud; it is paddling in the water; it is shovelling sand. You call it play, but you never worked half as hard in what you call your study; that is, you never put your faculties into anything with such intensity and concentration as that child is now doing.

He is learning thoroughly the qualities and relations of things; he is learning to know surface and substance, to distinguish between aëriform, fluid, and solid; to know what is ductile, what malleable, what flexible; he is becoming acquainted with lat-

eral strength, cohesive force, specific gravity ; he is
studying statics and dynamics ; the law of acceler-
ating forces ; the power of the lever, the inclined
plane, the wheel and axle ; he is learning equilibrium, rotation, angular motion, and the like. To
be sure, he does not learn all these fine words ; but
he learns the things meant by them. He learns the
things with delight in Nature's school ; by and by,
in ours, he shall learn their *names* with disgust and
difficulty.'

Nature gives delight in the use of all our faculties ; she makes also an additional pleasure to attend
every ACCOMPLISHMENT. When the child has learned
to break a stick, he will sit still an hour breaking
stick after stick. By this ingenious contrivance
she teaches him language. She also begins with the
easiest word, and the word nearest at hand, and in
this tremendous task of teaching him his first word,

---

¹ Let two little boys weigh each other on a platform scale.
Then when they balance each other on their board see-saw, let
them see (and measure for themselves) that the lighter one is
farther from the fence-rail on which their board is placed, in the
same proportion as the heavier boy outweighs the lighter one.
They will then have learned the grand principle of the *lever*.
Then let them measure and see that the light one see-saws farther
than the heavy one, in the same proportion ; and they will have
acquired the principle of *virtual velocities*. Explain to them that
equality of moments means nothing more than that when they seat
themselves at their measured distances on their see-saw, *they balance
each other*. Let them see that the weight of the heavy boy, when
multiplied by his distance in feet from the fence-rail, amounts to
just as much as the weight of the light one when multiplied by

she brings another powerful agency to bear, —
namely, LOVE. When the infant learns to say his
first word, and can actually articulate, " *Papa, Mamma*," there is very good reason why all the neighbors shall be called in (as they usually are) to hear
him say it. For if he shall live to be a Webster or
a Chatham, and speak with the tongue of men and
angels, he will never surmount a greater obstacle,
or take a longer step, or acquire a more wonderful
accomplishment. Nature brings three great forces to
bear on him in order to teach him to say " Mamma,"
—the pleasure of exercising a faculty ; the pleasure
of accomplishment, that is, of repeating over and over
what we have learned to do once ; and, lastly, the
exquisite delight of the mother, overflowing with
ecstatic love for her darling child, by which she
magnetizes his little heart, and attracts him to do
what gives him and her such joy. Her eyes shower

---

his distance. Explain to them that each of the amounts is in
foot-pounds. Tell them that the lightest one, because he see-saws
so much faster than the other, will bump against the ground just
as hard as the heavy one ; and that this means that *their momentums are equal.* The boys may then go in to dinner, and probably
puzzle their big lout of a brother who has just passed through
college with high honors. They will not forget what they have
learned ; for they learned it *as play*, without any ear-pulling,
spanking, or keeping in. Let their bats and balls, their marbles,
their swings, &c., once become their philosophical apparatus, and
children may be taught (*really* taught) many of the most important principles of engineering before they can read or write. —
From Trantwine's " Civil Engineers' Pocket-Book," — a book
which has been called the best practical manual for engineers.

affection into his, while she covers him with kisses. Dame Nature looks on, and says, "All right, — it will go now."

The child's eyes plainly say "I have done a big thing." And he has. After "Mamma" and "Papa" come other nouns of one syllable, — for "Papa" and "Mamma" are monosyllables repeated, — usually proper nouns. The people around the infant are the first objects of his interest, because they are actively interested in him. I have lately been watching a child learning to talk, and I observed that it gave monosyllabic names to each of the five or six persons around it. One was named "Bah," another "Gah," a third "Nee," a fourth "Ko," a fifth "Nee-nee." A cracker for eating was "Ka," and so on. Here we see the beginnings of language, and discover that the Chinese language is probably a primitive tongue whose development was arrested while in the monosyllabic stage.

After the proper nouns come sounds which resemble "milk," and "water," and "sugar," and other substantives, mostly relating to matters of diet, with which the child has made himself acquainted. Sentences follow. "I want" this. "Give me" that; only, as nouns take the lead of pronouns in this method, — it is usually *"Johnny wants"* this, *"Give Johnny"* that. Desire being the lever mostly used by Nature, the verbs significant of desire will arrive on the stage very early. Observe, too, the power of *repetition* in this system. The words first learned are never forgotten, for they are the words which are always in use, and so have to be repeated every day. Also notice that Nature in teaching grammar gives the rule first, and says nothing at all about exceptions till some time after. In our schools, we cram the grammars with every possible exception, qualification, collateral remark, and limitation, as though we were educating a Scaliger, and not a little Irish boy. Nature lets the infant form all his verbs regularly at first. He says, " I drinked the water." " I feeded the dog." " I runned out of doors." By and by, seeing that other people say "drank," *he* says "drank." So Nature teaches us grammar, — and most of the grammar we know we learn in this way.

Observe also that Nature *trains* while she teaches, she disciplines the powers while she imparts information to the intellect. We are too analytic; we teach only the memory, — she teaches all the primary faculties at the same time. Her synthetic method has great advantages over our analytic one. It is more vital, lively, interesting. While the child is learning the properties of bodies, he is at the same time training his own faculties. He is learning to measure; to weigh; and to distinguish forms, colors, and sizes. Moreover, he comes evermore into contact with a living and real world of substance, — not a dead world of words. Happy child! the roof of whose schoolroom is the blue heaven with its drifting clouds, and mellow tints of sunrise, and glories of evening, — whose bench is the soft grass, the gray stone, the limb of the apple-tree, — whose books are all illustrated with moving, living forms, — waving trees, dewy leaves, wild-flowers, all varieties of birds, and insects, and fishes, and animals, — how fast he learns, — finding " tongues in trees, books in the running brooks, sermons in stones, and good in everything."

" Well," but you may say, " what are we going to do about it ? Shall we shut up our schools, and send the children out into the fields to run about at random ? " No ! but patiently and reverently study the methods of Nature, and copy her principles in-stead of going in direct opposition to them. Do not drive the children by force, or fear; lead them by the attraction of joy. Let Mother Nature come into your school and be your assistant, — she is not too proud to be so. She will help you if you will let her.

" Ah ! " but you say, " children must learn appli cation, must learn to work, — they cannot always find study pleasant ; it must be unpleasant often, and so it is a discipline."

This is the old mistake of thinking that *hard* work must necessarily be *unpleasant* work Do children ever work as hard at school as they do at play ?

Is there ever more mental application displayed in any study than there is in a game of chess ? Is there more physical energy put forth in any kind of hard day-labor than there is in a game of football, or in a boat-race?

I do not propose that boys and girls should spend their time in play. But I propose to use the principle involved in play in acquiring knowledge. What are the objections usually made to games of chance, as cards, for example; or such games of skill as billiards? They are two: first, that there is no profitable result of the time and effort; and, second, that there is no useful discipline of any faculty. Let us suppose something as interesting, which disciplines the faculties, and also leaves the mind possessed of some valuable knowledge, and would you object to it because it was interesting and not dull? I should say you were rather dull yourself if you did. Let us suppose, for example, there were a Chronological game of cards (as there might easily be) as interesting as *Whist* or *Piquet;* by which the memory should be so disciplined as to retain easily some five hundred of the more important historic dates, and to have them fixed forever in the mind? Or suppose a Geographical game of cards, by which in like manner there should be fixed in the memory for life the names and localities of the principal cities, rivers, mountains; and their latitude and longitude. Would you object to it because it was a game, and because the children loved to play it, and would play it among themselves for amusement? Would you think it better for them to sit and loll at their desks hour after

hour, vacantly staring at their books, so as to learn
just enough of chronology and geography to pass a
decent examination, and then forget it again ?[1]

The principle I contend for is sometimes introduced into schools, but only occasionally, and as
though it ought not to be often permitted. The
whole school divides into two opposing sides, and
plays a game of spelling, perhaps, — to see which
side shall beat. The children become excited and
interested, and fix their whole attention on each
word, and learn more, I venture to say, of spelling,
in that fifteen minutes' game, than in many long
hours of half-stupefied inattention to their spelling-
book. In like manner I have seen Colburn's First
Lessons in Arithmetic made a play, in which the
children who answered right all went up, and those
who answered wrong all went down, — and so, in
an hour's recitation, a boy might get from the foot
to the head and back again once or twice. What
animation, what interest, there was in this exercise!
If study means the full tension of the intellect,
applied to some mental problem and concentrated
upon it with the whole force of the will, then I say,
I never saw harder *study* than that. But it was all
wrong, I suppose, because it was interesting; because it was like a play. In short, it was a natural
mode of study, and so not to be tolerated. Besides,

---

[1] The principle of arranging methods of study on the plan of
games was fully developed by Locke, in his Essay on Education,
and excited at the time much interest and discussion.

the dreadful principle of emulation was encouraged by it.

I am free to confess myself such a heretic to modern notions, as to believe fully in emulation as applied in teaching. We *do* apply it, we can't help applying it, — the question only is *how?* The difference in my opinion between the use and abuse of this faculty is in making the prize of excellence merely transient, and not permanent. Let the reward of excellence be the natural reward, the momentary sense and recognition that one *has* excelled. Do not offer prizes, which are to remain, and to feed vanity. Do not have *marks* for every exercise, to be added up each day, and kept from month to month, to determine who is to have the highest rank at the end of the year. Such things make children unnaturally and precociously attentive to their own interests, — make them selfish and mercenary. It is not a generous emulation, a desire of excellence, — but it is the wish for a prize, a high rank, or the praise of the outside visitors; all that, I think bad.

But let the reward of excellence be momentary, as when boys choose sides, and play football or base, and when they exert themselves for victory, as if the success of their life depended on it. But the game once over, there is an end. They will have forgotten, to-morrow, which side won. There are no ranklings left in the bosoms of those who are defeated, — no undue self-satisfaction in those who have won. So, in my opinion, the transient excitement and stimulus in the old plan of going up and down in recitation was good, provided the results of each day's success or failure ended with the day But I utterly abhor the system followed in some colleges, where everything goes to rank, — where recitations, behavior, presence at prayers, all are laid up for the final decision at the end of four years, and so some of the gentle youth are made unnaturally calculating, cautious, prudent, and are devoured by an envious and grasping ambition, — and others are equally made reckless and discouraged.

How good it is when the teacher gives lessons in Botany or Geology in the open air, — taking a walk with his class; guiding their minds, helping them to look, teaching them how to observe Nature, and giving them that vital interest which comes from contact with things themselves instead of with their names in books. The child who has found a beautiful orchid, or a group of harebells, or a bank by the roadside where the sweet Linnæa hangs its twin bells, never forgets them. The class which has seen Jupiter and his moons through the telescope, or which has studied out the constellations by its teacher's side during a summer's evening, has acquired a taste for knowledge which the dead letters in books can never give. There is something in contact with Nature herself which awakens a strange joy in the soul. The touch of water, the sight of a tree waving its multitude of branches in the summer air, the gray old rock covered with lichens and mosses, — these seem to carry knowledge *into* the mind, as books alone never can. So that I sympathize a good deal with the student in Goethe's Faust, who says, after thanking his instructor for his teaching, —

> "And yet, if I the truth might say,
> I would I were again away.
> Walls like these, and halls like these,
> Will, I fear, in no wise please,
> The narrow gloom of this low room,
> Where nothing green is ever seen,
> 'Mong benches, books, my heart is sinking,
> And my faded senses shrinking.
> I mourn the hour that I came hither,
> Ear, and eye, and heart will die,
> Thought, and the power of thought, will wither."

Our ancestors would sometimes get an Indian, and try to civilize him by sending him to college. He would study his Greek grammar and Latin grammar for a while, very faithfully ; but at last an irrepressible yearning for the woods would come over him, and he would disappear, — leaving " *Bonus, a-um,*" for the old wild life of the forest. Who could blame him, or wonder ?

There is, however, a serious objection to all this, which ought to be met, and I shall state it as fairly and strongly as I can.

" You propose to us," so says my opponent, " to make all study agreeable, to make education as interesting to children as play. You cannot do so, and you ought not to do so. Part of education is the discipline of self-denial, — it is denial of present pleasure for future good, — it is doing disagreeable things cheerfully, — it is doing not only hard work, but unpleasant work. It would be a bad thing to make all children's work pleasant; for there are a great many unpleasant labors before them in the world for which they ought to be prepared; and for which they will not be prepared if they are taught in youth on the principle that all study must be like play." That is the objection; stated as strongly as I know how to state it.

I reply, however, that if there is a great deal to be done by children which is unpleasant, I do not expect to make *that* agreeable. Not that which *cannot* be made interesting, but that which *can*, I try to make so. If you will admit that all the study which *can* be turned into pleasure shall be, I will be satisfied; and I will leave, for your comfort, all which must be disagreeable. If, however, you think that some good discipline comes to a child by having that study made stupid and hateful, which might be made attractive and pleasant, I differ from you. I admit that there will be always *some* work to be done, which will be harsh, — but I think that will suffice. If you think that the proper prepara tion for a hard, laborious life, a life spent in dis agreeable toil, is a youth and childhood also spent in harsh disagreeable toil, I differ from you as widely as heaven is distant from earth. God, also, differs from you, I am inclined to think; else why does He make childhood a season of pleasure, so far as we do not interfere to make it pain? Why does God make happiness so native to a child's heart, and give it such joy in everything? All young things are happy. They dance, they sing, they crow, they skip, they play. Give a child a heap of sand to dig, a few sticks to arrange, a piece of paper and a pair of scissors to cut it with, — give him a piece of string to make a whip with, or to play that he is driving a horse, when he fastens his string to the leg of a chair, — and he is happy. If God thinks grief the best preparation for grief, why did He not make little children unhappy to begin with? We *can*, if we try hard, I know, make them unhappy. We can collect them into a close room, and make them sit on a hard bench, and keep perfectly still the limbs which Nature has filled full of electricity, that they might be moving all the time, — and scold them when they move, — and we can, by hard effort, keep them in rather an uncomfortable state. But relax that effort; just say, "You may go out, children, into the yard!" and the whole tide of excluded and repressed pleasure rushes back again. You need not give them any playthings, or take the least pains about their being happy, — Nature will attend to that. See the little things scramble downstairs; hear their joyous outbursting glee, — see them running round and round, and laughing, and being as merry, as if to them there were no such thing as sin or sorrow in the world, — as indeed there is not. For, in my opinion, that deep sense of guilt which we call sin, and that permanent weight of gloom which we call sorrow, do not come naturally to childhood. Children do wrong, and repent of it, — they suffer sharp pangs of disappointment, and the like; but these are transient, and meant to be so. Sin and sorrow, the dark background of life, which tinge with permanent sadness our elder hearts, do not belong to childhood.

Those who oppose this doctrine have their quarrel, not with us, but with the Creator. He does not seem to think that the proper outfit for a life of pain is pain, — He has thought joy the best preparation for it. He does not think that the best way to prepare for a journey into the wilderness, where food and water are likely to be wanting, is to empty our knapsacks and canteens. No! but to fill them. A joyful youth is the best preparation for an earnest manhood. A youth of suffering and privation pre pare for discouragement and depression afterward.

It used to be thought that heat was a bad preparation for encountering cold. How often, when a boy, was I ordered not to go into the water when I was hot; but to wait till I was cool. But now we know that this is all a mistake. The hotter the body is, the better is it able to resist cold. The Russians go from a hot bath into one icy cold. The Indians used to take a vapor-bath sitting over some hot stones on which water was sprinkled, and then jumped into the cold river. Any one who doubts the wisdom of this may easily satisfy himself by going directly from a very hot bath into a very cold one. He will find that he scarcely feels the cold at all. In the same way people coming from the Southern States to New England do not feel the first or second winter as much as we do. In the Russian Campaign the Russian soldiers suffered more than the French from cold. The best preparation therefore for encountering cold is to be hot. The best preparation to meet famine is to be well fed. And the best preparation for a life of hard work, of trial, and difficulty, is to have a happy childhood and youth to look back to. It keeps up our faith in the goodness of God, it prevents us from being too much discouraged. We know that there is some real happiness in life ; for we have experienced it ourselves. The memory of a sunny, free, happy childhood goes with us all our way, — the memory of the good old grandparents who used to pet us and spoil us, — the memory of the ardent friendships of childhood ; of the beauty and bounty of nature ; the innocent pleasure furnished by earth and water ; by bird, and insect, and flower, and fruit, — all these leave their fragrance with us during life, and keep up our faith that love and happiness are the rule, sorrow and selfishness the exception.

The discipline of self-denial is good, both for old and young. All must learn self-denial, — it is one of the first and last lessons of life. But no one practises self-denial without a motive. The three principal motives for self-denial are the fear of pain, the hope of pleasure, and the sense of duty. In the discipline of Nature, Pain is a sentinel standing on the outside of the camp to define certain limits, which must not be passed over. But there is a vast deal more of self-denial daily practised from hope than there is from fear. The great majority of mankind deny the love of ease and of pleasure ; they labor and abstain, in order to acquire wealth, fame, power, or knowledge. Hardly anywhere, except in some very poor schools, and with slaves, is fear the chief motive for self-denial.

· No doubt children and men must also learn and practise self-denial from a sense of duty. We must do many things not very interesting in themselves, because we ought to do them ; — abstain from other practices, which are pleasant, because we ought not to do them. The duty may not always be agreeable. But to *do* it, *is* agreeable. And when the duty itself can be made agreeable, is it not desirable to do so ? Is it not well to have pleasant associations connected with our duties rather than unpleasant ones ? When we have once taught ourselves and others that a duty is always to be done, whether agreeable or otherwise, then it is best to surround our tasks with as much which is cheerful as possible.

This doctrine Wordsworth teaches in that marvellous ode, the most sublime poem since Milton, in which he declares that faith in immortality comes in part from the joy which God gives to childhood. In it he thanks God

> "for those first affections,
> Those shadowy recollections,
> Which, be they what they may,
> Are yet the fountain light of all our day.
> And yet a master light of all our seeing,
> Uphold us, cherish, and have power to make
> Our noisy years seem moments in the being
> Of the eternal silence ; truths that wake
> To perish never."

It is not then necessary to abridge at all the joys of childhood. Let us make our children as happy as we can. They will always have enough occasion for discipline and self-denial, — do not doubt it. I have known schools of two kinds. One, in which FORCE and WILL reigned supreme; in which scolding and threatening, harsh words and blows, were the normal incidents. I have known other schools, in which LOVE and REASON were Queen and King; in which a healthy and happy atmosphere was breathed by all the little ones; and a sense of peace, of order, of good-will, was taught to each child. Which of the schools did the most good ?. Which was the best preparation for time and eternity ?

Discipline is good, but discipline does not mean suffering or pain. I have seen schools in which there was much whipping, but very little discipline,

— while in others there was no whipping at all, but much discipline. Whipping is not discipline, — force is not discipline. I venture to say that, out of the army, there is no such strict discipline maintained anywhere else as is kept up in the games of children, — as in football, base, cricket, &c. A little fellow whose business is to "catch out" had much rather miss his Latin exercise in school under the sternest master, than miss being in his place to catch the ball. Play does not exclude discipline, but usually includes it. What admirable organization in a game of base! How perfectly every boy keeps to his place and his work! How wide-awake to the matter in hand! There is no indolence or inattention here, I think.

Nor does play exclude drudgery. When you go home to-day, you will perhaps find your boy, hard at work, whittling a stick into shape for a fishing-pole. He has been at it for an hour or two, and hard work it has been; but he has persevered bravely so that he may be ready to go fishing to-morrow. How hard children work at their play, or in getting ready to play. So you see that if we make study partake of the interest of play, by any ingenious arrangements, we shall not exclude hard work, nor drudgery, nor discipline, nor self-denial. As to self-denial, observe the young men of a boat-crew at Yale, or Harvard, in training for a match. They are studiously temperate or abstinent; they flee all college excesses; they renounce coffee, tobacco, wine, spirits, cake, and pastry; they go early to bed at regular hours; and, in short, lead the lives of anchorites. All of their own accord, for an end, — to win a temporal crown. Make study as interesting, make knowledge as attractive, and you will obtain the like results.

If, now, we pass from Instruction to Training, it is surprising how few of the faculties have hitherto received any discipline. Verbal memory has been cultivated; the power of calculation also; and I have seen exercises in Grammar Schools in addition, subtraction, &c., where a whole class would give the answer to a difficult question as soon as the teacher had asked it. But the perceptive organs, the powers which observe size, length, and breadth, those which observe weight, color, quantities, &c., have been much neglected. Object-Lessons will correct this to a great extent. It is difficult to say how far the quickness and accuracy of these faculties may be carried. The workers in Florentine mosaic can distinguish eight thousand varieties of red in their work. I have seen ladies who could correct by their eye a mistake made by a salesman in measuring cloth. He would measure it, and say, " It is just a yard." The lady would say, " Please measure it again, — I think it wants half an inch," — and he would find it so.[1]

---

[1] See, below, the Lecture on the Culture of the Perceptive Organs.

The highest object of Education is development; drawing out and unfolding the whole nature, physical, intellectual, moral, and spiritual. All things else come easily when the soul of man is well developed. An intelligent mind will learn everything easily, judge everything correctly. Develop the intelligence, arouse and quicken the understanding, O Teacher! and you have done the main work. In like manner, awaken the moral nature, by the love of what is noble, generous, great, pure; and moral conduct follows easily. We usually think it a hard thing to die, — requiring the preparation of a life. But how easily our young soldiers died in the Civil War, — how peacefully, tranquilly, submissively. It is because they usually went to the war with a generous and conscientious motive. They went as a duty, giving themselves to their country. The great crisis and peril of the nation aroused everything noble in their hearts; and they experienced a development of courage and self-devotion far above what would come in common times. Thus they learned fast, in those great hours, the true lesson of life. They learned that true life is not in length of days, but in quality of being; and that we may easily live long in a few years. They learned that our highest joy does not come from luxury, ease, success in this world, but from generous renunciation, self-forgetting devotion; surrender of all we have and are to the cause of virtue, liberty, justice, and humanity.

Education will at last become a high art, based on

a true science of Human Nature. Then the true teacher will be found to be one of the noblest bene- factors of his race, — the best follower perhaps of Him who asked that the little children might come to Him. So shall instruction in all valuable knowl- edge grow more complete and thorough ; and the boy or girl who has received a liberal education may be really presumed to *know* something of each im- portant branch of human science. So shall TRAIN- ING of all the faculties accompany INSTRUCTION, and the end of all be the full DEVELOPMENT of the man.

In the Lectures which follow, I have called atten- tion to the need and the practicability of unfolding to a much higher degree than has usually been thought possible, the primal faculties of man. I might have called these papers Lectures on Chris- tian Culture, for I have shown how naturally the Christianity of the Gospels allies itself with the full development of human nature. I hope that the frequent references to the spirit of Christ's teaching will not be thought out of place. This spirit seems to me both a strong incentive and a practical guide in education. While there is no dogma of any kind in the book, I do not think it will be less valua- ble for its purpose, for occasional references of this kind.

I.

MAN'S DUTY TO GROW.

MAN'S DUTY TO GROW

———◆◇◆———

G OD has placed us here to grow, just as he placed the trees and flowers. The trees and the flowers grow unconsciously, and by no effort of their own. Man, too, grows unconsciously, and is educated by circumstances. But he can also control those circumstances, and direct the course of his life. He can educate himself; he can, by effort and thought, acquire knowledge, become accomplished, refine and purify his nature, develop his powers, strengthen his character. And because he *can* do this, he ought to do it.

It is curious that Christian teachers should have so often neglected to inculcate this duty of self-culture, seeing that it is so plainly taught by Jesus in the Gospels. This is the doctrine of the parable of the talents and of the pounds. Both teach that it is not enough to render back to our Master what we have received, unimpaired and uninjured; but that we must bring back *more* than we receive, — that is, that we must add something, by our own industry and fidelity, to what God intrusts to us; that we are his stewards. The parable of the talents teaches the law of responsibility; that of the pounds, the law of retribution. The first shows that the more we receive, the more we are bound to do; those who have two talents must bring two more; those who have five, five more. The other shows that the more we gain, the more we shall receive; that progress is not according to arithmetical but geometrical progression; that it is a constantly accelerated progress.

Ten men have each a single pound. One gains two pounds, and receives two cities; one five, and receives five cities. Not merely two pounds, but two cities; the powers developed in a lower service are employed in a higher one. The man who is faithful in a few things here will be made ruler over many things there. Here, perhaps, his business was to make horseshoes; but he made them faithfully; he learned how to make better horseshoes, and more of them, as he went on. Consequently he may be found fitted, in another sphere, not to make horseshoes, but to help govern a planet. But, in both parables, the servant who brought back only what was given him, without improving it, is called a wicked and slothful servant, and loses what he first received. Improve your talents, or lose them, that is the austere law.

And this legislative enactment of the Divine Lawgiver, in the New Testament, has been confirmed by all the decisions of the Supreme Court of the

Deity in Nature. *Use and improve, or lose.* This is the sentence pronounced on each of us by all the courts of God, in the physical, intellectual, and moral world. Use and improve your muscles and your perceptions, or they will gradually but certainly fail. Use and improve your memory, your understanding, your judgment, or they will become feeble. Use and improve your conscience, or it grows torpid. Use and improve the powers which look up to an infinite truth, beauty, and goodness, and they lift you towards these. Let them sleep, and they cannot see this kingdom of God, this Divine element in the universe. The fool, who has not developed his spiritual nature, says in his heart, "There is no God." Nature reaches its hand to Revelation to maintain this law, and both, with concurrent voice, cry, "Use and improve, or lose."

If man has the power of self-improvement, then this power is itself a talent confided to him. Unless he improves, he does not use this power. But this power of perpetual self-improvement is one of the chief distinctions between man and the lower animals, between civilized races and savage races. Animals can be trained by man, but they cannot train themselves. They can be taught some accomplishments, formed to some new habits; but where man has not done this for them, they remain uneducated. Savage races reach a certain point of improvement under the influence of circumstances; and then they stop, their development arrested.

3

But, in the higher civilization of .Christendom, no such limit has been reached, and none such appears in the future. Christian civilization forgets the things behind, and reaches out to those before. Each generation is born on a little higher plane of attainment, in science, art, and social faculty, than that which preceded it. But this social progress depends on individual progress. Every man who improves himself is aiding the progress of society; every one who stands still, holds it back. The progress of society always commences in individual souls. A great advancing soul carries forward his whole age; a mean, sordid soul draws it back. That is a good reason why the talent should be taken from him, and given to another.

That man was made for progress appears evident from the fact that, without progress in some form, life itself becomes undesirable, almost unendurable. With a sense of progress, even of the lowest kind, the interest of life revives. As long as a man has hope, he can bear anything, endure anything, and be happy. Take from him hope, and his heart is dead before his body dies. Nothing that we have, or are, can satisfy us for more than a moment. If a man fixes his heart on pleasure, then he must have some new pleasure to-morrow beyond what he has to-day, or he is weary. If he fixes his heart on the acquisition of wealth, then he must have a larger property this year than he had last. So with fame, position, power, knowledge, — all tire us if we have to stand still. We must look forward, or die. We are like the man crossing a wild stream on a narrow log, — he is only safe while he goes on ; if he stops, he falls. The dreadful disease of ennui, of life-weariness, attacks all who have no aim, no permanent purpose, who are not looking forward, onward, upward. The only two classes of men who are safe from this poison of life are those who have an aim and those who are doing steady work. The great mass of men and women are contented because they are obliged to work. Of those who are not obliged to work, those only are contented who continue to work because they have some purpose, some object, something to which to look forward. The wine of life is the sense of progress.

The love of money, says the Apostle, is the root of all evil. So it is ; but it is also the root of a great amount of good. The love of money, in bad men and weak men, incites to cheating, lying, cruelty, meanness, reckless speculation, cold-blooded murder. But love of money, as the desire of getting on in the world, is a constant source of industry, foresight, prudence, economy. · It educates the whole community to these virtues. It furnishes hope to ten thousand homes. Stand in the street of a large city at evening, and see the very poor going to their houses. What are they ? Cellars, garrets, hid away in dark courts, dirty, without ventilation, with nothing of comfort about them, still less of beauty or taste. You say, " How can they bear life under

such conditions ? " Because in these poor homes
there is love, there is intelligence, warm social affec
tions. A great deal of strong thinking is done in
them. But, besides this, there is a sense of progress.
They are getting on, or hoping to do so. They hope
to lay by enough to buy a small house some day ; to
educate their children, and to leave them higher up
in the world than they are themselves.

Progress, in the sense of acquisition, is some
thing ; but progress in the sense of being, is a great
deal more. To grow higher, deeper, wider, as the
years go on ; to conquer difficulties, and acquire
more and more power ; to feel all one's faculties unfolding, and truth descending into the soul, — this
makes life worth living.

We all believe in education ; but what is it that
we call education ? A few years at school ; a little
reading, writing, arithmetic ; a few studies superficially pursued, — this is commonly understood to be
education. But education, in the true sense, is not
mere instruction in Latin, English, French, or history. It is the unfolding of the whole human nature. It is growing up in all things to our highest
possibility. This is. a life-work ; a work in which
our teachers are the heavens and the earth, day and
night, work and rest, nature and society, heavenly
inspirations and human sympathies, success and
failure, sickness, pain, bereavement ; all of this great
human life. And with this teaching, there must be
the earnest desire and purpose in our own soul to

grow, to become larger, deeper, higher, nobler, year by year.

For these reasons, we say that all should aim at self-culture. "Very early," said Margaret Fuller, "I perceived that the object of life is to grow." She herself was a remarkable instance of the power of the human being to go forward and upward. Of her it might be said, as Goethe said of Schiller, "If I did not see him for a fortnight, I was astonished to find what progress he had made in that interim." Every year she lived added depth to her thought, largeness to her comprehension, devotion to her soul. Being at first somewhat egotistic, disdainful, proud, she became, at last, modest, sympathetic, and kind to the lowest and humblest. This generous nature took its own way to perfection. Whether teaching young girls in New England, or nursing wounded Italian soldiers in Rome; whether studying with untiring energy the literatures of Europe, or scraping lint for the patriots who followed Mazzini, — she was always going forward and onward to the end of her days.

Consider, also, such a character as that of John Milton, who, having determined early to write a work "which the world would not willingly let die," thought within himself "that he who would truly write a heroic poem must make his whole life a heroic poem." He, therefore, describes his long devotion to that work of improvement, and tells us how his "appetite for knowledge was so voracious that from twelve years of age he hardly ever left his studies or went to bed before midnight;" then how he " passed seven years in the University of Cambridge," "with the approbation of the good, and without any stain on my character." And how, then, " being anxious to visit foreign parts, and especially Italy," he saw great kindred souls, like Grotius and Galileo, and the antiquities and arts of Florence and Rome. After defending the Reformed religion in the capital of the Pope, he returned to England, when he heard of the civil commotions there ; " for I thought," says he, " it base to be travelling for a moment abroad, while my fellow-citizens were fighting for liberty at home."

John Milton did make of his whole life a heroic poem, and at last, old and blind, fallen on evil days and tongues, he sat in his obscurity and composed his immortal poem, which the world will never " willingly let die." We reverence him most of all, because he was himself greater than his poetry.

"But we cannot all be Miltons," you say. Not every man by any amount of culture can become a Milton ; not every woman can become a Margaret Fuller. No, nor is it so intended. But we can all be as faithful in our measure as they were in theirs. Each of our souls may be unfolded into something as beautiful, as necessary to God's world, as the souls of the great heroes and saints. It would not do to have too many heroes and saints. An army made up wholly of generals would win no battles.

Soldiers are as necessary as generals in the battle of
life. —

> "A battle, whose great scheme and scope
>   They little care to know,
> Content, as men at arms, to cope
>   Each with his fronting foe."

I do not believe that we are able to make of ourselves anything we please. But we can make of
ourselves what God pleases we should be. In every
soul he has deposited the germ of a great future.
Every soul is a seed. It does not yet appear what
it shall be,—it is bare grain. Of some seeds may
be born beautiful roses; others will become modest
violets: some will tower into graceful elms, whose
branches shall bend and wave in the summer air,
and beneath whose far-reaching shadows the cattle
shall stand resting in the hot days. Others shall
become grasses for food, herbs for the cure of disease
and solace of pain, — "to every seed its own body."

Formerly we were told of the formation of character, and this was inculcated, as though each man
could carve himself into what he pleased; that by
sheer force of will he could make himself a character to suit himself. I have heard some prosaic
persons say that, no doubt, if they had taken the
trouble, they could have learned to write as good
poetry as Lord Byron. I believe in no such possibility. I rather would believe that in every man's
organization there was decreed, before the foundation of the world, every man's destiny. Every one

of us was made to be something noble, good, lovely, useful, but not all the same.   Instead of the formation of character, we now speak of development, which is a much truer word.   There is a seed of the future in each of us, which we can unfold if we please, or leave to be forever only a stunted, half-grown stalk.   We are free to do, to become, or refuse to become, what God means us to be and made us be.   One shall be a rose in God's garden, "angry and brave;" another a buttercup or a sweet-pea. One shall open as a tender morning-glory, and give the poet a hint of a strain so sweet that it shall comfort all mourning mothers' hearts; and another be a daisy, turned up by a Scottish plough, and, dying so, be born again into an immortal song. Why shouldst thou envy thy brother because he is more wise, or has more genius, more business faculty, than thou?   Why envy thy sister because she is more fair, more brilliant?   The buttercup does not envy the rose, nor the prairie vine complain because it is not a Virginia creeper.   God has made every thing beautiful in its time and place; let it only be contented to unfold into that which he intends it to become.

But the power of circumstances, you say, are so great that they prevent self-culture.   We have no time, no opportunity, to make anything of ourselves. We are obliged to work for our daily bread; we are fettered by unfavorable circumstances; how can we ever unfold ourselves into anything of value?

These are the arguments of cowardice and unbelief. Look! O thou of little faith, at the great workers in the world, and see how they have fought their way to triumph against all sorts of opposing obstacles. Milton wrote "Paradise Lost" in blindness and poverty. Luther sang in the streets to buy bread as a child, and before he could establish the Reformation had to encounter the prestige of a thousand years, the united power of an imperious hierarchy, and the ban of the German Empire. Linnæus determined to devote his life to the study of plants, and had only about forty dollars with which to get his education. He was so poor as to be obliged to mend his shoes with folded paper, and often to beg his meals of his friends. Columbus was not sent to discover America in a steamship; but beset and importuned in turn the States of Genoa, Portugal, Venice, France, England, and Spain before he could get the control of three small vessels and one hundred and twenty men. Marlborough and Wellington won their great battles in spite of the perpetual opposition and resistance of the governments for which they were fighting. Hugh Miller, who became one of the first geological writers of his time, was apprenticed to a stone-mason, and, while working in the quarry, already began to study the stratum of red sandstone lying below one of red clay. Where other men complain of circumstances, the man or boy who has an idea and a purpose compels these untoward circumstances to serve him. Where

others see nothing but bare rock, he notices analo
gies and differences. George Stephenson, the inventor
of the locomotive engine, was a common collier,
working in the mines. James Watt, the inventor
of the steam-engine, was a poor sickly child, not
strong enough to go to school. John Calvin, who gave
a theology to the seventeenth and eighteenth centuries, which it has hardly yet outgrown, was tortured
with disease all his days. So was Robert Hall, the
greatest preacher of his time. What favorable circumstances helped the peasant girl of Arc to deliver
France, when kings and great generals had failed?
In what cradle of easy circumstances were Pascal
and Shakspeare, George Fox the Quaker, Spinoza and
Charlotte Bronté or Harriet Martineau, rocked into
success? They were pillowed on hardship, taught
by poverty, made strong by neglect, made pure by
loneliness. All the great founders of religious sects,
Buddha and Mohammed, Augustine and St. Francis,
Wesley or George Fox, have been denounced, perse-
cuted, and reviled through long years of fierce oppo-
sitiou. Have we not seen, in our own day, the
antislavery reformers forcing their way to triumph
against the combined opposition of churches, political parties, commerce and manufactures, and the
saloons? When were circumstances ever favorable to any great or good attempt, except as they
were compelled by a determined purpose to become
favorable?

I have given well-known instances of those who

have struggled up to fame and influence in spite of the most unfavorable circumstances. But these famous people, often gifted with that mastering and irrepressible quality which we call genius, are not the best illustrations of the power of growth in man. Go out into any New England village and look around you. In each such community you will find men and women who have developed power of mind and heart by simple fidelity to truth and conscience, until they have become sources of light and comfort to all the neighborhood. Do any need advice, sagacious counsel, wise help, in difficulty ? — they go to this village Franklin, to this Oberlin or Algernon Sidney of the hillside, and find new courage and new hope. Is there a poor woman, half driven to despair by untoward fortune ? She goes to the mother-confessor of the town, and tells her tale of woe, and finds sympathy, advice, and help. This woman, who has taken no vows in any sisterhood, and wears no garb indicating that she is set apart to religion, is yet the true patron-saint of the little neighborhood. Long experience in well-doing has developed a wonderful gift of helpfulness. Sorrows of her own have taught her to feel for others. Blessings precede, attend, and follow her footsteps. Perhaps she is poor, perhaps unattractive in appearance or manners, and yet a sweet halo of generous kindness spreads soothing influence around her. Her cheerful patience and hope, and unfaltering courage, are a perpetual inspiration. She, by patient continuance in well-doing, has grown up into all she was meant to be by her Creator.

I gave an address in Central New York one summer in which I described such a woman as this, and, after the lecture was over, the people of the town declared I had been painting the portrait of one of their neighbors. Of course I had never seen her nor known her, but this shows how many there are who by faithfulness inherit the promise, "Give and it shall be given you."

> " Far from the madding crowd's ignoble strife,
>   Their sôber wishes never learn to stray ;
>   Along the cool, sequestered vale of life
>   They keep the noiseless tenor of their way."

A man cannot make of himself anything he chooses, but he can carry out God's intentions concerning him, if, with a single eye to doing what is best, and becoming what he was meant to be, he makes use of all circumstances, favorable or unfavorable.

But perhaps you may say, Is not self-culture, in the last analysis, a selfish aim ? Is it not better to make it one's aim to do the nearest duty, or to do all the good we can to our fellow-creatures, rather than to cultivate our own powers and unfold our own nature ? This objection is a serious one, and deserves to be considered before going further.

No doubt there is a danger in making self-culture an exclusive aim. There are rocks ahead, no matter in what direction we may steer. The rock ahead, if we steer toward self-culture, is selfishness. The man who devotes himself to the cultivation of any faculty, talent, or taste, is in danger of separating himself in his sympathies from the mass of his fellow-men, in whom that faculty or taste is dormant. Graver still is the danger which comes from making one's self the object of all one's thoughts. This has often been seen in religious experience, where too much stress has been laid on making personal salvation the great object of life. This may end in a morbid self-included aim. The Westminster Assembly therefore wisely declared that the chief end of man was to "glorify God," as well as "to enjoy him forever." And the Hopkinsian School of Theology went further, and so subordinated the desire of personal happiness here or hereafter to the love of absolute goodness, as to declare that no one was capable of being saved till he was willing to be damned for the glory of God.

But in all extremes there are dangers. The modern equivalent for "the glory of God" would be Truth, Goodness, Humanity, Universal Progress, or some such generalization. But the same danger of egotism emerges also here. Men whose lives are devoted to these large abstractions, patriots, philanthropists, and reformers of all sorts, are often forgetful of daily duties, neglectful of home ties. This at least, is their risk, — if they fall, they fall in that direction.

Thomas Carlyle, at one period, satirized this tendeney of world-reformers with the whole force of his sharpest satire. The aim which he suggested and urged was the opposite to all this. " Do your nearest duty !" A large class of his admirers immediately adopted this maxim as their motto in life, and began courageously to do their nearest duties. And certainly this, too, is a very useful rule, if not carried to an extreme, and not made an exclusive one. But there is evidently danger on this side too. Persons who are confined altogether to home cares and family duties become narrow. It is very well to talk about " fireside virtues," — but how many men and women have had their mental and moral growth stifled by limiting their obligations to their business and home. The danger from this aim is narrowness. If those who adopt it fall, they fall in that direction. " Doing good " is another aim. To do the greatest good to the greatest number, to help all who need help, is often, in our time, thought the true " imitation of Christ." The modern Christian does not retire into a cell to pray, but goes about doing good. He thus avoids the risk of narrowness, which attends the man who desires only to do the " nearest duty." But there is a danger here also, — that of shallowness. The man who is always giving, never receiving ; always helping others, and never feeding his own soul, is in danger of becoming empty. His virtue leans that way, and if he falls, he will fall in that direction.

No single aim, exclusively pursued, is without its

risks. Moral forces are polar forces, and every virtue has its antagonist virtue. We admit, therefore,
while advocating self-culture, that it should not be
pursued to the exclusion of other aims, but including them, as necessary adjuncts and helpers. While
seeking to develop one's powers in an integral way,
we must bear in mind also one's duty to God and
man. To live in THE WHOLE, is the way to live
wisely in any part.

He who devotes himself to self-culture should
therefore bear constantly in his mind the justifica-
tion of this method of life. It is justified, if he
seeks thus to advance the good of others as well as
his own ; to use his developed powers for the cause
of justice, truth, and humanity ; to become a better
friend to his friends, a greater help and blessing in
his home, to do the common duties of life more
ably ; and thus to serve God and man better than he
could do without such culture.

In my youth I knew two young men who adopted
for their aims, the one, self-culture, the other,
philanthropy. The one sought to educate himself;
the other, to do good. After a while, the youth who
sought self-culture found that to get it he must quit
the still air of delightful study, and go out to help
his brother man. He found that he needed work,
sympathy, society, in order not to freeze ; and so, in
order to gain self-development, he became a man of
usefulness. The other, who began by doing good,
found himself at last growing shallow. He had

emptied himself, and had to stop to fill himself full again. He said, " I must be something, in order to do something. I must gain, in order to give." So, from motives of philanthropy, he proceeded to cultivate his mind and develop his faculties.

I do not think that making self-development an aim will ever lead to selfishness, if this aim is pursued in the spirit of the two parables to which I have referred. If we cultivate all the powers of body and soul in order to use them as talents in the service of God, not in order to gain for ourselves glory, or merely to excel others, but because God has made us to grow and intends us to grow, that we may be plants in his garden, every blossom a censer swinging its perfume on the air for him, every fruit ripening that it may bless and help his creatures, — then I believe that this aim will be in all respects a true and good one.

These, then, are the conditions, and these the possibilities of growth. We are put here to grow, and we ought to grow, and to use all the means of growth according to the laws of our being. Hereafter we will consider further what those laws are, and what are the means of our progress.

We grow only when we become more and more ourselves, our best selves, our truest selves, the selves that God made us to be. We do not grow when we try to be like this man or that, to strive for this man's wit or that man's scope, to become like this saint or that genius. The rose grows when it unfolds into a rose, not when it tries to become any other shrub or flower. The palm springs erect to heaven, and grows up a palm; the vine creeps, and hangs, and swings in the air, and pours fragrance on the breeze, and grows into a vine. Thus God has made each of us to be something, to have a real place, and do a real work in this world, and that our own work, which no one else can do. If we are faithful to the inner light of our own conviction, and to the daily duties which God sends to us, we shall grow. With glad surprise we shall find ourselves becoming genuine and real plants, of use or beauty, in the garden of our God.

II.

TRAINING AND CARE OF THE BODY.

II.

TRAINING AND CARE OF THE BODY.

———◦◦◦———

IN many of the ancient religions the body was thought to be the enemy of the soul. The duty of a religious man, therefore, was to weaken the body, as far as was possible, without destroying life. The body was to be kept under by means of mortifying practices, — fasting, want of sleep, poor clothes or none, by living out of doors, and, finally, by self-inflicted flagellation. Only one ancient nation — the Egyptian — appears to have had much respect for the human body. The Egyptians took care of the body during life, and preserved it after death. They saw something divine in all living organizations. In worshipping animals and vegetables they worshipped the mysterious principle of organization, that vital power which is to us, as it was to them, utterly marvellous and inscrutable. The Egyptians thought it religious to adore and worship the body; other nations thought it religious to despise and ill-treat the body. Christians have, therefore, followed the Brahmins and Buddhists more than the Egyptians in their view of the body, and have thought that the greatest saint was the man who lived in a cave, half-starved, and very dirty. But there is no such doctrine taught in the New Testament. The Son of Man came eating and drinking. Neither Paul nor John nor Peter advised their disciples to become monks and nuns. When Peter repented of denying his master, he did not proceed to inflict flagellation on himself, punishing his body for the sin of his soul. The letter and the spirit of the New Testament teach that we are to glorify God with our body, as well as our spirit. And I proceed now to show how we can glorify God with our body; or, to speak in modern language, how the body may be made the means of self-culture.

We glorify God with our body by keeping it in good health.

Good health is the basis of all physical, intellectual, moral, and spiritual development. Men and women, permanent invalids, have, no doubt, been sometimes distinguished as thinkers and workers. A powerful soul will triumph over bodily disease; but usually a sick thinker has something sickly in his thought. Calvin, whose life was darkened by disease, had a morbid and gloomy element in his theology. Emaciated and sickly saints usually have a sickly piety. I believe that Jesus was healthy in body as in mind; all his faculties active, and so full of vital power as to awe and control even his opponents, who came expecting to put him down.

For a certain amount of vital energy is needed to give weight to the best argument. To be a great prophet it is necessary, not only to have inspiration and conviction, but also to possess a body able to endure fatigue, instinct with magnetic force and physical energy. I repeat, then, that bodily health is the foundation of all rounded self-culture, all integral development. I fully admit the power of the soul, under great spiritual and moral excitement, to compel a weak body to do its bidding. This is one of the most eminent proofs that soul is the king, and body its subject. A great soul *may* inspire a sick body with strength ; but if the body were well, it would obey yet more promptly and effectually.

I do not sympathize with those reformers who say that we are always to blame for being sick, and that if we obeyed all the hygienic laws we should be always well. Some persons are born diseased, with congenital and inherited poison in their blood; some take disease from the air, and from unavoidable exposure. But, no doubt, a vast amount of sickness comes from bad living ; from intemperance in work, in eating and drinking; from breathing bad air, living in damp, dark homes ; from bad food, poor clothing, want of recreation and amusement. In New England we are not a healthy people. We are, to be sure, free from the scourge of the Middle and Western States, — fever and ague ; nor are we as liable to inflammatory disease as in other places. Our demon is consumption, and the natural preven-

tion and cure for consumption is pure air, and
enough of it.   But the great mass of our people shut
out the sunshine, shut out the air, shut themselves
up during our long winter months with air-tight
stoves in air-tight rooms, using the same air over
and over again.   Ventilation is a lost art.   No one
knows how to ventilate a public building or a railroad car.   Along the shores of Maine, where the air
is pure and balmy, and merely to breathe it is like
drinking the wine of life, if you go into the houses
you will find the people pale and sickly.   The ex-
planation is the air-tight stove and the indigestible
food.   Whoever will teach the people of New England
the advantages of good food, fresh air, and sunshine,
will renew the physical constitution of the race.

But the work of physical degeneracy is begun in
our schools.   We put a crowd of little children
together in an imperfectly ventilated room.   We
task their immature brains with from five to eight
hours of •mental application.   We stimulate them
by a system of prizes, promotion, and praise.   We
make them study at home, in the evening, by lamp-
light, after having been confined at school half the
day.   When the child's natural tendency to move
about, to smile, to talk, manifests itself, we repress
it by the brutal application of the rod.   So we treat
our children, and wonder at the mysterious Providence which sends them disease and death, while
the vagabond newsboys, half clothed and half fed,
but moving about in the open air all day, are comparatively well.

Some years ago, I was placed on the State Board of Education. A friend told me that the health of the scholars in the Normal schools was suffering from over-study. Like others, I refused to believe it; like others, I took for granted that the system was about as good as it could be. At last my pertinacious friend urged on me so strongly that it was my duty to look into it, that I could refuse no longer. Accordingly, I went to two of the State Normal schools, in each of them called all the pupils together into the large room, and said that I wished to talk with the pupils without the teachers taking any part in the discussion. I then proceeded to ask the following questions : —

1. How many hours do you study out of school ?

2. How many of you are usually well, but with occasional headaches, weariness, and sleeplessness ?

3. How many are perfectly well ?

4. How many have a good appetite ?

5. How many sleep well all night ?

The result was that, in both schools, the majority studied between four and five hours out of school, beside the five hours in school ; only one-sixth were perfectly well ; less than one-half had a good appetite for their food ; while about two-thirds to three fourths slept well. On these facts being brought before the Board of Education, they voted that eight hours' work, including all the time in school and out, should be the maximum allowed ; and even this is a great deal too much. As regards younger children, it has been proved by carefully collected facts, presented to the British Parliament by Mr. Edwin Chadwick, that children working on half-time (that is, studying three hours a day, and devoting the rest of their time to out-door work) really make the greatest intellectual progress in the year. Walter Scott said he could never work with his brain more than five hours a day, and all physicians of standing, without exception, agree that children ought never to be confined more than an hour at a time, or study more than four hours a day.

Nervous diseases, also, are becoming very frequent in New England.   These result, probably, in a great degree, from too much brain-work, too little social reaction, too great anxiety and care.

If a healthy body contributes to the health of the mind, so, also, a healthy mind keeps the body well. Cheerfulness, interest in life, interest in our work, enough to do, without haste or rest ; pleasant society, friendship, — these react favorably on the body. The haste to get rich, and the intense struggles of business rivalry, probably destroy as many lives in America every year as are lost in a great battle. Patience, equanimity, trust in Providence, contentment with our lot, these keep the body from disease. A good conscience is better medicine than all the druggists can supply.

Again, whatever defiles and corrupts the body is a sin against God.   Intemperance in eating and drinking, licentiousness, these defile the temple of

God. One of the greatest evils of our time and land is intemperance. A large part of the misery and crime in our community comes directly from this source, and all the influence of religion, education, and law should combine to deliver the community from this frightful scourge. Every day we hear of some poor woman beaten to death by a drunken husband; some man made insane by poisonous liquor, sold him by those whom we license. For the sake of a few dollars, men spend their lives in making and selling these dreadful poisons. Self-protection requires that society shall put an end to this evil. How this shall be done is one of the most difficult, but also one of the most important, questions of the time.

There is another form of sensuality which constantly endangers the health and peace of the land, which demands our best wisdom to control. I fear that our community is not aware of the pains taken to corrupt the morals of our children, both boys and girls, by corrupt exhibitions, publications, pictures. It is seriously asserted that there is, in every room of our public schools, some scholar who is hired by the publishers of improper photographs and books to sell them among his companions. Ignorance of the laws of life, and the dangers to which they are exposed, cause our children to be led astray. Young girls are left unprotected, exposed to temptations of which they know nothing, and against which no one has warned them. The amount of suffering so caused, of families filled with misery, of innocence misled, is far greater than is generally known. Owing to the disgrace attending such evils, they are concealed. We apply instruction to prevent and cure all other vices and sins; but this we leave to grow in darkness. What we need is to have our children carefully taught, either at school or at home, or both, the laws of life and health, and the dangers of all kinds of excesses. Only so can these miseries be abated or prevented.

God has so bound society together that if one member suffer, all suffer. If we leave the poor in their alleys exposed to disease, that disease finds its way to all our homes. Year after year, our Board of Health has told us that the tenement-houses of Boston are a disgrace to the city. There are twenty-seven hundred of these houses in Boston, visited by the Board of Health, many of which are left by their wealthy owners in a condition which creates disease through defective drainage and dirt. Another cause of disease is the wholesale adulteration of almost all kinds of food, and the sale of provisions unfit for human use. A late report of the Board of Health told us that there was scarcely an article of food or drink which was not adulterated by some worthless or injurious material. One-third of the manufacturers of the candy sold to children had put the deadly poison, chromate of lead, into their colored candies, and several cases were reported recently where death soon ensued from innocently eating such substances. Out of forty samples of colored candy submitted to examination, thirty-six contained this active poison. I speak of all these evils here, because enlightened public opinion is the only power which can cure them.

But we glorify God with our body, not merely by keeping it free from disease, but also by developing all its faculties. Education has, been confined too much to the intellect. We have sought to discipline the brain to remember, compare, deduce, analyze, generalize; but it has not occurred to us that the body is as capable of education as the mind. Yet we see in special cases how this can be done. A singer trains her voice to express exactly every cadence and inflection of her song; why should we not learn to modulate our voices to an equal accuracy and delicacy in reading and speech? Unconsciously every educated person acquires a certain flexibility and refinement of utterance, and you can tell in the darkest night whether two persons whom you meet are rude or refined, if you only hear the tones of their voices in conversation. But why not cultivate the power of speaking well? Robert Houdin, the celebrated French juggler, tells us in his memoirs that in educating his son to the same business he made him walk slowly past the shop windows in Paris, until he was able to remember every article exhibited in a window from once going by. This shows to what quickness of perception the eye can be trained. There might be such an education of the perceptive organs in our schools, that young children should, in a little while, be able to tell by their eye the length or height of a room, or of a house, tell within an inch the size of a table, tell the shades of color in a bunch of flowers, in skeins of worsted, or in a carpet; tell the weight of an object by holding it in their hand; tell at a glance the exact number of objects suddenly shown and removed, just as they now are taught rapid processes in intellectual arithmetic. No one, in fact, can tell how far the perceptive faculties can be educated, because no systematic attempt has ever been made to educate them.

Every organ may be trained, every member. Paul says, if the foot should say to the hand, "I am not of the body, is it therefore not of the body?" We shut up our feet in tight shoes, and so prevent the muscles from developing. But there is a gentleman in Paris who has lost his arms, who uses his feet as if they were hands, and may be seen in the galleries copying pictures. Only one nation has ever tried to develop the body in its integrity. The Greeks, by their games and gymnastic exercises, brought out the force, grace, and symmetry of the human form, and their sculptors have preserved these types in immortal marble. These are the natural forms of the human being. Give man air, sun, proper food and clothing, ample and varied exercise, and there is no curve of grace in ancient statuary which would not be reproduced to-day.

The miracles performed by Christ have always seemed to me prophetic. They show us what man, when he reaches his perfect state, will be able to perform. Jesus was the perfect man, sent to reveal to us man as well as God, and to show what humanity is to be when it has conquered its weakness, risen above its sinfulness, and attained its full development. Jesus cured disease by a word or a touch. He thus shows that the soul is superior to the forces of external nature, master of the body, and that the laws of matter are flexible before the powers of the mind and heart. This is the lesson of his miracles, of his transfiguration, of his resurrection. "Greater works than these shall ye do, because I go to my Father." What we call miracle is only the natural supremacy of soul over body, the prophecy in one divinely ordained example, in one providential person, of what humanity, in the coming centuries, is to attain.

While a healthy body makes a healthy soul, the reverse is still more true. Mind lifts up, purifies, sustains the body. Mental and moral activity keep the body healthy, strong, and young, preserve from decay, and renew the life. As a rule, those who exercise and unfold their higher nature are long-lived. Wentworth Higginson made out a list of thirty of the most remarkable preachers of the last four centuries. It contained such names as Luther, Melancthon, Beza, Knox, Barrow, South, Jeremy Taylor, Tillotson, Paley, Blair, Priestley, Massillon,

Bossuet, Fénelon, Robert Hall, Chalmers, Wesley, Channing. He then proceeded to find the average length of their lives, and discovered it to be just sixty-nine years. The life and activity of the soul sustains and renews the body. Consider John Wesley, with his perpetual labors, preaching every morning at five o'clock, travelling every week hundreds of miles, never knowing rest or leisure, and living till eighty-eight, in full possession of all his faculties. Dr. Joseph Priestley, whom Coleridge calls "patriot and saint and sage," was a philosopher, an inventor, a discoverer in science, a radical in theology, and he wrote more than eighty books. He began life a sickly child, and lived to be seventy-one. And, at fifty-four, he said, "So far from suffering from application to study, I have found my health steadily improve from the age of eighteen to the present time."

In our day gymnastic exercises for young men have become a fashion, and I am glad of it. But devotion to mere muscular development in rowing, ball-playing, lifting weights, &c., is not integral education. The mind and heart and soul must be exercised also, and more than the muscles, if you wish to keep the whole man in health. Health descends into the body from the soul, though it may also ascend in the opposite direction. We must not rush into one error while avoiding another, and because bodily exercise has been neglected think that it will make up for every other exercise. Bodily exercise, without mental, profiteth little.

The moral and conclusion of what we have said is this : We shall not get to heaven by ill-using and ill-treating the body, as the old saints hoped to do. Nor must we neglect it, and think it of no cousequence compared with the mind. We owe to our body, the wonderful temple of the soul, care, culture, temperate usage, due training, pure, virtuous treatment. We must not defile it with vice, nor brutify it by sensual indulgence, but treat it as a divine work, to be reverenced and cultivated, like every other talent. The body must have its due exercise, food, sleep, because it is the temple of the soul. The body is to be raised by the power of Christianity to a higher condition, no less than the soul. There is a natural body and a spiritual body, a terrestrial and a celestial body. Even in this life we often see the spiritual body shining through the natural one. When the soul is active with thought, with noble purpose, with love, it transfigures the body, and " o'er-informs its tenement of clay." In an infant's smile of pure joy, in the expression of generous, noble purpose in youth, in the sweet patience which sits serene on the brow of the suffering saint, we see, even here, the body which is to be. Milton, in his poem concerning the " aidless, innocent lady," tells us · —

> " That, when a soul is found sincerely pure,
> A thousand liveried angels lackey her,
> Driving far off each thing of sin and guilt,
> And, in clear dream and solemn vision,

5

Tell her of things that no gross ear can hear ;
Till oft converse with heavenly habitants
Begins to cast a beam on the outward shape,
The unpolluted temple of the soul,
And turn it by degrees to the soul's essence,
Till all be made immortal."

To conclude, Montaigne expresses the sum of it all when he says, " Our work is not to train a soul by itself alone, nor a body by itself alone, but to train a man ; and in man soul and body can never be divided."

So many books have been written on the care of the health, and so much attention has been called to hygienics within a few years, that it is not necessary here to go into details. Let us briefly summarize the substance of all in the following rules :

Take exercise every day, in the open air if possible, and make it a recreation, and not merely a duty. Eat wholesome food. Drink pure water. Let your house and room be well ventilated. Take time enough for sleep. Do not worry.

Watch yourself, but not too closely, to find what exercise, air, diet, &c., agrees with you. No man can be a rule for another. One man can eat all things ; another, who is weak, can only eat herbs. Experience, in this regard, is better than rules.

If you consult a physician, it is better to do it before you are unwell than later. Prophylactics are better than therapeutics.

The time will come, let us hope, when all boys

will be taught the use of tools, and all girls the
principles of cooking. A carpenter's bench and
tools in a house will furnish as good exercise as
dumb-bells. And is it not a little discreditable to a
well-educated man to have to send for a mechanic
when anything is out of order in the house. Ought
we not to be able to ease a door, make a shelf, stop
a leak in a leaden pipe, milk a cow, harness our own
horse. An hour spent in such work about the house
or stable every day would not only exercise the body,
but relieve the tension of a student's brain.

Consider this : No carpenter will go to his work
without seeing that his chest of tools is in good order. The musician examines his instrument every
day to keep it in tune. We have our horses carefully
groomed. Let us do as much, at least, as this for our
own body. That is our wonderful box of tools, —
our organ with thousands of pipes. It has, no doubt,
a remarkable power of self-recovery, of repairing its
own lesions. But do not try it too much. It is the
faithful servant of the mind : but let the mind treat
its servant tenderly and wisely.

The body constantly acts on the mind : this is
now universally recognized. It is not as often
noticed how the mind acts on the body. A mind
strengthened by truth and a determined purpose
will support a feeble body, and enable it to do wonders. Mental excitement often cures bodily disease.
There are authentic cases of persons given over by
their physicians, who resisted death and saved their

lives by a strong determination not to die. Any influence which rouses the mind to action will often
cure the body. One day we shall have a mind-cure
hospital, where bodily disease will be relieved by
applications to the mind. Meantime, how much can
be done for invalids by visits from cheerful, bright,
entertaining visitors, — by religious influences which
inspire faith and hope, not doubt and fear. Whatever takes the mind out of itself, causes it to look
up, interests it in great truths, helps the body too.
Hospitals for invalids, especially for the insane,
should be carefully constructed on the principle of
surrounding the patient with sunshine and beauty,
and removing all harsh sights and sounds. Then,
let those radiant natures, to whom God has given
the power to charm and inspire, employ this gift
(so often wasted on circles which have everything
else) in visiting the depressed and the forlorn, the
sick and the weak, — and they will wonder at the
good they can do.

III.

THE USE OF TIME.

III.

THE USE OF TIME.

———◆◇◆———

FEW of the facts of our life are more mysterious and inexplicable, more paradoxical and contradictory, than the commonest and simplest of all, — that is, the progress of time. Time is the most rigid, and at the same time the most elastic, of all things. Time is a stream which bears all creatures on at the same rate. All beings who live on the surface of the earth are living in the same day of the same month and year. Time and events happen alike to all. No one can hold back longer than the rest; no one can hurry forward so as to get a month, a day, an hour, a minute, a second, in advance of the rest. Why should it not be so? Why should not sluggishness of hand and laziness of mind drop back, and be left a month or a year behind in time, as they would be left a mile or ten miles behind in space? Why should not genius and energy get on faster, and arrive sooner? But no! We are all immersed in the same *now*. The same moment arrives at once to all the thousand millions of beings on the earth. Ah, if we could only go back when we choose, and live the past over again! What a gift, more wonderful than that imagined in any fairy story, this would be! If some angel should come, and say you may be as you were a year ago, before that fatal crime was committed, that terrible mistake made; before that opportunity came which you threw away and lost forever; before that dear friend was taken from you by death, so that you could show him the love you felt in your heart, but neglected to manifest in action! If in the light of those results, of that experience, which is the divine judgment here on all human actions, we could begin our lives anew!

No. The moment which has not yet come is perfectly fluid. It is open to us all. We can put into it what we please. It arrives out of the future a shadowy possibility; it crystallizes in that infinitesimal moment we call the present, around whatever we think, or feel, or say, or do, and is gone forever, unalterable, holding in its adamantine grasp the changeable, irrecoverable action. What is done, is done forever; what is omitted, is omitted forever. The good action is sealed up, and made immortal; the bad action is sealed up, and can never be recalled, though we seek to repent of it diligently, and with tears. No awful fate, no tremendous doom, no iron necessity, can compare with this relentless grasp of Time, which seizes and retains, inexorable, unforgiving, all that passes into its irresistible embrace. So that time, of all things the most airy and impalpable before it comes, seems to be of all things the most solid and substantial when it has gone by.

Yet, on the other hand, this same element of time is a very flexible and elastic material. How it stretches out to some persons! How much more a day, an hour, is to one person than to another! How much more some people put into a month or a year than others do! Yes, how much more to each of us are our few hours of fiery inspiration and insight than the months in which we hammer mechanically this experience into opinion on the anvils of logic! How much more we live in the deep, momentary experiences of faith, generosity, love, than in the dreary years of routine which follow them! We see then what is meant by *redeeming* time. It is to fill the hours full of the richest freight; to fill them with the life of thought, feeling, action, as they pass by.

It is to live so as to be glad, not sad, when we look back. It is to conquer in the great struggle with the devil, with incarnate evil, and to have the sentence pronounced by the Rhadamanthine voice of the past, — Well done! This is the safety vault into which we can put our treasure, sure that no thieves can break in and steal. One moment of self-conquest, one good action really done, one generous deed actually performed, yes, one effort to do right really made, has the seal of time put on it, and no power in heaven nor all the fires of hell can melt that wax from the eternal bond. This last year, one man has made a fortune, and invested it in the best securities, — in mortgages, in houses, in railroads. But houses burn; thieves steal your bonds; robbers of a worse kind, who walk about State Street and Wall Street with unblushing faces, devour the property of the stockholders in a sham corporation. Another man has given his wealth for a good object, and that is safe forever; no thief can touch it, and no railroad president or bank teller can ever run away with that money.

What a difference between two lives, equally long, of which one has been wasted, the other redeemed! One has gone on without a purpose or aim; the other, steadily directed to some noble object; the one, empty of love, thought, action; the other, crowded with hours of glorious life; the one, in which, as we look back, we can see nothing but eating and sleeping, and mechanical, empty labor; in the other, the lowest toil made bright by a good and generous purpose, the humblest lot gilded and glorified by high thoughts and large loves. This is the real everlasting punishment, — to remember the irrevocable past. Just as far as we have wasted our time we go into everlasting punishment, for what shall ever annihilate the black record of the evil we have done? I suppose that even the most blessed saint must sometimes go into this kind of everlasting punishment. And just as far as we have redeemed time we go into everlasting bliss; for the record of good is equally indestructible. One man looks back — yes, we all look back sometimes — with a sense of utter loss, like that of Coleridge. Coleridge, in one of the most pathetic passages in English literature, speaks of the

> "Sense of past youth, and manhood come — in vain!
> And genius given and knowledge won — in vain!
> And all that I have culled in wood-walks wild,
> And all that patient toil has reared, and all
> Commune with thee has opened out — but flowers
> Strewed on my hearse, and scattered on my bier,
> · In the same coffin, for the self-same grave."

And sometimes we look back, thinking of one good act done, one great truth seen, one deep affection experienced; and then we can use the lofty strain of Dryden, in his noble translation of Horace, and say : —·

> "Happy the man, and happy he alone,
> He who can call the hour his own,
> He who, secure within, can say,
> 'To-morrow do thy worst, for I have lived to-day!
> Be fair, or foul, or rain, or shine,
> The joy I have possessed, in spite of Fate, is mine!
> Not heaven itself upon the past has power;
> For what has been has been, and I have had my hour.'"

Life becomes solemn enough when we look at it from this point of view. It becomes vastly more solemn than death; for we are not responsible for dying : we are responsible for living. Why talk of a judgment to come on some great day in the future, when every day is a day of judgment; when every moment, as it goes by, judges us; when the act we put into it is carved into this terrible past in letters more lasting than those which have resisted for five thousand years the sands and the revolutions of Egypt. Carved on the granite there, you may read the actions done fifty centuries ago; you may see the task-masters, by the command of the great Rameses, beating the poor Hebrew slaves at their work of building his cities. Those stones may decay at last, and that record be lost. But not an idle word, not an unkind word that we say, not a moment of our life, but gives an account of itself in the imperishable record of the past.

As regards self-culture, all depends on the use of time. All those who have unfolded great powers have been hard workers. Genius itself is nothing but an immense power of work. It is the power of immersing one's self in work, but making it all play and joy by the quantity of life put into it. Genius always "redeems the time."

There were four men who lived during the last century, who all lived to be very old, whose lives were contemporaneous during the largest part of the period from 1700 to 1800, who were different in many respects, but who were all alike in this power of turning time into thought and action. They were Swedenborg, Voltaire, Wesley, and Franklin. Swedenborg died in 1772, aged eighty-four; Voltaire died in 1778, also aged eighty-four; Franklin died in 1790, also aged eighty-four; Wesley died in 1791, aged eighty-eight. Perhaps no four men of the century exercised a greater influence on the age than these. Swedenborg's thought has been slowly filtering into philosophy and theology, spiritualizing both. To him, the whole world, both in this life and the life to come, is a shining web of divine laws, — God descending into nature, into the soul, into the body, and making everything divine. His thought, so subtle and so deep, is gradually conquering the materialism of philosophy and theology, and so bringing down what he called the New Jerusalem, or the sight of divine truth incarnate in all actual facts and laws. But what a vast amount of thought and study; what patient labor on works which no one in that day, and but few even in ours, have cared to read; what entire confidence in the power of truth; what fidelity to his thought, persistency in his purpose, cool ardor, patient energy, marked the life of the solitary thinker! He was the most lonely man on the earth in his day; hardly a soul sympathized with him, or understood him. Yet he worked on, without haste or rest, an incarnation of thought, sure that somewhere men would be found to read and understand what God told him to say. Surely *he* "redeemed the time."

How different was Voltaire! The man of society, the man of the world, the man who wrote for the day and hour, — whose every book and pamphlet had an immediate answer and welcome; the critic, the wit, the superficial but acute thinker on all subjects under heaven, but who seldom lifted his eyes to the heaven itself; the man from whose soul religious sentiment seemed to have been eliminated, in whose organization reverence was omitted. He also did his work, — to expose shams, to dethrone superstitions, to attack hoary abuses, to claim for man justice, freedom, opportunity. He worked, not by faith, but by sight, in the present moment, but with indefatigable energy, redeeming the time. And if, as the preacher says, "there is a time for everything," that time was certainly the time for Voltaire, when the world was so full of evils and abuses, which needed such stinging scorn as his for their correction. The pulpit has used Voltaire only as the type of the worst unbelief and sin. But do him this justice, he put his whole soul into his rather barren work of destruction. It was the best he knew, and he did it. And he did it well.

How different again, both from Swedenborg and Voltaire, was Wesley! No mystic like Swedenborg, but with an intense practical desire to turn all the doctrinal truth he saw into instant life, he made the new heavens and earth in England of which the Northern sage dreamed. No man ever so fully believed that "now is the day of salvation" as John Wesley. No man ever went so entirely out of the religion of form, doctrine, and ceremony, into that of life, as he. His profoundest conviction was this:

that no human being lived on earth so bad or base, so stupid or worldly, so utterly corrupt and worthless, but that, if he could believe it, God was ready to kindle in his soul a fire of love which would wholly consume this evil. His business was to make men believe it. For this faith he lived. In this faith he worked, redeeming the time. He saw the dead in sin coming to life all around him, he passed his happy years in this divinest of labors; he died a soldier with his armor on, having done a work which neither God nor man can ever willingly let die.

And now look at the fourth whom I have named, Dr. Franklin, — differing from the three, with none of the mysticism of Swedenborg in his nature, yet with none of the sneering scepticism of Voltaire. A practical man, bent on doing work, — not living, like Voltaire, for literary success, not feeding on flattery and popular applause. He had also his share of hard trial and opposition, and lonely struggle. But he rose out of it, higher and higher, by the steady strength with which he did his work, — plucking the lightning from the clouds, and the sceptre of America from the hand of obstinate, stupid, conscientious George the Third. When he stood before the English Lords in Council, the object of abuse and ridicule; when he stood in the midst of the glittering court of France, the object of praise and admiration; when he stood in the American Congress, with his calm good sense directing its counsels; and when he tried experiments with his kite and his key, — he was still the faithful servant of his highest thought, he also was "redeeming the time," and he redeemed it well.

We see then how it is. We see, by these examples, that if a man will be faithful to his highest conviction, to the best thought which God gives him to say, the best act given him to do, he will change time into life. He will bring forth fruit in youth, and in age will be still green and flourishing, like all the four men I have named. This is the first condition, then, of making the most of time, that we shall be always true to our best thought, that we shall do with our might whatever our hand finds to do. We must understand the value of the present moment. We must not spend our days in grieving over the past, but forget the things that are behind. We must not look with anxiety or fear to the future, but let to-morrow take thought for the things of itself. On this point philosophy and Christianity are at one. Jesus says, "Take no thought for the morrow," and Horace, the epicurean, says the same. "What may happen to-morrow, do not inquire, but whatever Fortune brings to-day count as clear gain."

Yes; time may be kept. Those who have wrought one hour in a sincere fulness of life may accomplish as much as long years of common toil. Therefore, all that we said at the beginning of this lecture of the inflexible and unchanging past is indeed true. But it is also true that we who know how much of time we have wasted, may begin to work now in such a spirit that we may redeem our past years from their emptiness by the overflow of our present fulness. So it sometimes happens that a single bright and generous act serves to atone for the abuse of years. So, in what is perhaps the best story of Dickens, the man of wasted life gave himself to die in the place of another in the Reign of Terror, and so by a sunset of glory and purity gilded the clouds of his dark and stormy day.

John Newton, friend of the poet Cowper, author of some of the Olney hymns, led a wild and troubled youth. He deserted from an English man-of-war; was caught, flogged, and degraded; commanded an African slave-trader during four years, during all which time, he says, "he never had the least scruples as to its lawfulness." But who thinks of that evil career, obliterated and swallowed up as it was by his long subsequent life of devoted usefulness?

But while we value every hour of life, it is important also to remember that there is time enough for all that is to be done. The first rule is to do everything with our might. The second rule is not to hurry. It is better to do a single thing as well as we can, than to do a great many things imperfectly. It is better to read one good book thoroughly, than a great many superficially. I recollect hearing of a young man who thought of preparing himself for

6

the ministry, a farmer's son, with only a common-school education, who came to a minister and asked for some book to study in his leisure hours. The minister gave him "Locke on the Understanding." At the end of six months, he told his friend that he was discouraged by his own stupidity, for he had not half read it. At the end of twelve months, he brought it back, and said, "I can never be a student, for it has taken me a whole year to read this book." But, on examination, it was found he knew everything in the book perfectly, and his friend told him that to read one book thus was to be a scholar. That would help him as long as he lived.

As I look back and remember the books I have read, I find those that have done my mind the most good are not those I have gone over superficially, but those which I have eaten and drunk, and made a part of myself. It is an old saying, that the most terrible thinker and scholar is the man of one book, *homo unius libri.* Let a person know all about the Bible, let him know all of Shakspeare, or let him be perfectly familiar with the best of Lord Bacon's writings, or of Leibnitz, or of Swedenborg, or of Plato, or Dante, or Goethe, — any one of them, and he will be a highly accomplished man. But we waste our time doing too many things, reading too many books, seeing too many people, talking too much. Therefore we do nothing well, read nothing thoroughly, know no one really, say nothing that is worth hearing. Let us 'write in our souls this maxim, — quality, not quantity, never hurry; take time to do what you ought to do as well as you can do it. That is the only way to take time.

⌐ ˉMuch time is wasted in schools, academies, and colleges, by wrong methods. In my youth, both at school and ·in college much time was lost by the ⌐recitations. In college we had three recitations, each day, of each division; each lasting an hour. Thus we spent three precious hours every day in hêaring other young men recite, more or less badly, what we had spent already some hours in studying ourselves. If we had learned the lesson properly, we could learn nothing more by hearing it recited by others. If the teacher had explained or illustrated the difficult passages, that would have been an advantage; but in those days he regarded it as his sole business to hear the recitation, and to mark on a paper by his side the degree of accuracy attained by each scholar. This took his whole time. A better method has been introduced in some places. Teachers now have learned that it is their business to teach, — a fact of which, in those days, they seemed wholly unaware. I have known teachers of the better sort, who would not allow a class to go through an Algebra or Geometry without making sure *that every one of the class understood everything in the book.* That was teaching. Rapid progress is made by the help of a teacher who is ready to assist the pupils over difficult places, and interest them in what is wonderful, remarkable, beautiful in the science or the book.

In the study of languages much time is wasted by insisting on too much grammar and dictionary. Instead of the dictionary, students should use translations or interlined text-books. The grammar should lie near at hand, to be consulted while translating, but should not be committed to memory. All pedants will cry out against such suggestions; but I have on my side the wisest writers on education, such as Milton, Locke, Montaigne, and a multitude of others. In Milton's Prose Works there is a Latin Grammar in about twelve pages, which he declares enough for practical purposes in learning Latin; and Milton was the great Latin scholar of his day. Locke, in his treatise on Education, advises that, in teaching Latin, no grammar be used at all, but to have a teacher able to teach Latin by conversation, without the perplexity of rules, just as a child learns his own language. "For," says Locke, "if you will consider it, Latin is no more unknown to a child than English is, when he comes into the world. And yet he learns English without master, rule, or grammar." But Locke recommends, when the right person cannot be found to teach Latin by talking, as the next best method to use an interlined translation; and in this case it may be necessary, he adds, to learn the formation of verbs, and the declension of nouns and pronouns.

But the chief rule for saving time in study, is to study only what interests the mind, and when the mind is interested. Time is wasted in dawdling over studies into which we put no heart. This also the sagacious Locke constantly dwells upon; as do other writers of insight. Thus Herbert Spencer insists, as a fundamental principle, that instruction must be always made interesting. "Nature," he says, "has made the healthful exercise of our faculties, both of body and mind, pleasurable." He adds that with all, except the most complex, which come into activity the last, "the immediate gratification consequent on activity is the normal stimulus." The method of study which produces delight is proved, he says, by all tests, to be the true one.

Of this we may be sure, that every method which can be devised to make study interesting, saves time to the student.

"I would fain," says Locke, "have any one name to me that tongue that any one can learn or speak as he should do, by the rules of grammar. Languages were made not by rules of art, but by accident, and the common use of the people. And he that speaks them well has no other rule but that." "I know not why any one should waste his time and beat his head about the Latin grammar, who does not intend to be a critic, or make speeches in it." It is lamentable to think of the amount of time wasted by children in committing to memory useless rules of grammar, when in the same time they might have learned to read the language with ease.

D'Arcy Thompson, in his excellent book called "Day Dreams of a Schoolmaster," says that all the Latin grammar which need be committed to memory by a boy could be contained in twenty-four pages.

The Latin grammar has been made absurdly complicated and difficult, but the absurdities of the English grammar taught in our common schools almost exceed belief. If grammar is "the science of language," it is a very difficult one, and ought never to be taught to children. But if it is "the art of speaking and writing correctly," then nine-tenths of what is usually taught is worse than useless. We do not learn to write and speak correctly by committing to memory unintelligible definitions and rules, but by reading well-written books, and conversing with educated speakers.

Learning to spell by means of spelling-books, orally recited, is another foolish way of wasting time. No one ever wishes to spell orally, — he only needs knowledge of spelling when he writes. Spelling, therefore, should be learned at the same time as writing, — by the teacher giving out sentences to be written down containing the words usually mis spelt.

No work which we do trains the powers, except that which we do thoroughly. Imperfect and slovenly work leaves a slovenly result in our own mind. Our thought becomes vague, and our judgment loses its definite outline. Therefore let us avoid hurry.

It is not the longest lives that have been the most full. Rafaelle died when he was thirty-seven, while Michel Angelo lived to be ninety. During his thirty-seven years, Rafaelle seems to have done as much as Michel Angelo did in his ninety years, though the genius and industry of the latter were, perhaps, fully equal to those of the other. For a single work perfectly done is enough to make a full life. Handel lived to be eighty ; Mozart died when he was only thirty-six. But who remembers how many years they lived ? As you listen to the music of Mozart, and as you look at the infants of Rafaelle, you find that each of them attained that marvellous summit of human experience in which joy and grief become one. They solve the problem of evil by showing that the deepest sorrow may be one with the highest joy. When we look at the face of the infant Jesus in the pictures of Rafaelle, and listen to the music of Mozart, we perceive in both a perfeet union of pathos and joy, of sadness and gladness, of gloom and glory, of light and shade, of sunshine and shadow, of tender pity and triumphant praise. That which no philosophy and no theology can do, art has done, to show us the element of good in evil, to show that evil is the black carbon out of which Nature manufactures her most brilliant diamonds.

The death of Christ has given this faith to the world. Jesus lived only thirty-one or thirty-three years ; the first thirty years were years of

preparation, of silence, obscurity, apparent inaction.
Then came one year of real life, which has trans-
formed the world, created a new faith in God and
man, caused us to believe in good in spite of all
appearance, and by means of this undying faith
in good has made goodness real. What a meaning in the death of Jesus is this, — that the most
cruel and wicked action has been so transfigured
and glorified that we forget all the horror of the
cross, and make it the symbol of triumph! I
presume that the cross which Constantine saw in
the skies was not miraculous in the common meaning of that term. But can anything be more miraculous in reality than this fact, — that, in three
hundred years from the death of Jesus, this instrument of a slave's torture should become the standard
of the Roman Empire? This miracle was but one
of the results of Christ's single year of labor.

To make the best use of time, we must have
life in the soul. He who is something will do
something; he who is more will do more, and he
who is most will do most. Jesus, in a single year
of active life, has done the greatest work which has
ever been done in the world; hence we may infer
that his was the fullest soul that has ever been in
the world.

Therefore, it is not a quantity of time that is
needed in order to do a great work, but the power
of using time. What we need is the eternal youth
of the heart, the undying love of truth, which will

lift us above the hard conservatism which refuses to see what it has never yet seen, and so never learns anything new.

To make the best use of time we must keep the old and accept the new. There are two kinds of men who can make no progress, — the conservative who is so conservative as never to accept the new births of time, and the radical who is so radical as to drop the old truth in order to take the new one. This obstinate conservatism, which shuts its eyes, and closes its ears, and hardens its heart against every new revelation of the divine spirit, is typified by the friend of Galileo, who refused to look through his telescope to see the satellites of Jupiter, because, according to his theory, there ought not to be any satellites there. " Look and see them," said Galileo. " I will not look," replied the other. " What is the use of looking ? I know that there are none there." But the emblem of that radicalism which can only get on new ground by deserting the old ground is the little child, whose hands are so small that he drops the apple he already holds, in order to take another. True progress is in keeping all the old truth and accepting all the new truth. So we save the time, and go on from good years to better years.

We must be something in order to do something, but we must also do something in order to be something. The best rule, I think, is this : If we find it hard to do good, then let us try to be good. If, on

IV.

SELF-KNOWLEDGE.

———◦◦◦———

THE subject of this lecture is Self-knowledge. Is it desirable, is it possible? And if so, how is it to be attained?

"Know thyself," was the maxim of Thales, the old Greek realist; a maxim thought so divine that the ancients said it fell from heaven. "Search and try your ways," said the Prophet of Judea. Modern Christian teachers have insisted on self-examination as the perpetual and universal duty. "Thomas à Kempis," "Taylor's Holy Living," all books of practical piety, inculcate it without end. "See what your motive is in everything," says Jeremy Taylor, "for the holy intention is to the actions of a man that which the soul is to its body, or the form to matter, or the root to the tree, or the sun to the world, or the fountain to a river, or the base to a pillar; for without these the body is a dead trunk, the matter is sluggish, the tree is a block, the world is darkness, the river is quickly run dry, the pillar rushes into flatness and ruin; and the action is sin-

IV

SELF-KNOWLEDGE.

————◦◦◦————

THE subject of this lecture is Self-knowledge.
Is it desirable, is it possible? And if so,
how is it to be attained?

"Know thyself," was the maxim of Thales, the
old Greek realist; a maxim thought so divine that
the ancients said it fell from heaven. "Search and
try your ways," said the Prophet of Judea. Modern
Christian teachers have insisted on self-examination
as the perpetual and universal duty. "Thomas à
Kempis," "Taylor's Holy Living," all books of practical piety, inculcate it without end. "See what
your motive is in everything," says Jeremy Taylor,
"for the holy intention is to the actions of a man
that which the soul is to its body, or the form to
matter, or the root to the tree, or the sun to the
world, or the fountain to a river, or the base to a
pillar; for without these the body is a dead trunk,
the matter is sluggish, the tree is a block, the world
is darkness, the river is quickly run dry, the pillar
rushes into flatness and ruin; and the action is sin-

ful, unprofitable, and vain." Not only religious teachers, but philosophers and poets, have taught the importance of self-knowledge. Burns says, —

> " O wad some power the giftie gie us,
> To see ourselves as others see us ! "

And Pythagoras advised that "sleep should not seize upon the region of the senses before we have three times recalled the conversation and incidents of the day," in order to know what we have done or omitted to do.

In a moral point of view, the importance of self-examination is that we may not deceive ourselves, imagining we are better than we are. Man has the curious power of deceiving himself, when he cannot deceive others. It is sad even to tragedy to see how some persons are puffed up, like the frog who thought to make himself as large as the bull by swelling. People deceive themselves about their capacity, their motives, their character. How many persons persuade themselves, whenever they wish to do anything, that it is their duty to do it. Some persons go through the world believing all the time that they do just about what they ought, and because they have some rule or principle of action, think they are conforming to it. They " cast the mote out of the eye " of their brother, and do not perceive the beam in their own. They " compound for sins they are inclined to; by damning those they have no mind to." Then we call them hypocrites.

But they are not so, not deliberate hypocrites. They are not cheating us, they are cheating themselves. They are walking on straight toward a day of judgment, utterly ignorant of what they really are. They are like the cruel jailer in Charles Reade's story, who tortured his prisoners in the most horrible way, and then went to his room and cried over "Uncle Tom's Cabin," and did not think it possible there could be such cruelty as Legree's in the world.

But for purposes of intellectual self-culture, as for those of religion and morality, self-knowledge is necessary. Before we can really acquire any accomplishment or develop any power, we need to know what we can do, and what we cannot. For men are not made alike; they are made differently.

There is a theory, I know, which assumes that all persons are alike at first, and become different from force of circumstances, or from their own efforts. No father or mother who has brought up a family of half a dozen children will believe such a doctrine as that. The little things, as soon as they are born, show symptoms of the traits which they continue to have all their days. One child has a strong will, but is easily guided by his affections; another is cold; one is quick, but changeable; another slow, but persistent; one is reserved, another open; one has a taste for music, so that he sings from his cradle; another a tendency to construction, so that he makes all his toys himself; one, like George Washington, cannot tell a lie, and another, poor

little thing! finds it hard to tell the truth. Just as
a young duck runs to the water, young children run
to the work or play, the pictures, the poetry, which
they are made for. Every observing father and
mother sees this, and laughs at the philosopher who
tells them that children are born alike, and made
different by circumstances.

No; "every man has his special gift from the
Lord,— some after this fashion, and some after that;"
and the point is to find out what we are, what we
are made to be, and to do. This sort of self-knowl
edge prevents discouragement. Children are often
thought to be stupid, and think themselves that they
are so, merely because they are trying to do something they are not fitted for. Other children are
thought infant prodigies, because they happen possibly to possess a fine verbal memory, and can repeat, like parrots, what they hear. So they grow
conceited upon their one faculty; and find out, too
late, that the memory of words is only one part, and
a very small part, of intellectual power. Walter
Scott was considered a very stupid boy, out of whom
nothing could be made. He was a kind of fruit
which ripened slowly; the best kind often does so.
I heard Dr. Spurzheim say that a young man had
that day told him, "Dr. Spurzheim, you do not
know me, but you were the greatest benefactor to
me on one occasion You came into the school
where I was. I was considered the greatest block-
head in the school, and believed it myself, and did

not think it worth while to try to learn. You put your hand on my head, and said, ' Perceptive organs small ; he does not do much now. Reflective organs very good ; when he comes to the studies which ex ercise those faculties, he will be one of the brightest boys in the school.' This gave me courage, and I found it was really so. When I came to the studies which required thought, instead of mere memory, I went to the head of my class."

When, therefore, I speak of self-knowledge, and of self-examination in order to self-knowledge, I do not mean merely the knowledge of our sins or our virtue. I do not mean a continual searching into our motives, and a constant picking to pieces of our own soul to see how it works. This sort of self-examina- tion may be carried a great deal too far. Most books of piety and morality make that mistake. They inculcate a self-scrutiny which is fatal to healthy moral life. (To watch one's soul all the time, seeking for moral disease, is as bad as to search one's body all the time, seeking for physical disease. We know what that leads to.) It produces hypo- chondria. A man comes to fancy that he has every possible malady he is looking for.' Every part of the body, in turn, becomes the seat of pain ; the head seems about to burst ; the heart about to stop ; and the symptoms which simulate all diseases ap- pear. These hypochondriacs are the torments of their physicians, and think they are insulted if their com- plaints are called imaginary. There is a spiritual hypochondria of the same kind. A man who is searching his motives to find how much sin and selfishness there is in him, will find a great deal. He torments himself with all sorts of fears; he is afraid he has no piety, no genuine charity; that his prayers are false, his repentance insincere; he thinks he has blasphemed the Holy Ghost, and committed the unpardonable sin; and if his spiritual adviser denies this, he thinks himself being misled, and very badly treated. One danger of the Roman' Catholic confessional is the tendency to produce this disease, and sometimes the opposite state of spiritual pride and self-deception. Blanco White says that in the Spanish nunneries this spiritual disease is very common, and even has received a special name. It is called *Los Escrupelos*, the "Scruples." The physician who has a hypochondriac patient, and the Roman Catholic confessor who has one of these self-tormentors in his confessional, are equally to be pitied.

By self-examination I mean something different. I do not mean this sort of daily self-inspection which tends to egotism and which freezes the heart. You must not keep pulling up the seeds to see if they are growing. If you do this, you kill them. The tree is known by its fruits, not by its roots, nor yet by a chemical analysis of its sap and fibre. When the great ocean steamer is battling with the Atlantic, they do not put out the fires every day in order to examine the boilers. They give them one careful examination in port. When at sea, if the engine works well, and the steam-gauge tells the proper story, they conclude that all is right.

I do not believe in any minute self-scrutiny. I believe in a general self-examination, once for all, or once in a great while, and then in looking to see whether the engine is doing its work; in daily self-examination, not of the motives, but of the conduct, of the actual life. Do not look within, to see whether you have sinned against the Holy Ghost, or whether your feelings are right; but look without, to see what you are doing for others; what you are saying; what your temper and spirit are to those about you. If the engine is looking well, and the vessel is running, you may assume that the boilers are in good order. Look up, also, for higher light, and for more life.

But we need a certain general knowledge of human nature in order to gain a special self-knowledge. To know what our particular capacity is, what our special defects are, we need some systematic knowledge of the soul. It is true that, without any such system of psychology, we get a knowledge of human nature from life. We also learn a great deal about mankind from history, biography, the drama, poetry, novels. Probably these teach us more, and more truly, on the whole, than any system of moral or mental philosophy. A play of Shakspeare's, or a novel by Dickens, shows us human beings in action; human faculties at work and alive : metaphysics shows them inactive, and taken apart. The one is like the study of muscles in an anatomical museum; the other, like studying them in a gymnasium. But I think that, as, in order to know the body, we must see it in both ways; so, in order to know the soul, we must not only read history and poetry and see actual life, but it is also desirable to have some methodized system of human nature; for only thus can we be prevented from being one-sided; from laying too much stress on some qualities, too little on others. We ought to have a knowledge of the whole soul while studying its separate faculties.

And of all systematic divisions of human nature into faculties and powers, I think that of phrenology, on the whole, the most convenient, merely as the basis of self-examination. I think so for several reasons; first, because it is founded on actual observations of life, and therefore is true in the main. I am not now speaking of craniology, or the shape of the head, but of phrenology, or the arrangement of human powers. I like it, though it does not give us the depths and heights of human nature. But it presents a good sketch, for working purposes, of the various powers of the human soul. It has nothing to say of the soul itself; it only speaks of its organs, its faculties, its tools. It has nothing to say of freedom; that is assumed, or not, as you will. The phrenological arrangement of human faculties leaves all these questions just where they were, neither asserting nor denying anything in regard to them.

I recommend the phrenological arrangement of human powers simply as a convenient one in self-study. If a man wishes to know what he is fit for and capable of, this gives him a useful method of investigation. It divides, for example, all our powers into mental, moral, and passional, — intellect, morals, and affections. To the intellectual region belong, first, the perceptive faculties, by which we take notice of outward objects; observe their size, form, weight, and color. Then the reasoning powers, by which we compare objects to see if they are alike or unlike, if they are cause and effect, if they are congruous or incongruous. Then there is the imagination, which makes a picture of the whole while examining the parts. Then, again, come the moral qualities, — sympathy, reverence, conscience, firmness. Then follow the passional and energetic powers, which supply movement and force, as self-reliance, the desire of approbation, the desire for home, the love of family and friends, the passion for battling with difficulties, the passion for destroying evils, the passion for collecting property in all its forms, the desire of construction, which is the basis of all art. Now, this may be, or may not be, the best classification of human powers; but it is, at least, a nearly exhaustive classification. Add, as the basis of it, the soul itself, and its freedom, which is the essence of the soul, and this classification shows well enough what our faculties and powers are.

One advantage of this classification is that it helps us to make very useful distinctions in self-study. For instance, the old mental philosophy recognized only one kind of memory. A person had a good memory, or a bad one. Now, we know that there are a great many different kinds of memory. One person remembers names, but forgets faces; another easily remembers lines of poetry, but not prose; another recollects single facts and dates with remarkable tenacity, but has little memory for causes, reasons, or arguments. I, myself, can remember ten thousand lines of poetry, but, though I have lived in Boston since I was a little boy, I cannot describe the looks and size of the buildings on Washington Street, between Milk Street and State Street. And yet I can give you a general picture of any city in Europe which I may have seen during only a few days. Phrenology explains all this by teaching us that every organ has its own memory. A large organ of time remembers time. A person who has a great deal of this can often tell what o'clock it is without a watch; a large organ of tune remembers music; a large organ of language remembers names; a large organ of configuration remembers faces and forms; a large organ of imagination remembers the general aspect of a country, of a story, of a face.

One advantage of this system is that it shows us how every power has its use and its abuse; how God has made everything in us good, but that we can abuse everything by excess. It also shows how one faculty may correct the excesses of another, or supply its deficiencies. Thus what the phrenologist calls the organs of combativeness and destructiveness are most important and valuable in their proper sphere. They help us to wage the battle of life, to conquer difficulties, to meet opposition, to resist and destroy evil and wrong; in short, to fight the good fight, and finish the work given us to do. No man can be an eminent philanthropist or a martyr without them. But they can easily be carried to excess, or exercised in a wrong direction. Then they make us quarrelsome, controversial, satirical, vindictive, lashing others with tongue or pen, and striking them with the dagger of sharp, poisonous, bitter, unkind words. They make termagants and scolds, fault-finders and Papal inquisitors. On the other hand, the best moral tendencies may be excessive, or misdirected. The lovely power of sympathy, which causes so much happiness, which makes men enter into the feelings of others, rejoice with those who rejoice, and weep with those who weep; which constitutes so much of the sweetness and comfort of life; this, also, may be excessive or one-sided. Then it makes persons weak and false, yielding to the present influence, loving the person who is near, forgetting the one who is absent, neglecting past promises, and so tending to insincerity. Therefore this tendency needs to be restrained by firmness, self-esteem, and conscientiousness. But these, in turn, though good, are also easily carried to excess. Self-esteem produces self-reliance, which is one of the most essential features of character. Without it, character can hardly exist. It is the organ of sincerity, of independence, of personality. Yet it tends to dogmatism, to egotism, to assumption of superiority, to overbearing manners, forgetting the claims of others; and it makes the character hard and cold. Even the conscience may be diseased. Conscience may be too irritable, or too scrupulous; it may be always tormenting the soul with questions about imaginary sins; it may make us so afraid of doing wrong that we shall never do anything right. Firmness may become obstinacy; the love of order may grow into pedantry; the love of home take one away from social and public duties. Even reverence may become a fault. It is the crown of the whole moral nature, and has been therefore fitly found .by phrenologists on the summit of the head. It produces that beautiful modesty which, when accompanying manliness, is so charming; it creates that respect for all that is above us, which lifts the soul; it is the great incentive to nobleness; it is the power which enables us to rise above ourselves in the worship of goodness, whether human or divine. Shakspeare calls it "that angel of the world;" Goethe calls it "the crown of the whole moral nature." It is the power of moral harmony; which makes a concord of all discordant things, by opening the soul to the highest and best of all.

And yet even this great and wonderful power may be abused. It may, if not enlightened by reason and truth, lead to gross superstitions and worship of the letter and the form. It may become idolatry. It is essentially the religious organ, but it leads, when unenlightened and unregulated, to the worst abuses. All the cruelties practised in the name of religion have been the results of an unenlightened reverence. If we reverence a being as God whom we believe wilful, cruel, unjust, or partial, then our reverence tends to make us, also, wilful, cruel, and partial. The special abuse of reverence is idolatry, which is worshipping the letter instead of the spirit. To worship a form, a name, a letter, instead of the spirit, hurts the soul. To worship the letter of a creed, of a church, of the Bible, injures the spirit. That is why the Apostle declares that "the letter killeth."

The great advantage of any self-study which shows us what are our special organic defects and corresponding gifts and powers, is that it makes us both humble and hopeful. Self-conceit comes from a vague imagination of possessing some great genius or superiority; and not from any actual, precise knowledge of what we are. Actual knowledge of one's self will always show us that some temptation besets every success; that some opportunity comes with every failure; that our weaknesses have a strength hidden in them; that our strength has also its weak side. "Every one," says the French proverb, "has the defects of his qualities;" every one, also, has the qualities of his defects. "Our virtues and vices," says a great thinker, "grow out of the same roots." And does not Jesus intimate as much in that parable which teaches that, in trying to pull up the tares, we may run the risk of pulling up the wheat, too? That is the risk which those run who try to root out and destroy every natural tendency in man, because of the abuses which it occasions. Christ, who did not come to destroy anything, but to fulfil everything, said, "Let both grow together till the harvest." We cannot always root out an evil tendency; but we can often grow it out. Give more life, more growth, more sun and rain, more truth and love, — these powers of growth will conquer the evils in the soul and in the heart.

These considerations, as I have said, make us both humble and hopeful. We are humble in thinking that our best success and our highest gifts have their danger. We are hopeful when we see that even the worst thing in us can be turned to good. So God, in his great geological workshops, makes diamonds out of carbon and rubies out of clay. Man's brain is a self-compensating machine, an automatic, self-correcting apparatus. God has set in it two against two; every power has its antagonist power. He has placed in man a tendency to hope, and another to caution, as its counterweight. He has given self-reliance, and also sympathy; he has inspired the wish to battle with wrong and evil; he has added the tendency to reverence and submit to good. He has given us powers which take us outward into the world of things and men; others which draw us inward to the world of imagination and reflection.

But man is not a mere machine, nor is organization the whole. The body, after all, is only the chest of tools which the soul uses. And just as one man with a jack-knife can do more than another with a whole box of tools, so we see some men of comparatively small natural powers accomplish more in the course of life than others of great genius, who have neglected their gifts or abused them. The power which modifies all organization, and lifts us above the control of matter and structure, is the power of conviction, of a living faith in truth. Self-knowledge is an immense help in progress, but it is a small thing compared with the knowledge of God, truth, duty, and goodness. In the history of the world we have seen the most richly endowed nations sleep on, undeveloped and inactive, through long centuries, and then, inspired by some great conviction, flame up into magnanimities and heroisms without example. So it was with the Arabs in the time of Mohammed; with the Greeks in the age of Miltiades and Pericles. So, in biography, we find vast results proceeding from the soul of some man not very greatly endowed, not very richly organized, but who has been fired by a sublime conviction. The founders of religions, the movers of reformations, have usually been men with some special organic gifts, indeed, but, more than that, men magnetized by a deep conviction.

I recollect that once, when I lived in the West, there came a phrenologist to the town and examined the heads of all the clergymen in the place, and found us all deficient in the organ of reverence. More than that, we all admitted that the fact was so; that we were not, any of us, specially gifted with natural piety or love for worship. Then he said, "You have all mistaken your calling. You ought not to have been ministers." But I, for one, protested against that sentence, for I knew that, though I had no natural tendency to worship or pray, I had come by experience to know that I could not live well without prayer. Though I did not pray from sentiment, and feeling, I was able to pray from conviction and faith.

The sight of truth is the necessary supplement to the power of structure. Without the sight of truth, man is the slave of his organization. Study his head, and you can, perhaps, tell what he may be. But, endowed with truth, he is the master of his organization; he makes it serve him. He is able to see what are its defects, and supply them. If he finds himself too hopeful, he studies to supplement his hope by a greater caution; if he sees that he is too timid, he encourages himself to do his work more bravely. If his sympathy runs away with him, he meets this by educating his self-reliance. If his imagination is too active, he supplies the fault by a habit of increased reflection, and by more devoted attention to facts. He is thus like the man who steers a ship, with the compass before his eyes, showing which way the vessel is moving; with the chart in the cabin, telling which way it ought to go; with the helm in his hand, enabling him to turn it to the right or left as need requires. But the mighty winds of divine truth coming from above; the mighty fires within, of a divinely-gifted organization, — these supply the motive-power; and what he has to do is to keep the course in his mind, and to keep the compass in his eye, and to keep his hand on the helm, always steering the ship in the right direction.

This is human freedom, and these are its limitations. We are not free to become anything we choose, or to do anything we wish. We are limited outwardly by circumstances, inwardly by our own organic tendencies. But, if we have any sure convictions of what is true, right, and good, we can steer that way. We can study our complex nature, and when we come to know it, we can encourage and cultivate what is best, discourage what is likely to lead us astray. We cannot make circumstances, but we can select those which are favorable. We can make use of the power of habit to fix and solidify all our good qualities. And, above all, if we believe in an ever-present God, and a divine influence from him, we can trust ourselves to his care, and open our hearts to his inspiration, and so be lifted up into the serene atmosphere of peace and purity, away from whatever is dangerous to the soul.

V

EDUCATION OF THE POWERS OF OBSERVATION.

V.

EDUCATION OF THE POWERS OF OBSERVATION.

———✦◆◆✦———

I HAVE to speak next of the perceptive organs, — the faculties of observation in man, — and their education.

The immense importance of these faculties appears from the fact that by means of these, and of these alone, the soul comes in contact with this whole external universe of God.

I am not now merely speaking of the bodily senses, — the eye, the ear, the smell, the touch, the taste. Behind these senses are the organs which use them ; and behind these, the soul itself, with its faculties. We must not confound the organs of observation with the senses, for then we limit the power of their education. Perhaps the eye and ear cannot be trained to very much greater quickness and power, but the faculties which use the eye and ear certainly can.

Hitherto we have neglected too much the education of the faculties of observation. Yet the power of noticing and remembering the outward phenomena

8

of the world is one which may be very highly educated. The North American Indian had no better
eyes than the white man; but he had trained his
powers of observation in a certain direction, till no
sign of the woods escaped him. A turned leaf, a
broken twig, the faintest film of smoke against the
sky, betrayed to him the passage or presence of an
enemy. But the white man readily learned this
art, and the hunters of Kentucky were soon able to
match the Indian in his knowledge of the signs of
the wilderness.

In-door life and mechanical inventions dull the
powers of observation. Instead of noticing the shad-
dows of the trees to find the hour, we look at the
clock; instead of observing the movement of the sun
to and from the north for the seasons, we examine
the almanac; instead of looking at the movements
of the clouds for the weather and winds, we look at
the barometer, and examine the Probabilities in the
newspaper. With all our book knowledge, our school
culture, we are conscious of a certain inferiority
when we meet a man taught by Nature, — one who
knows the woods, the birds and beasts; one who can
help himself when lost in the forest or overtaken by
tempests. A gentleman once told me that he went
to visit his brother, who had long lived in Texas.
His brother introduced him to an old settler, rough
and ready, who looked at him, and said, in a friendly
way, "You'll learn something by and by; your
brother was very green when *he* first came here."

We live too much in-doors. The out-door races — the Indians of America, the hunters of the West, the Arabs of Asia and Africa — have a more exhilarating life than ours, because always in contact with air and sun, sky and plain. But we need not turn Arabs or Indians in order to commune with Nature. We can have all the blessings of a high civilization, and yet retain the health of body and mind which comes from being immersed in God's great world of external phenomena, if we will educate the powers of observation.

We begin the mistake in our schools. There we teach chiefly words, seldom things. Even object-teaching, in the primary schools, which promised to supply this defect, has, in many places, relapsed into the teaching of words. I have seen object-teaching of this sort. The skeleton of a dog or cat is placed on a table. The teacher says, "This is a skeleton. What is this?" Then the children repeat, "A skeleton." The teacher touches the skull, and says, "This is a skull. What is this?" Then the children repeat, "A skull." Now, it is true that the children here see an object, while its name is given them; but what they learn is the name. They do not learn to observe.

I know it is difficult, in a city, to teach the children of the schools to observe outward facts. Yet much may be done by museums, gardens, and green houses, in which specimens of plants, minerals, and animals are arranged and classified, as in the great collections in Europe. And, in the country, why should not the children be taught to make collections themselves of grasses, fungi, lichens, leaves, bark; of the different stones and earth; to observe and describe insects, birds, fishes. I think a text-book might be prepared for the schools, which should contain descriptions of the Mineralogy, Flora and Fauna of New England; that is, of all the common weeds, flowers, trees, birds, insects, animals, and the geological formations just around us here. Every child ought to know, first of all, the wonderful creations of God in the midst of which it lives. Think of the absurdity of spending so much time at school, and then of not knowing the difference between a beech and an oak, between a piece of quartz and a fragment of marble! Yet such is the result, often, of our system of education, which devotes years to learning the names of towns in India and China, or the absurdities of English grammar, and not an hour to the common things which lie around us.

It would seem from the study of the brain that man has distinct organs for observing individual facts and events, the shapes and forms of things, words and names, the pressure and resistance of objects, the progress of time, the tints of color, and melodies of sound. Each of these faculties can be trained and developed. By careful practice all can be greatly improved. The members of a family might agree to remember and relate every evening the events of the day, to describe the persons they have seen, to repeat the striking remarks they have heard, and to cultivate habits of careful observation. Drawing from memory faces and figures, making rapid sketches in walking or travelling of picturesque scenery, educate the organs of form. Drawing from memory outline maps, as practised in schools, does the same. By practice, a person can learn to tell the height or length of a room within a few inches; the weight of an object held in the hand to within half an ounce. By practice, a list of a dozen or twenty names, heard a single time, can be remembered. Such accomplishments, once acquired, give pleasure in the exercise; for this is a law of human nature, which causes what is once gained to be secured. Study which does not result in accomplishment is bad, for we forget easily what does not root itself by means of useful attainments and skilled processes. One reason why a language is learned so rapidly in the country where it is spoken is this: that everything so learned is turned instantly to use, and becomes an accomplishment. If, in France, I learn to ask for a plate or a napkin, there is a certain pleasure in this, and I repeat it as an accomplishment, and so fix the knowledge.

One of the best methods of educating the perceptive powers is by the study of some science, as botany, geology, zoölogy, or some form of natural history. These ought to take us out of doors, put us in the fields and woods, show us Nature, open our eyes and awaken observation. The botanist walks on, hour after hour, searching for some plant, till he detects its *habitat* by the side of a stream, or on the damp borders of a quiet lake. The ornithologist steps with the light tread of an Indian over the rocks and leaves, following the whistle of a thrush or the cry of a cat-bird, till he detects the little lady, sitting in maiden meditation, fancy free, among the leaves, and watches her gentle movements till he comes to know her by heart. Then the student of geology walks over hill and plain, reading a great history of one hundred thousand years in the swell and roll of the meadow, in the rounded escarpment of rocks, in the long level of the plateaus.

I rejoice much in the increasing interest in such studies. They bring us into loving relations with the great universe of God, that roaring loom of Time which forever weaves the garment of the Almighty, the garment by which he becomes visible. They educate those powers which half perceive and half create (as Wordsworth says) the world. One of my friends spent four months in a visit to Japan, and used such diligence as to bring back hundreds of specimens of curious living beings. Another friend, instead of passing his winter at dinner-parties and in clubs, goes to dredge in the Gulf of Mexico for the lower forms of life. One summer, at the sea-shore, I found a school of students, with their microscopes, diligently studying varieties of the sponge. And, last summer, sitting on our piazza in the evening, we were mystified by the appearance of a lantern,

moving to and fro in a neighboring field, with uncon-
firmed intent, till late at night. At last, we went
to see what it could be, thinking the man was look
ing for something valuable which had been lost;
and, behold! it was a naturalist catching night-moths.
Now this new interest in all the lower forms of life
is certainly a good thing. Since the Creator has not
thought it beneath his dignity to make them, we
must not consider it beneath ours to study them.
Last night, we watched from our roof that lovely
phenomenon, the approach of Venus to the moon, till
a cloud received them out of our sight. Have we not
reason to admire the goodness of God, who has given
us power of observation, by which we can perceive
the motions of these majestic luminaries, millions of
miles away in the depths of space; and, also, study
the minute animalcules which pass their days in a
spoonful of water, and, no doubt, enjoy that small
existence in their way, as we do ours.

A certain amount of out-of-door life is necessary
to bodily health, and without bodily health how can
we have mental vigor, moral purity, or spiritual
peace? What people think to be sin in themselves
is often only disease, dyspepsia; what we censure
sharply in others, as a fault of temper, is only the
want of fresh air. The minister recommends a girl
or young man to spend certain hours in his closet at
prayer, when what he really needs is to take a long
walk in the country. It is difficult for a sick man
to fulfil his social duties; good health, therefore, lies

at the basis of morals, manners, and religion. But
the conditions of health are simple; they depend on
this prescription, composed of five parts, to be taken
daily: (1) Sun; (2) air; (3) exercise; (4) plain, nour-
ishing food; (5) a contented mind. Given these five
conditions, and if we are not well, neither patent
medicines, nor those famous doctors who can only
stay in Boston a few days longer, will avail us anything.

But what is to take us out into the air and sun,
and give us exercise, and the healthy appetite which
enjoys plain food? Only some attraction. We cannot be driven out from a sense of duty; we must
be drawn out by an interest in some out-of-doors
pursuit.

I knew a man in Brattleboro', a shoemaker by
trade, who was rapidly going into consumption. His
wise physician said to him: "Nothing will save
you but to be out of doors six or eight hours every
day. But you will never stay out of doors this
length of time unless you have something to attract
you, and that something must be some study. Choose
some study, and pursue it." The man chose botany,
and became familiar with all the plants of his region.
In winter, he studied lichens and mosses, and he
not only recovered his health, but became one of the
first botanists in New England, and, as far as I could
see, his business as a shoemaker went on as prosper-
ously as before.

This leads me to say that less time given to

business would often enable us to do it more effectually. Men stupefy themselves by staying all day
in their shops or counting-rooms. Every human
being needs a change, and God has meant that a
part of our life shall be spent out of doors, in observing the magnificent world which he has created
for us.

Consider, also, the moral influence of the study of
the natural sciences. Nature feeds the soul inwardly
with content. She satisfies us with herself. Go
into the fields and woods; row your boat on the
ocean, or the river, or lake; spend a day in climbing
a mountain; pass a week in the wilderness, — and
all cares seem to drift out of your mind and heart.
What has become of all those anxieties about our
life, about our success and failure? What has become of our ambitions, our desire for social triumphs,
our rivalries, our small vanities? They have all
been washed away by this bath of mountain air.
That tall pine-tree, with its voice of silvery music,
speaking to us as out of a period before the flood,
has calmed our heart. We envy no one, we are
jealous of no one, while we see that angry cardinal
flower by the side of the brook. Or, when, by night,
we watch the stars, and study the vast constellations; when we see, through a telescope, the double-
stars, purple and gold, shining like emeralds and
rubies in the immense depths of the sky; when we
see the nebulæ composed of a million solar systems, but seeming like a soft cloud in the profound

abysses of space, — our anxieties, our heats, our foolish fears and fond desires pass out of us. What no moral training can do, this communion with God in his universe of Nature accomplishes.

Last summer I met, in the middle of New York, a famous politician. To my surprise and pleasure, during the day or two which I passed in his company he had no word to say about politics, but described with unfeigned joy his early experience in the Adirondack woods, where he spent winters in camp, sleeping in his blanket on the snow, and enjoying the winter forms of forest and mountain. No doubt he had collected there some of the force and facility which he afterward used in the affairs of state. I thought of what Mr. Emerson said in his first printed book : " The poet, the orator, bred in the woods, whose senses have been nourished by their fair and appeasing changes, year after year, without design or heed, shall not lose their lessons in the roar of cities and the broil of politics. Long hereafter, amid agitation and terror in national councils, these solemn images shall reappear in their morning lustre, as fit symbols for the language of the hour. At the call of a noble sentiment, again the woods wave, the pines murmur, the river rolls and shines, and the cattle low upon the mountains, putting the spells of persuasion, the keys of power, into his hands."

There is also a religious side to our subject. God has set the members every one in the body as it has pleased him, — eye and ear, touch and taste and smell. He has given us faculties of observation, organs of perception, by which to observe his work in the world. He has also created for us this dome of heaven, these solemn fires of night, these drifting, changing clouds by day. He has made this earth so rich and so lovely, with its sights and sounds, its mountain precipices, its rolling prairies, its vast blue lakes, its tumbling cataracts, its ocean with long swell, rolling night and day on the shore, like the perpetual beating of the human heart. He has made the varieties of plants, leaves, flowers, trees ; the birds, fishes, insects. Since he has thought it fit to create this vast and wonderful world, shall we not think it worth our while to see it. Is there not an irreverence in this ? Will not the idolaters who worship the sun and moon and stars, seeing something of God in his works, rise up and condemn us, who spend all our week-days in our shops, and go to church on Sunday for a sermon, but never lift up our eyes on high to see who has created all these things ? Wordsworth, in one of his finest sonnets, rebukes this neglect of Nature thus : —

"The world is too much with us ; late and soon,
  Getting and spending, we lay waste our powers !
  Little we see in Nature that is ours ;
  We have given our lives away, a sordid boon !
  The sea, that bares her bosom to the moon,
  The winds, that will be howling at all hours,
  And are regathered now, like sleeping flowers ;
  For this, for everything, we are out of tune.

It moves us not.   Great God!   I'd rather be
A Pagan, suckled in a creed outworn ;
So might I, standing on this pleasant lea,
Have glimpses that would make me less forlorn ;
Have sight of Proteus, rising from the sea ;
Or hear old Triton blow his wreathéd horn."

But the powers of observation are educated by the study of art, as well as by the study of nature. Every child ought to learn to draw, as well as to read and write.   Not in order to draw poor figures and bad landscapes, but in order to sketch easily and readily whatever object he sees and wishes to remember.   The power of drawing in perspective, which can be acquired in a week, is a satisfaction during all one's life.   Sketching picturesque objects — trees, forms, faces — leads to observation, cultivates observation.   Many of us go through the streets, and see hundreds of faces, and never notice them.   Yet God has made each human face with its separate expression, its own story.   In each one is written a prophecy of possibilities, a history of successes and failures.   Are not these worth noticing?

I recollect, when I first saw portraits by the great masters, — an Ignatius Loyola, by Rubens; a Grotius, by Rembrandt; and those tender and noble faces and forms by Vandyke, Titian, Sir Joshua Reynolds, and Gainsborough, — I seemed not only to have found an art I never dreamed of, but also to have been introduced into a deeper knowledge of human nature.   A face by Titian is like a character of Shakspeare, — it is so much added to humanity.

You read in it a poem of the soul; some large and generous purpose, or deep resolve; or a struggle continued patiently, hopefully, against overwhelming obstacles. You look at those portraits and go away, and then wish to go back to study them again. There are faces in European galleries that rise before me now, like the features of a long-lost friend. But what is the secret of that skill, but that the artist saw — what we might, also, have seen and did not see — the hidden interior expression, the face behind the face, of the real man. If we cared enough for our fellow-creatures, we should look at them and see them as they really are. Every face, which now appears to us as commonplace and tame, would thus become profoundly interesting. In the humblest and poorest we might find some romance and some charm. To the person who knows how to look, the mask drops off, and the real man and woman appear. Love reads every secret in the changing expression of brow, lips, and eyes. Love watches the cloud, unapparent to others, which for a moment darkens the sunshine of the smile. If we loved our fellow-men we should notice them, and so humanity and sympathy would educate the powers of observation.

Thus Christianity, which teaches us to love God with all our heart, mind, soul, and strength, and to love our neighbor as ourselves, tends even to cultivate the perceptive faculties. This benign influence, descending into the lowest details and crannies of human life, ennobling all nature, throwing a glory and a glow over all earthly interests, calling nothing common or unclean, will vitalize science, art, literature, the intercourse of man with man, and teach us how to take an interest even in reptiles, insects, and weeds, since these, also, are creatures of God.

We have already mentioned how the ancient Egyptians, the most sharp-sighted of men for out ward facts, looked with awe on the mystery of organic life. To them there was something sacred in the growth of a plant out of a seed, and the strange forms and instincts of animals. In this they were surely wiser than we are, if we neglect to notice these mysteries of creation, and think it not worth while to look at those things which God has thought it worth while to place around us. " In wonder," says Coleridge, " all philosophy begins, and in wonder it ends." He who does not see, with admiring curiosity, how wonderful the world is, does not see the world at all.

There is one remarkable physical power in man, the only one perhaps in which he excels all other animals. This is the balancing faculty, by which he is able to stand upright, though naturally top-heavy, — a faculty which manifests itself also in a variety of other applications. It is the sense of momentum, of equilibrium, of resistance. It operates by means of the antagonist muscles, which restrain each other, modulating all motion, preventing it from being jerky. Jerkiness in movement is awkwardness; modulated movements are graceful. This power modulates the voice in speaking or singing, making speech fluent and not abrupt. In writing or drawing it gives uniformity of pressure. In music it produces delicacy and precision of touch on the stringed instrument, and a measured pressure of air in the wind instrument. It is, therefore, a very important faculty, and deserves to be carefully developed. It is capable of being trained to a high degree of perfection, as we see in the case of rope-dancers, who will stand with one foot balanced on a single wire, and keep four or five plates in the air revolving on the points of as many sticks held in the hand. Mountain-climbers, sailors who lie out on the yard-arm when the vessel is rolling in a gale, slaters who walk on a sloping roof, — all have trained this faculty. Its education begins with the first attempt of a child to stand upright. This is a much more difficult operation than we usually suppose; for man is so top-heavy in his structure that his centre of gravity is almost always outside of the base. A statue of a man standing on his feet could hardly be made which would not immediately topple over. It is evident, therefore, that we are always holding ourselves up when we are standing, though by an unconscious action of the will.

The advantage of training this faculty is that it gives grace to all human actions. It modulates our walk, speech, and writing. The man who walks ungracefully throws his foot forward with a jerk; while the graceful walker *puts* it forward with a restrained movement, which is not merely mechanical, but dynamical. The soul goes into every act to make grace. If one remembers this, and avoids all jerky movement, he will learn to walk gracefully He will not pitch himself forward in walking, but go on with a balanced attitude of the body. It has often been remarked that those who carry weights on their heads acquire a graceful movement. The reason is that they are obliged to balance themselves at every step. Dancing has the same result. In our common conversation we can give pleasure and escape sharp tones, by avoiding jerkiness in speech. Such are some of the practical uses of this sense of equilibrium, a physical function which has hitherto been scarcely noticed.

Let us, then, thank God for these powers of ob servation, and employ them to his glory, by educating them to finer uses, and becoming better acquainted with his creation.

VI.

THE EDUCATION OF THE RE
ELECTIVE POWERS.

VI.

THE EDUCATION OF THE REFLECT IVE POWERS.

M AN acquires knowledge in two ways, — by per- ception, or intuition ; by looking out through the senses, or looking in by his intuitions. By means of his perceptive organs he becomes ac- quainted with the external world ; he comes in con- tact with nature, society, history. By means of his intuitions he sees the truths of the eternal world, the laws of spiritual being, abstracted from phe- nomena. By the perceptive powers he comes in contact with the actual universe ; by the intuitive faculties he lays hold of the ideal universe.

Knowledge, therefore, is acquired by these two methods ; knowledge of the external universe, by perception ; knowledge of the internal universe, by intuition.

The reflective faculties have a different function to perform. They do not give us any new truth ; they give no knowledge. But they arrange, classify, sys- tematize, put in order, make accessible, the truth re- ceived through these other channels. They take the crude material and manufacture it, so that we not only have it, but possess it; not only know it, but know that we know it, and are able to use it.

We do our thinking by means of the reflective faculties. And the chief intellectual difference between men is, that some think and others do not. Some men put their minds to all they do; others, not. But thinking is hard work, perhaps the hardest work that is done on the surface of the planet; and by means of thinking all other work is accomplished. Therefore, among all men, the thinkers are the laboring classes. Thought is the most practical and powerful of all the forces now acting on the globe, to modify its aspect. Civilization is another name for thinking. Civilized man is thinking man; the uncivilized races are men perfect in body, in powers of perception, in muscular and vital force, in physical energy; but they do not think. Thinking man has conquered nature. By thought, iron has been taken from the mine, and turned into every implement; by thought, steam, a giant with a hundred arms, makes cloth, planes, bends and cuts metal, manufactures everything we need. It drives ships over the ocean and cars over the continent. Thought builds cities. Thought tells the lightning to run its errand; and the lightning, an obedient fairy, puts a girdle round the earth in forty seconds. Thought tells the sun to paint its pictures; and the sun, in Europe, Asia, Africa, America, photographs everything we wish to see. Thought weighs the mountains in scales, and the hills in a balance; takes for a measuring tape the distance between the earth and the sun, and with that line measures the enormous spaces which separate the sun from the stars. Thought takes the globe in pieces and sees how it was made; unfolds it, leaf by leaf; reads how, hundreds of thousands of years ago, it was covered with an armor of ice ; how, before that, it was enveloped in hot vapors. Thus thought shows us each act and scene of the mighty earth drama, and introduces one set of performers after another on the stage ; enormous saurian reptiles in one act, strange fishes and birds in another; till, at last, man arrives " to close the drama with the day."

When I heard Dr. Spürzheim lecture on phrenology, he taught us that there were two reflective organs in the forehead, and that all our thinking was done by the use of these two little convolutions in the front of the brain. One of these he called " comparison," and the other " causality." Next to " causality " he placed an organ which he called " mirthfulness." Not having looked into the subject for some years, I do not know whether the present phrenologists retain the same location and nomenclature. But I remember being puzzled by finding this sense of mirth, which is a mere feeling, having its habitat by the side of the grave reflective faculties. This led me to examine the subject more narrowly, and I came to the following conclusion : There are not *two* organs merely of reflection, but *three.* These are the powers by which, as we say, we "put this and that together." The organ of "comparison" has for its function to put things side by side, and examine them to see whether they are alike or unlike. It observes resemblances and differences; it classifies and distributes; noticing fine resemblances it becomes wit. In literature, it gives rise to images and illustrations; it colors style, it prevents vagueness, it detects the sophistry which puts one thing for another. This power of comparison gives definiteness and clearness to thought; we never can understand anything well but by comparing it with something else. All sciences rest on this as their basis; and we see the power of this faculty especially in the modern sciences of comparative philology, comparative geography, comparative theology, and the like.

The second of the reflective powers in man, "causality," does not put the two facts side by side to see whether they agree; but suspends one on the other, to see if it can be supported by it or not. When we perceive an event, we instinctively demand a cause. By a primitive law of the mind, we assume that nothing can take place without a reason. By this power we penetrate into nature and human life, discovering the hidden causes of all phenomena. As science rests on "comparison," which is the faculty of exact observation, and which gives us distinct phenomena, so it takes its second step by "causality," by which it discovers law.

For law in nature means the regular action of causes, producing always the same results.

But now comes the third organ of reflection, which the early phrenologists, noticing only one of its outcomes, hastily called "mirthfulness." It ought rather to be named the faculty of "adaptation." It examines two phenomena, to see if they are adapted to each other, if they fit each other as the two parts of a common whole, if they are congruous or incongruous. As the sight of incongruity produces the sensation of mirth, this organ, unfortunately, was believed to have this for its function. But this form of its activity was not central. It is by this power that we both perceive and exercise design. It is the fashion, at present, to ignore final causes ; but this fashion must be temporary, for teleology is rooted in the very structure of the reasoning intellect. The whole human race is occupied from morning till evening in adapting means to ends, and the power which discovers this adaptation is the third of the great reflective faculties in man. All inventions, and so all progress, arrives through this activity.

All these reflective faculties are exercised in the common business of life, as well as in the highest actions of which man is capable. Applied to every-day concerns, they constitute what is called common sense, or practical wisdom. Let us take a very humble operation to illustrate this, — that of a cook preparing dinner. She must exercise her powers of perception with the organ of comparison in choosing her materials; she applies the causal faculty in applying the processes of making dough, beating eggs, mixing ingredients, and in determining the amount and duration of heat. With this process the faculty of adaptation conjoins itself, making the congruities of the meal in its various parts and in its relation to the number and quality of the guests. The faculties do not the less act, because they act instinctively and unconsciously. Sound thinking consists in putting facts side by side to see if they are alike or different, to see if they depend on each other or are independent; and to see if they are congruous or incongruous.

In order to know the outward world, it is not enough to perceive, we must also reflect on what we perceive. The perceptive faculties, without the reflective, do not give us knowledge, but only the material of knowledge. The sharpest pair of eyes, looking through a tropical forest, cannot see what is there, unless there be a thinking brain behind them. It sees a confused mass of trees, flowers, insects, birds, animals; sees them, but brings away little knowledge about them. But the mind which has been taught to think, to compare, to distinguish, to analyze, to generalize; which has learned to classify its facts, and knows what to look for, — this can put each observation in its place, and bring away a store of knowledge. The same divine law applies everywhere, " To him who hath, shall be given." He who has studied, reflected, learned, and arranged his knowledge in system and order, is able to gather other stores of knowledge, and add them to those already acquired. In order to knowledge, therefore, reflection is indispensable.

The reflective faculties, we see, are eminently practical. They are not so much for speculation as for life. Not even the simplest work can be well done without them. You send for a mechanic to do some work about your house. Suppose that he goes to work with his hands and not with his brains. He then pulls down your walls, tears up your floor, and finds, at last, that he has done it for nothing, — he ought to have done something else. Another man comes, and before doing anything he stops and thinks. He looks, and then reflects ; he tries carefully an experiment, and watches the result. He finds, at last, the cause of the difficulty, and immediately proceeds to remove it. That is the chief difference in all working-men ; some put their brains into what they do, others do not. It is so with woman's work, too ; with sewing, house-keeping, cooking. How invaluable is thought in all this, and, alas ! how rare. That is why we say, let boys and girls in our schools be taught to think ; let them not be drilled so much in remembering as in reflecting ; lay more stress on processes than on results.

There is an objection often urged against these higher reflective faculties in their exercise for common objects, — that they give theoretical rules which are not practical. Thus, if one not actu ally engaged in teaching suggests any new view intended to improve the processes of education, he is apt to be told that this is not "practical." It is sometimes even assumed that theory and practice are opposed to each other. We often hear it as serted that a notion may be "true in theory but false in practice;" that is, useless for practical purposes. I, for one, esteem practice. I trace all real knowledge to experience. I care for no theories, no systems, no generalizations, which do not spring from life and return to it again. I feel perhaps undue contempt for the vague abstractions we often listen to, idle figments of an idle brain, speculations with no basis of sharp observation beneath them. Yet we are in danger of going too far in this direction, and of undervaluing theory in its proper limits. People often eulogize *practice* when they only mean *routine;* boasting themselves as practical teachers, intending thereby that they only do what always has been done, and do not mean to do any better to-morrow than they did yesterday. Practice and theory must go together. Theory without practice to test it, to verify it, to correct it, is idle speculation; but practice without theory to animate it is mere mechanism. In every art and business theory is the soul and practice the body. The soul without a body in which to dwell is indeed only a ghost, but the body without a soul is only a corpse. I some times pass a sign on which the artisan has painted, "John Smith" (or whatever the name may be), "Practical Plumber." I should not wish to employ him. When the water-works in my house get out of order, I want a theoretical plumber as well as one who is practical. I want a man who understands the theory of hydrostatic pressure ; who knows the laws giving resisting qualities to lead, iron, zinc, and copper; who can so arrange and plan beforehand the order of pipes that he shall accomplish the result aimed at with the smallest amount of piping, the least exposure to frost, the least danger of leakage or breakage ; and this a merely practical man, a man of routine, cannot do. The merest artisan needs to theorize, i. e. to *think*, — to think beforehand, to foresee ; and that must be done by the aid of general principles, by the knowledge of laws. An intelligent man, a man of general culture, whose mind has been quickened with ideas, will often be able to show a mechanic how to do his own work. When we are young, we have a superstitious faith in the knowledge each man is supposed to have of his own business. We outgrow this after a while. If you wish anything done about your house, send for a mechanic; but overlook him, do not leave him to himself. You will presently find that you can suggest something to him in his own work which he has never thought of. All success depends on practice, but all improvement on theory. Let neither despise the other.

The saying that anything "is true in theory but false in practice" involves an impossibility. The theory indeed may be plausible, but false, and then it will not work; and its not working is the proof of its being false. It is neither true in theory nor in practice. On the other hand, a theory which is true may not work at first, because the true way of working it has not been found out. It is not *false* in practice, but practice has not come. All great inventions and discoveries have failed at first, but you cannot say they were "true in theory but false in practice." They had not been really put in practice. If anything is seen to be certainly true in theory it will come right by and by in practice. Fulton's steamboat would not work at first, nor did Stephenson's locomotive, nor Daguerre's sun-painting, nor Morse's electric telegraph; and no doubt a great many people said, "Oh! that's true in theory but false in practice."

Least of all should teachers undervalue theory; they whose whole art aims at guiding life by ideas, inspiring the soul with the love of truth, awakening the intellect by the sight of universal laws, and even while communicating the smallest details of knowledge, teaching them by the light of vital principles of wisdom. We cannot teach a little ragged boy his alphabet as we ought, unless we do it with the idea of his being an immortal soul, made for eternity; and that is a *theory.*

Practical men need outsiders to suggest improvements to them. We are all much benefited by lay criticism. There is lay criticism in all arts, and it is always needed. We saw in the civil war that merely military men were not always the most successful in military matters. Some of the graduates of West Point began by objecting to the volunteer soldiers and generals; but they ended by being compelled to see that in war, as in all other things, it is good sense, devotion, and loyalty which succeed. Outsiders, laymen, can always benefit experts by *suggestions*, if in no other way.

Let us not suppose, however, that the education of the reflective faculties consists in studying metaphysics, logic, or intellectual philosophy. These can, indeed, be learned so as to make the best possible display at a school exhibition, and yet no power of thinking may be acquired thereby. It is not by committing to memory descriptions of the reflective faculties that we learn to reflect; it is by reflecting.

We cannot obtain knowledge without reflection. Still less can we acquire wisdom. Wisdom is knowledge in its application to the exigencies of human life. Wisdom puts everything in its proper relations; sees the due perspective of objects; knows how to distinguish what is essential and non-essential, primary and secondary. It judges each case by its own merits, not by any abstract rule. The wise physician, for example, is not one who has a number of theories about diseases and their cures, which he applies to all cases. Rather, he is one who watches carefully the constitution and condition of his patient; narrowly observes symptoms; follows the indications of. Nature; notices everything, and reflects on what he notices. The wise mother is one who carefully studies the character of her children; who knows how to gain and keep their confi-' dence; who is their best friend, to whom they go for counsel. She is cautious, but not too cautious; gives them liberty, but not too much of it; watches them, but not too narrowly; in short, observes, and then reflects. The wise statesman rises above party, conquers his partialities and prejudices, takes a broad view of the state of his nation, and so steers the ship of state on its majestic voyage. The wise friend is he who sees both the good and evil of his friend; does not become his blind admirer, but loves him with intelligence, and so helps him to correct his faults, and to put forth courageously his good powers. He is one who encourages all that is good in us, discourages all that is evil, gives us confidence in what is best, exalts our purposes, inspires us with a generous ambition, and so gives us faith in God, man, and ourselves.

What a blessing in any family, community, neighborhood, is a person who has cultivated this large and genial wisdom! If there is one who has trained his powers of thinking, who is able to apply his mind to any difficulty, how much good he can do by his counsel! To him men resort in their emergencies, and he gently untangles for them the skein of their life. By a large experience of the world, by a careful study of the particular case, by a habit of reflection, he is able to guide the poor, lost souls who have gone astray in the wilderness of life, and to set them again in the right way.

There have always been some men and women who have possessed this wisdom of life in an eminent degree. The ancient Germans selected such wise women for their advisers in all grave national difficulties. The mind of man and that of woman acts differently in reflection. The man looks at the case in hand, judges it in its details, takes it to pieces, examines it part by part, and reasons out carefully the necessary remedy or relief. The woman's mind is more apt to work sympathetically; she sees the case as a whole, and keeps it before her mind till there arrives a distinct conception of what the difficulty is, and how it can be relieved. Both methods are good. Where there is a long journey to go, the masculine method, step by step, is better. Where a judgment is needed at once, the feminine method is surest. The best method is that which we call common sense, — not because it is common, for it is rare, but because it needs no special discipline of school or college to develop it. It comes from the training of life, and all practical persons have it in a greater or less degree.

One book of the Bible is devoted to the celebration of this kind of wisdom; that practical wisdom of life, in its form of prudence, which says, "Neither too little, nor too much." The Proverbs of Solomon, from first to last, glorify prudence. Their object is "to give subtilty to the simple, and to the young man knowledge and discretion." This book points out, graphically, the evils into which men fall who do not "consider their ways." "A fool," in this book, is the worst sort of man. Men are saved — this is the doctrine — by wisdom. "When wisdom entereth into thy heart, and knowledge is pleasant to thy soul, discretion shall preserve thee, understanding shall keep thee. To deliver thee from the way of the evil man, whose ways are crooked; to deliver thee from the strange woman, whose house inclineth unto death. That thou mayest walk in the way of good men, for the upright shall dwell in the land." The result is temporal prosperity and inward satisfaction. "Length of days, and long life, and peace, shall they add to thee." "And thou shalt find favor and good understanding in the sight of God and man." "Honor the Lord with thy substance, and thy barns shall be filled with plenty." Solomon urges obedience to parents. "My son, keep thy father's commandment, and forsake not the law of thy mother. Bind them continually upon thy heart, and tie them about thy neck." And, certainly, there is no surer safety from the extravagances of youth than this respect for the experience of parents. Honesty, chastity, cautiousness, carefulness in speech, consideration before action, — these are the gods of the Book of Proverbs. They are not the Most High God, but they are very important virtues.

One thing may be noticed in the Book of Proverbs. Its acuteness often becomes wit, and makes one smile. Thus, notice such sentences as these · " The legs of the lame are not equal; so is a proverb in the mouth of fools." He does not see its application to himself; one side of the proverb limps. Again : " As a thorn in the hand of a drunkard, so is a proverb in the mouth of a fool." The drunkard does not feel the point of the thorn, nor the fool the point of the proverb. " Bray a fool in a mortar, his foolishness will not depart from him." That is, no amount of experience will teach a man who does not reflect. " A continual dropping in a rainy day and a contentions woman are alike." This outcrop of wit in the heart of the Bible suggests this remark: All the three reflective faculties have a mirthful side to them. They all put two things together to see their relations. Comparison puts them together to see if they are like or unlike. Now, the perception of fine resemblances and minute analogies constitute what we call wit. If you examine the sayings of Charles Lamb, Sydney Smith, and other great wits, you will perceive that what amuses you is the sudden perception of some fine resemblance. Then the organ of causality, the second reflective organ, which puts two things together to see if one depends on the other or not, is the source of that somewhat egotistic and hard-hearted amusement which we take in sarcasm and satire. Causality is the organ of controversy and argument, and has always a light

10

sneer on its lips towards its opponent. It is almost impossible to carry on a controversy and treat your adversary with respect. It seems necessary to turn him into ridicule, and to prove his position not only false, but absurd. That is the evil of argument. "Knowledge puffs up," and no kind of knowledge more than formal knowledge, verbal accuracy, logical precision. When we prove another to have made a mistake in his statement, we are always tempted to exult over him. He may be right in the substance; he may be essentially right; but if he is verbally wrong, we decree ourselves a triumph, and look down on him with great self-complacency. The third reflective organ is that of system. It arranges, classifies, generalizes, sees the adaptations of part to part, sees that which is congruous. Its mirthful side is to see the incongruities, and this creates what we call humor. If a well-dressed man, who evidently prides himself on his perfect neatness of costume, suddenly slips in the street and falls into a mud puddle, men laugh. It is hard not to laugh, because of the incongruity between his satisfaction a moment before, and his utter confusion afterward.

But not only virtue in its lower form of prudence, but in its higher aspects, depends on the culture of the reflective faculties. Our virtue is only secure, only safe, when it is rooted in convictions. Take an innocent boy, brought up in the country, taught to be good, good by habit, but not taught to think for himself, not taught to see the reason why he should do right. As long as his surroundings encourage and support his virtue, he is virtuous. But now let him come to a city, far from his home; let him enter a new society of gay and reckless young men; let him hear his old opinions ridiculed as absurd, antiquated, puritanical. His conscience, which had only been guided by the serious public opinion of his village into right doing, is now guided the other way by the new opinions which surround him. So he drifts into extravagance, intemperance, licentiousness; his former opinions were not rooted by thought, and so were not *his* opinions at all.

Only by habitual reflection do our opinions, our purposes, our sentiments, root themselves in the soul, and become convictions and principles. The frivolity, the superficial life which men satirize as frequent in women, is usually due to the absence of culture of their reflective powers in youth. Men first insist that women shall not pursue serious studies, but only external accomplishments, and then they condemn them for being so frivolous and empty. A woman may learn to think and to exercise her judgment without growing masculine, or becoming a pedant or a bookworm. If she does not learn to think, she necessarily drifts and floats on the surface of society, a pleasant object while she is young, pretty, and fascinating; neglected, when she has lost these charms.

The world can never become very much better without a greater exercise and culture of the reflect-

ive powers. It requires some thinking to become
very good. One may be conscientious, — his con
science may be sensitive, tender, active ; but if not
guided by judgment it will often become bigotry,
fanaticism, and cruelty. How much wrong is done,
what harsh judgments uttered every day in the name
of conscience ! Men think it their duty to treat with
indiscriminate contempt those who.differ from them
in opinion. They think it their duty to be intoler-
ant, relentless, and unforgiving. A large part of the
misery of life comes from narrow and unenlightened
conscientiousness. So, also, unreflective good-nature
often does as much harm as good. Sympathizing
persons with no judgment, hurt those they are trying
to help. Blind sympathy turns poverty into pauperism by inconsiderate gifts. It weakens instead of
strengthening those it tries to help. Instead of helping them to help themselves, it encourages them to
lean for a time on others, and then, at last, is sure
to tire of supporting them, and to withdraw its help,
and so leaves them worse off than it found them.

And, most of all, in religion are the exercise of
the reflective organs needed ; and. most of all, in this
highest sphere, have they remained unexercised.
Men have been taught that it is wrong to think for
themselves on religious subjects, because thought
leads to doubt. The title for unbelief has been
" Free-thinking," as if freedom to think must necessarily end in disbelief. But though free thought
may sometimes, for a season, produce scepticism, it

must in the long run lead to the sight of truth. God, who has revealed truth, has given to us our reason with which to examine, investigate, define, and arrange it. The best and highest view of Christianity must come from the general exercise of reason in regard to it.

We have been taught that there are mysteries in Christianity above human comprehension. So there are in nature. But it does not follow that the student of natural science must stop, and cease his investigations, because he meets with something mysterious. On the contrary, this excites him to more active thought. Mystery in nature stimulates inquiry ; why should it not do so in religion ?

The truth is, that no form of Christianity will convert the world to Christ but rational Christianity. By this I do not mean the opinions of any existing sect or school, but I mean the Christianity which encourages thought and has no fear of inquiry ; which recognizes law as universal ; which does not ask for assent, but asks for conviction ; which does not claim submission to authority, but demands personal faith. In all sects, in all churches, I see the advance of this rational Christianity. I hail its approach as the surest proof of the triumph of Christ, and the coming of the kingdom of God. The name of the wicked woman in the book of Revelation was " Mystery," and she was the mother of abominations. But the name of Christianity is Light. Christ is " the Light of the world." Christians are children of the light and of the day. Those who are true " come to the light," and only those who do evil hate the light. In the depths of Christianity, as in the depths of nature, are mysteries, secrets, problems. But when we find a secret in nature, we do not say, " This is an awful mystery ; let us humbly adore it, and not try to understand it." On the contrary, we accept it as a challenge to investigation ; as a summons from the God of truth to the fullest inquiry. The God of nature is also the God of Revelation, and in neither of these spheres does he ask for any blind acquiescence, or any torpid lethargy of thought, but for the fullest, freest exercise of all our reflective powers. We must love God not only " with all our heart and soul and strength," but also " with all our mind and all our understanding." " Care is taken," says Goethe, " that trees shall not grow up to heaven," and there is not the least danger that we shall ever grow too knowing or too wise.

You will observe that I have given no distinct directions for the culture of the reflective powers. I have all along implied that they are best developed by practice. The right way to unfold thought is by thinking. The study of metaphysics has its use, but it does not necessarily train the thinking powers. But the habit of putting your mind to each question as it arises, and thinking it out, is the best discipline. Everything which exercises the reasoning powers, whether it be the study of a science, a debating society, a game of chess, or an intellectual game of questions and answers, helps to develop these faculties. Perhaps one of the best methods is to read books in which important questions are discussed, and carefully to examine the reasons and arguments as you proceed ; not hurrying, but going very slowly, thinking out everything as you advance. Conscientious work of all kinds requires reflection, and to do any piece of work conscientiously brings its reward in culture and strength of thought. No business, in which we deal with men or with things, can be rightfully conducted without thinking. But it is always hard work to think, and the tendency and danger is to take for granted, to assent without investigation, to believe as others believe, to drift with the stream. Nor is the inde pendent thinker always agreeable to others ; for most men like those best whom they can easily bend to their will.

The highest influence which comes to educate the power of thought is the serious and earnest love of truth. This alone enables us to conquer our indolence, to resist the tendency to conformity, to oppose public opinion and the fashion of the hour, and seek for what is real, looking for it with our own eyes. This is the heroic element in human nature, which makes those who possess it the salt of the earth and the light of the world. To awaken and cherish this love of truth in ourselves and in others, to follow after it as long as we live, this is what has created the prophets, saints, heroes, and martyrs of history; and this is what, in private life, has purified souls, and made them the source of strength and light in the humble spheres of conscience and duty. This enthusiasm for truth makes the eye single, and so fills the whole body full of light. This is

> " The life of whate'er makes life worth living
>   Seed grain of high emprize, immortal food,
>   One heavenly thing whereof earth hath the giving."

Truth quickens the soul in all its faculties. This is one of the divine elements in human nature: the other is the divine element of love. The two belong together, and neither is fully itself without the help of the other. Truth spoken in love, truth acted in love, truth sought for lovingly, truth held lovingly, these make the complete man.

VII.

THE INTUITIONAL NATURE.

VII.

THE INTUITIONAL NATURE.

I PROPOSE next to speak of the Intuitions of the Soul, and of that power in man which is capable of perceiving ideas.

Outward facts we perceive through the senses; inward facts through insight, or higher intellect. There are many who adopt a sensational system, deriving all knowledge from sensible experience, and denying that the soul furnishes any part of our cognitions. Locke argued against innate ideas, and derived all our knowledge from sensation and reflection. But as reflection or reasoning furnishes no new intellectual matter, but merely orders and arranges what we possess, it follows that Locke was a sensationalist. It is not my intention to enter into any metaphysical discussion of this subject. I shall merely endeavor to show, from plain and evident facts, which all can appreciate, that all our knowledge is not derived from sensation, but that some of it comes to us from the action of the mind itself.

For example, take the idea of cause. I see a boy strike a ball with a bat, and the ball immediately flies through the air. I say that the blow by the bat was the cause of the motion of the ball. How did that belief come to me ? Not through the senses, certainly. All I perceived with my eye was the phenomenon of the blow, followed by the motion of the ball; two phenomena, one following the other. I saw no cause, I saw no force even, passing out of the bat into the ball. I only perceived succession, and I inferred causation by an act of reason. The idea of cause did not come from without, through the senses; it must, therefore, have come from within, through the reason itself.

If it is said that a long observation of such facts, showing the invariable succession between impact and motion, gives us, at last, the idea of cause, I reply, first, that little children who have scarcely seen any phenomena have as lively a conviction of cause and effect as the adult man or woman. Little children, as soon as they can talk, begin to ask, " Who did that ? " " Who made that ? " And if you should tell them that the action did itself, or that the thing made itself, they would hardly be satisfied.

But, beside, invariable succession is not the same thing as cause. We have seen, every year we have lived, night invariably succeed day, and day invariably succeed night ; but we have never believed one the cause of the other. Sleep invariably succeeds wakefulness, wakefulness invariably succeeds sleep; but no one thinks that sleep is caused by wakefulness, or wakefulness by sleep. Death succeeds life inevitably and invariably. Does any one suppose that life is the cause of death? Invariable succession is not, then, the same as cause and effect. When we perceive, by our senses, any phenomenon taking place, any event occurring, then immediately, by an inevitable act of the reason, we infer some cause.

The idea of substance, in the same way, is given by the reason, though not by reasoning, and cannot be derived from sensation. I perceive some material substance, — a stone, for example, a tree, a book. I perceive by my eye only form and color, outline and shadow. · I touch it with my hand; I perceive resistance and extension. These are all sensations in my own mind. How do I know that there is some real substance outside of me in which these qualities inhere? It is an inference of my reason, inevitable, necessary. When we perceive by the senses these material qualities, then, by a spontaneous act of the reason, we infer a substance, or some thing standing under them. We infer cause and substance, however, not by the reflective powers, but by the intuitive reason.

All men believe in infinite space and infinite time. We cannot conceive of space coming to an end anywhere. We cannot conceive of time beginning or ending, for then there would be a time when there was no time. But certainly the senses cannot perceive the infinite. The senses only perceive what is finite and limited. Consequently, the idea of the infinite must come from the mind itself. We perceive finite space, and infer infinite space beyond it. We observe the succession of minutes, days, years, and infer a past eternity behind, and a future eternity before. This, also, is a spontaneous and inevitable act of the reason.

Those ideas of the human mind which cannot be derived from sensation are intuitions of the reason. They do not come from reasoning, for they are the basis of all reasoning. They are first truths, without seeing which we could not see anything else. A piece of reasoning is like a suspended chain, in which link is joined to link by logical dependence. A weight hangs from the last link; that link is sustained by the one above it, that by the next higher up. But, as we ascend the chain, we at last come, not to a link, but to a staple, which is driven into the wall. So all reasoning at last brings us to a first truth, a truth of intuition, which is a staple fastened into the very structure of the mind. All great thinkers have recognized these original and fundamental truths, the heritage of the soul itself, the birthright of man, which constitute him a rational being. These truths are self-evident, are believed naturally, necessarily and universally. They are incapable of demonstration. Proclus says, " He who thinks that all things can be demonstrated, takes away demonstration itself." Epictetus says, "Whoever denies self-evident truths cannot be reasoned with; he has no intellectual modesty." Aristotle, no less than Plato, asserted the existence of these first truths behind all reasoning. They are distinguished by two characters, — universality and necessity. If there is any idea which we find in all men, working either consciously or unconsciously, and which is so necessary that they cannot help having it even when they try not to have it, that idea is an intuition of the reason.

If I am asked, then, what I mean by intuition, or the intuitional faculties, I reply that, beside the powers with which we look outward and perceive the external world, we have other powers, by which we look inward and observe another world of ideas. Locke fought stoutly against the doctrine of innate ideas, and justly. A man is certainly not born with ideas of the inward world, any more than he is born with ideas of the outward world. Both are developed by means of experience. We have no innate idea of justice and goodness, any more than we have innate ideas of color, form, substance, and mathematical proportion. But just as there is an outward world which all men can recognize, so there is an inward world which all men can recognize. Just as all men, by experience, come to know weight, extension, form, color, as realities in the external world, so all men, by experience, come to know justice, love, purity, as realities of the spiritual world.

I have dwelt on these intellectual intuitions to show how solid and real is the knowledge which comes from looking in; to prove that just as real as the outward world which we perceive by the senses is the inward world which we perceive through the soul itself. For as all our knowledge of intellectual realities rests on intuitions of the reason, so all our knowledge of goodness rests on intuitions of the moral nature, and all our knowledge of religion on intuitions of the spiritual nature. The Apostle Paul says that spiritual things are spiritually discerned. Just as physical things are physically discerned through the senses, moral things are morally discerned through the moral nature, and spiritual things are spiritually discerned through the religious nature.

The intuitions above mentioned are intellectual, but another class are moral intuitions. There is a moral sense by which we perceive the distinction between good and bad, right and wrong, just as by the physical sense we perceive the distinction between black and white. The idea of right and wrong is universal. There is no man so bad as not to recognize evil in another, if not in himself. All the world over, in all lands and all languages, men use the words " duty," " justice," " right," " wrong," " ought," " ought not." Everywhere there is found in man traces of conscience, rewarding him when he does what he believes to be right, punishing him with remorse when he does what he thinks to be wrong.

People differ as to what is right and what is wrong. The standard varies, the law differs. Yet there never has been a nation or race which did not approve courage, truth, generosity, honesty; did not despise cowardice, falsehood, selfishness, dishonesty. A North American Indian, a Spanish inquisitor, a Southern slaveholder, or an absolute despot, will torture human beings from pleasure, from principle, or, as he thinks, from necessity; but not one of them approves cruelty in the others, or in general. So men will lie, in business, for their religion, for their friends, for their own safety; but no one approves of lying in itself. Each man disapproves it in every one but himself, and in every case except his own case.

In all souls there is this instinctive sense of right and wrong. If there were not, morality could not exist, and society would be impossible. For morality is nothing if it is not respect for right and duty, apart from all rewards they may bring. A man who only does right because he is afraid of punishment if he does wrong, or because he hopes for some reward here or hereafter for doing right, does not act conscientiously at all; he merely acts selfishly. Society is held together by conscience. See that laborer, uneducated, poor, who has been working ten hours a day since he was a child, and can only just support himself. What makes him industrious, temperate, honest, orderly, instead of being an idle wretch, ready for any crime? Is it the fear

11

of the police and the prison ? No. The great mass of men support order and law, because they think it right to do so ; because conscience tells them to do so. A few scoundrels are kept from being too scoundrelly by the police and the prison ; the great mass of men never think of the police or prison, but do right because duty tells them to. It is an evil for a nation when conscience takes the side of rebellion, when law seems tyranny ! The deep corner-stone of republican institutions is faith in a universal conscience. You give all the power to the majority of the people. What is to prevent them from tyrannizing over you ? The majority are poor, only a minority are rich. What is to prevent them from voting themselves your houses and lands ? Nothing but conscience, the instinct of right. Now we have proved in this country that there are no institutions so stable as a democracy. In proving this, we have at the same time proved transcendentalism : that is, that all men have a conscience.

Besides the intuitions of reason and those of the moral nature, there are also the religious intuitions. Man has the power of looking into the spiritual world, and of perceiving there God and immortality, divine beauty and infinite wisdom.   •

We do not know God by argument, by reading books of evidences or books of theology : we know him just as we know the external world, — by experience. We know God by intercourse with him, by looking up instead of down, by looking through the wonders and beauties of nature to the infinite spirit beyond.

> "One impulse from the vernal wood
>   Will teach us more of man,
> Of moral evil and of good,
>   Than all the sages can."

Sometimes we can learn more of God by a walk in the woods or by the shore, than by all the arguments of theology. See the infinite tenderness of the lights and shadows on the leaves, the grass, the trunks of trees. Notice the soft tints on the clouds which drift over your head above. Hear the sighing of the winds, as they sing their everlasting song in the tree-tops. Sit on the rocks and see the perpetual rush and roar, the swell and heave, of the ocean. Then you say, " Lo ! God is here, and I knew it not ; this is none other than the house of God, and this the gate of heaven."

We talk of inspired men, of men who walk with God, and see him face to face. These, however, are only more highly endowed with that power of intuition which we all possess. In every heart there is a door which opens inward to God. We leave it closed. We look out, and not in. So we lose half of our inheritance.

Some men, we know, have more active perceptive powers than others. Some will notice outward things more easily ; observe faces, forms, events, with great facility. Others, in like manner, are born with more active intuitional powers than others ; they have a quicker sense of beauty, a more ready perception of right; they are more shocked by injustice; they are more elevated by the sight of goodness; they have more ardor for truth. We take men with active perceptive powers as our guides in respect to outward things. They see what we cannot see in the outward universe. But instead of taking the men of intuitions as our guides in the inward universe, we are very apt to call them sentimentalists and visionaries. They are visionaries; but the visions which come to them are of infinite truth, beauty, justice, of the great realities of the spiritual world.

Woe to the land and time in which there are no such visionaries as these! In such days moralists repeat by rote their old maxims; preachers recite their lessons like school-boys: there are only conventional morals and manners, plants with no deep roots. Such a time is mentioned in the Old Testament, "The word of the Lord was precious in those days; there was no open vision." In such times the old formulas and creeds are idolized; men cling to them as their only support. But in the midst of this dreary waste the Lord sends some new prophet, — some Socrates in Greece, some divine singers like Dante or Milton, some man of good sense like Dr. Johnson or Benjamin Franklin; some teachers of religion who do not repeat by rote, but speak what they know and testify what they have seen, like Luther, George Fox, John Wesley, Swedenborg, Channing, Parker, Martineau, — and then it is like a breath of fresh air blowing in a stagnant miasma; new life, love, hope, speedily comes in. All men feel this power; all rejoice in it.

This is the secret of the great influence exerted by such men as Channing in this country and Schleiermacher in Germany. They were both men of spiritual insight, men of intuitions, coming in the midst of a generation whose minds were saturated by the well-worn commonplaces of theology and morals. Men had been preaching from hearsay; repeating over and over what their fathers and grandfathers had said before. But now there was another open vision of truth; no wonder that it filled men with joy as they listened, and they said, " How beautiful on the mountains are the feet of those who publish glad tidings!"

Bunsen, in his work called " God in History," declares Dr. Channing to be one of the prophets of his time. Dr. Channing came at a day when religion had become very much diluted, had gone into the sphere of opinion, which consisted of cold and dry formulas. He caused a great revival of faith by looking with his own eyes at the truth. He was a man of a powerful intuitional nature. He saw ideas, and he saw them so plainly that he caused others to see them. He saw the better side of man; saw the dignity of human nature saw that God had made man little lower than the angels; saw, in spite of all the degradation and sin of man's actual condition, that he had divine and immortal capabilities, and was destined to a great future. Hence he rejected, with the utmost horror, all doctrines of total depravity and human inability which darkened this great idea. Hence he opposed human slavery, chiefly as a wrong done to the nature of man, turning man into a thing.

It is not merely delight and joy which such men bring. They fasten anew to human hearts the chain of moral truths which bind us to eternity and God. They lay once more, deep and strong, the solid foundations on which the interests of society, morality, the worth of man, depend. These are the men who "speak with authority, and not as the scribes." These are the seers who help us to see. They help to make a new heaven and a new earth in which dwells righteousness.

In some periods all spiritual truth seems to be lost or fading away. It is like the fatal time thus described : —

> " I dreamed a dream, last Christmas eve,
>   Of a people whose God was Make-Believe,
>   A dream of an old faith sunk to a guess,
>   And a Christian church and people and press
>   Who believed they believed it — more or less."

In such doleful days as these God sends us men of intuitions, and then, all at once, the whole spiritual and moral world comes out fresh and fair, more real than aught beside. We see through their eyes, are nourished by their enthusiasm, our intuitional nature is awakened by theirs, and we, also, begin to

see that God is a living God, and that Christ is a
living Saviour; that beauty, holiness, virtue, honor,
are not names, but things.

We have had two such men of intuition in our
times, — two men who have led the English thought
back to that divine spring which flows fast by the
oracles of God; two men still living, — I mean
Thomas Carlyle and our own Emerson. Their power
over their age consists in their possessing in a
high degree this capacity of intuition. They do not
argue nor reason, but they simply say what they see.
We may not agree at all with their conclusions. We
may differ greatly from their doctrines. But we are
willing for a season to rejoice in that light of which
God has made them mediums, a light which reveals
to us the vast inward realities of the world of conscience and faith. They do not, perhaps, consider themselves religious teachers, and are not so
considered by others. Carlyle has become cynical
in his later years, soured and harsh. But we cannot
forget his early and better days, when he did not
worship the God of Force, but the God of Justice, and
when his soul brought inspiration to men, convincing
them of the realities of an eternal and infinite world.

There is an intuition of immortality, there is an
organ of hope in the brain which perpetually looks
forward. It is the instinct of the future. It teaches
us that there is not less life for us after death, but
more; not less of power, knowledge, love, work,
beauty, joy, but more. This belief in the future life

does not rest on knowledge or argument, but on the habit of looking forward in faith and trust. Some have more of it, some less. It may be strengthened by exercise. We may look at the dark side or the bright side of things, as we choose. We may look down or up, we may look at our sorrows and trials, or at our joys. All depends on this. By looking at the dark side, everything looks worse and worse; we lose the power of seeing good. We see only what is selfish, cold, and hard in men; only what is dark and terrible in the universe. Seek and you shall find. You have what you look after. As a man sows, so shall he reap. A man may think that he believes in a future life because of the arguments in its favor; he may think that he disbelieves it because he has been convinced by the arguments against it. No. He believes it because he has established the habit of looking at the good side of things; because he has exercised and educated his organs of faith and•hope. He disbelieves it because he has not exercised and educated them.

There are prophets, seers, inspired souls, in all religions and in all nations. They are those in whom these intuitions of conscience, faith, hope, and love are strong. They are the men of intuition, who see through their inward eye, not their outward eye. They have not believed as every one else believed, but have looked into their own souls for truth, and have found it. They have seen God face to face, and he has talked with them, as a man talks with a friend. In the darkness of night they have seen the approaching twilight and the rose of dawn, and have announced to all men the coming day. They hold up the heart of nations; they come, in great emergencies, to add faith and fire to noble resolutions; they suffer and die for their convictions, and so inspire others with a like resolution. These are the prophets who have been since the world began; the prophets, unrecognized in their own time, despised and rejected of men, but heralds of every great advance of the human race. Their power lies in the strength of their intuitions. They see God, truth, justice, and beauty as realities, not as probabilities. Inspired by these visions, they are ready to speak their word, whether men will hear or whether they will forbear. They die in obscurity, perhaps, and defeat; but their lightest words live and conquer the world, and grow up into great trees, in which all the birds of the air find rest.

But the gift of prophetic vision is not merely to make great teachers of the human race; it is for practical daily life and common duty. Some men see only the outside of the world; others see all that, and see, also, the ideas which rule the world. Those who are commonly called worldly wise are only half wise; their wisdom has no roots and principles; it grows from the shifting sands of temporary expediency. But everywhere in society there are men who see, not only outward facts, but also ideas and truths. They see justice, goodness, honesty, integrity as realities, not merely as conventional arrangements. These men are the only really moral and religious men in the land; the only ones whose religion and virtue have roots. They would believe in truth if all mankind beside themselves disbelieved it; they would do right if the universal custom was to do wrong. Such men and women, wherever they are, are the salt of the earth and the light of the world.

The intuitional nature needs education, and can be educated, like the perceptive powers. We are helped to spiritual insight by communion with the souls whom God inspires to see realities. Their faith arouses ours. It is a true instinct which causes mankind to cleave to its prophets, poets, seers, and great moralists. Their life feeds the world. Men eat and drink them, and become spiritually alive themselves.

But our intuitional nature is also educated, and that most efficiently, by obedience to our insights. The man who listens to the voice of conscience in his soul hears it afterward more distinctly. If he refuses to listen to it, his ear becomes dull to that divine melody. He who never looks up to a living God, to a heavenly presence, loses the power of perceiving that presence, and the universe slowly turns into a dead machine, clashing and grinding on, without purpose or end. If the light within us be darkness, how great is that darkness!

The best culture of the intuitive faculties consists

in using them. The same law applies to these as to all our other faculties, — use, improve or lose. A man who always looks down, never up, loses, at last, the power of looking up. A man who always looks out, never in, loses the power of looking in. We must look at the things not seen; we must accustom ourselves to visions of infinite majesty, beauty, and truth. All in this life is not logic; all is not sensation. There is a place in it for faith, hope, and love.

VIII.

THE IMAGINATION.

VIII.

THE IMAGINATION.

M ANY persons think the imagination deserves
rather to be repressed than to be cultivated.
They regard it as dealing only with dreams, not realities, and so tending to unfit a person for actual
life. Its realm they suppose to be the world of
fairies, and of other impossibilities. At best, they
will allow its use only to artists and poets, and they
conceive its principal function to be the production
of rather commonplace pictures and poems.

But the imagination is one of the faculties which
God has given to all men. It is a part of human
nature, and was certainly put into us for some
important purpose. My object now is to find what
this purpose is, for what end the imagination was
given, and how it is to be used; what are its abuses,
and what its dangers; how it is to be cultivated, and
how restrained.

But first we must try to say what the imagination
is. It is the ideal faculty, that which perceives
ideals, and helps us to realize them. It is the

power which makes a picture or image in the mind
of something not perceived by the senses; a type of
something more perfect than the reality, and a type
which is necessary for all work which requires skill
and aims at excellence. It gives us a vision of the
perfect in the midst of imperfection, of pure beauty
amid what is rude and homely.

The importance which the Creator attributes to
the culture of the imagination appears from the
great activity given to it in childhood. The plays
of children all exercise and educate this power. A
little girl playing with her doll, — what is she
doing? She imagines the doll to be alive, imagines herself to be its mother; she talks with it,
feeds it, puts it to bed, dresses and undresses it; in
short, carries on a little drama, imagining herself
and the doll to be the actors. See children at
play; everything is imaginary; they put together
chairs, and imagine them to be ships, or railroad
cars, or houses, or forts. They imagine themselves
into all the concerns of life; they play at weddings,
funerals, wars, trade. Thus the plays of children
are endless imitation, and the constant exercise of
the ideal faculty.

And this is, all of it, a preparation for their work
in life. For all work, to be done well, requires the
use of this power. All work which is not mere
routine and drudgery must be done with an ideal
held before the mind, as a pattern.

I therefore believe that the imagination is a very

practical, useful, and important faculty, given to all men, and necessary to all men; and, moreover, that it is a faculty which can and ought to be educated.

Without attempting to define the imagination, then, we can see what it is in its operation. As the object of the perceptive faculties are forms, colors, sounds, perfumes, or outward sensible phenomena; as the object of the reflective faculties are the laws of likeness and unlikeness, cause and effect, adaptation and incongruity, — so the object of the imagination is beauty. The senses perceive facts, the reason perceives laws, the imagination perceives the ideal or the perfect in all things, — physical, mental, moral, spiritual.

We may also say that while, as an intellectual faculty, the imagination gives us the knowledge of the beautiful, so as a practical power it creates art. In its method it belongs to those high functions of the soul which tend to union, instead of division; which do not see things scattered and separated, but harmonized and united. Thus the reason sees truth as one law binding all things together; the moral nature sees one goodness uniting all souls in love; and the imagination sees one perfect beauty pervading nature and life.

The work of the imagination, I said, is art. But art is simply doing a thing as well as it can be done; doing it according to an ideal in the soul; having in the mind the image of the whole while working on the parts. There is no work which can be done well without a constant exercise of the imagination. A carpenter cannot build a house without keeping in his mind the idea of the whole house while working on the parts. A blacksmith can make a horseshoe only by the help of imagination, for he must hold in his mind the image of the horseshoe to guide him while hammering it out on the anvil from the rude bar of red-hot iron. Thus the commonest labor may become a work of art. The common sense of mankind has put this into a proverb, — "Whatever is worth doing at all, is worth doing well." But you can do nothing well unless you have an ideal of how it ought to be done; and this comes by the action of the imagination.

It is a mistake to suppose that, in order to be an artist, it is necessary to paint pictures, carve statues, build cathedrals, or write poems. Beauty is by no means confined to these objects; wherever there is proportion, finish, harmony, thoroughness, unity, there is beauty. What more beautiful than a ship under sail! What fine proportions, what exact symmetry, in the moulding of the hull, in the rake of the masts, in the symmetry of the spars, in the drawing of the sails! A splendid ship under sail is as beautiful as the Apollo Belvidere, and a great deal more beautiful than most of the statues with which we adorn our public grounds and public buildings. For a ship means something: it means the power which yields to the storm and sea, and so conquers them, and compels them to serve it; which rides on the mighty billows, and shows the triumph of mind over matter. But most statues mean nothing at all.

When the great Gothic cathedrals were built, no one thought of calling them works of art. Nor were the Greek temples built as works of art; they were built for worship. The Gothic minsters, also, were built for worship, and their form came from a desire to carry out an ideal in the best way and at the smallest expense of materials. Their builders were no more thought artists than we consider a ship-builder one. Nor were Shakspeare's plays regarded as works of art by his contemporaries. They were delightful amusements for an afternoon, that was all. But to build a ship, a cathedral, or a play, one must put his imagination into it; have the image in his mind of what he wants to accomplish, and hold firmly to his ideal while he works out the details. The result is unity in variety, a harmonious whole; in short, beauty.

In dealing with men, imagination is a very practical faculty, and very necessary. By imagination you enter into their state of mind; see how they feel, what they think, and what they mean to do. For example, in war, the general must put himself in place of his enemy, and by force of imagination discover his plans. All great generals — Hannibal, the Duke of Marlborough, Napoleon — have had this gift in a high degree.

All inventors and discoverers are obliged to use the imagination. They see their invention as an ideal and image long before they are able to put it in practice. This image is so luminous that it encourages them to persevere, in spite of ridicule and repeated failure, and at last success comes. Few of the great modern inventions would have been made if man had been destitute of this faculty.

All occupations, to be done well, require the constant use of the imagination. By means of it the physician puts himself into his patient's place, imagines how he feels, and so discovers what he needs. The lawyer puts himself into the place of his client, the judge, the jury, and the opposing counsel, and imagines, in turn, what each will think and feel. The orator puts himself in the place of his hearers, in order to move them. The merchant makes a picture in his mind of the world's needs, and puts himself in the place of his customer. Without imagination, social intercourse grows dry and hard, and human life is despoiled of charm.

So, in science, the imagination foresees the law which is to bind the phenomena together long before it can be established by proofs. Kepler and Newton had a vision of harmony in the heavens, of vast laws regulating the movements of the planets, years before they were able to demonstrate them. The imagination, in science, is John the Baptist preparing the way for law, which is to come after. It also partakes of the nature of faith, and is the evidence of things not seen. The undiscovered invention, or law, which we are seeking, seems so beautiful in vision that we believe it must be found, and so persevere till we find it. The ideal marches before the mind, a cloud by day and a pillar of fire by night, guiding us into the promised land. The imagination is the prophetic soul which dreams of things to come, and is always making a new heaven and a new earth.

It would be a great gain to theology if the interpreters of the Scriptures had usually more imagination, and were able to throw themselves into the state of the times, and make a picture of the condition of things. They are apt to explain the Scriptures by dictionary and grammar. But merely by the help of grammar and dictionary one cannot enter into the mind of Christ, or into that of Paul. How much mischief has been done by prosaic commentators interpreting texts in too literal a way! If a teacher tells you that such and such a book will feed your mind, you know well enough what he means by help of your imagination. But when Jesus says, "You must eat me and drink me in order to get any life out of me," men have supposed he is to be literally eaten, and have burned and tortured thousands for doubting it. If you hear a man say, "There is no end to the evil which comes from such conduct," or if he says that "man's passions are a fire which nothing can put out," you simply suppose he means that the consequences are very grave and terrible. But when Jesus says that those who refuse to feed the hungry and clothe the naked will go into eternal punishment, and that their fire will never be quenched, the theologians, with dictionary and grammar, insist, perhaps too peremptorily, that he must necessarily teach never-ending punishment hereafter. When an ambassador says, " If you show disrespect to me, it is showing disrespect to my government," we do not understand him to say that he is the government. But when Jesus says that " all men must honor the Son even as they honor the Father," the dictionary and grammar theologians declare that this is the only legitimate inference. If a patriot says, " I can forgive you for ill-treating me, but I cannot forgive you for betraying my country ; that is an unpardonable sin," we do not hold him to the letter; but we take Jesus literally when he says, " If you say anything against me it can be forgiven, but not if you are false to the spirit of truth in your own soul. That is an unpardonable sin in this world and every other world." This is why Paul says " The letter killeth." It has been remarked that nothing lies like a fact ; so, we may say, nothing is so false as the interpretation which sticks in the letter. We never can understand the Scripture until we give up the notion that Jesus is always in a pulpit preaching a sermon. He walked in the streets, and talked with common people in their own way ; and till we throw ourselves, by force of imagination, into the scenes and the time, we fail of seeing his truth.

In morals, also, the imagination is very necessary. You cannot be just to another person if you merely observe what he says and does; you must put yourself in his place, and see things from his point of view. Prosaic persons are often unjust, hard, cruel, unforgiving, simply from this defect. They cannot identify themselves with the offender so as to understand the force of circumstances and the power of the temptation. They only see what is done, not what is resisted. To sympathize with a person who is different from yourself requires an act of the imagination. You must " put yourself in his place;" then you feel with him, and so can feel for him. A great deal of the selfishness of the world comes not from bad hearts, but from languid imaginations.

The imagination is not only a moral, but a religious faculty. God is revealed not only by the prophets who teach his truth, but by the universe which shows him in its beauty. We do not see God as we ought, if we only see him in the Bible and not in nature. God has filled the world with beauty to overflowing, — superabounding beauty. He has manifested himself in suns and storms, in stars and flowers, in the majestic order of the universe, in the infinite variety of creation. And if we do not see this, we do not see his working. Nature plies evermore at the roaring loom of time to weave a garment by which we may see God. And then, because

"the world is too much with us," we are out of tune
for it all, and it does not move us. Therefore, the
great Christian poet declares he had rather be a
Pagan suckled in an outworn creed, for then he
might catch a glimpse of something divine in nature,
— of Proteus rising from the sea, or Triton blowing
his horn.

To see God in the order, variety, majesty, tenderness of the universe will save us from superstitious
terrors. This gives us a sense

> "Of something far more deeply interfused,
> Whose dwelling is the light of setting suns.
> A motion and a spirit, which pervades
> All living things, all objects of all thought,
> And rolls through all things."

And this will drive away the foul terrors of hell,
and the narrow doctrines which make God a tyrant
and man a slave. Our bigotry fades away as we
look at the midnight stars and at the rising sun;
our anxiety leaves us as we feel the gentle gradations
of autumnal tints, and the slow decay of the dying
year. God seen in nature corrects the superstitions
born of the narrowness of human creeds.

The imagination may be educated by the sight of
beauty, and by making all our own life beautiful;
that is, by receiving and giving the beautiful.

All men have the power of seeing beauty. If we
love it, and look for it, we shall see it everywhere.
The great law, "Seek and ye shall find," applies here
as in other things. Some men pass their lives in

ugliness, seeing only ugly objects everywhere. Others are always surrounded by beauty. The reason is that some have cultivated the habit of looking for it, others not. Milton lived in London, but he saw more beauty in one morning's walk in the country than many country people observe in all their lives. It is not necessary to go to Switzerland in order to find the Alps. You can see them after any thunderstorm in summer. Then the departing masses of cloud, bathed by the western sun, swell into vast snow-mountains, and roll up into great glaciers and fields of ice.

We also educate the imagination by creating good things and beautiful things. Every man is an artist who tries to do his work perfectly, for its own sake, and not merely because of what he can get by it. He gets a great deal more this way than he will in any other. Every man can turn his life into poetry, romance, art, by living according to an ideal standard. He may be a day-laborer, a mechanic, a sweeper of street-crossings ; but, if he puts his soul into his work, his work becomes a fine art. No one may notice it, but he notices it himself, and I think that God and the angels notice it also.

There is an old Norse story of a blacksmith who sold himself to the devil on condition that, during a certain number of years, he might be the best blacksmith in the world. So over his shop-door he wrote, " Voland the Smith, Master of Masters." One day Jesus Christ came in, and said he could teach him something he did not know, and showed him a better way of shoeing a horse than he had ever seen. Voland, in delight at seeing this better way, forgot his vanity and pride, and asked to be allowed to be a scholar, and sit at the feet of this greater Master. Then Jesus said: "Now you have escaped from the power of the devil, for you have learned a better way than he could teach. He only made you a master from pride, in order to be better than all others; you have learned of me to be a master for the sake of the work itself, and in order to learn you have been willing to humble yourself."

Perfect expression becomes beauty. Truth, perfectly expressed, becomes beautiful poetry, rhetoric, oratory. Goodness, when it is so perfectly expressed in life as to rise above all effort and struggle, becomes the beauty of holiness. Nature, being a perfect expression of God's will, is a revelation of the divine beauty. The imagination is the faculty by means of which we grasp this beauty, and hold it before our mind while we attempt to realize it. Every human action done well partakes of this element of beauty. When books were all written with the pen, before the invention of printing, many manuscripts were so beautifully written as to become works of art. A piece of good handwriting is still beautiful; good reading is beautiful. This element of beauty descends into the most humble acts of human life, and gives a charm to every human work when it is done according to an ideal standard.

If we limit beauty too narrowly, we fall into the danger of becoming fastidious. This is a disease which affects many artists, and grows into an irritable and nervous dislike of everything not in the best taste. It is a bad thing to cultivate the love of beauty when it makes common things, people, life, distasteful to us. It need not do so, as appears from the example of such great poets as Burns, Wordsworth, Whittier, who have known how to glorify common life and every-day people with the charm of romance. These great masters make the humblest flower immortal in their song; walk in glory and in joy, following their plough along the side of the mountain; and impart some random truth from the common things which lie around us.

No man can be wholly unhappy who is accustomed to look for beauty in nature and in human life. His is a joy which never wearies. As we grow old many of our senses grow dull, but the sense of beauty becomes a more perfect enchantment every year. Each new spring seems to open in more exuberant, miraculous grace, tenderness, and charm than the last. Every new rosebud seems the most perfect one we ever saw. The tender lights and rosy coloring of the auroral dawn; the drifting feathery *cirri* clouds in the depths of the blue heavens; the grace of a kitten playing on the carpet; the wonder in the eyes of an infant; the innocent snow, with its soft curves, drifting over fields and weighing down the laboring trees; the splendor of

sunset, when the king of day holds his court, surrounded by his magnificent cloud-courtiers, appar-
elled in all gorgeous colors; the forest and wood,
with their delicate mosses below, and their lights
and shadows above, — how the goodness of God
seems to descend into our human heart through all
these messages, saying how he loves us, and what a
home he has made for us!

Let us thank the great poets of modern times who
have taught us to discover a divine presence in the
charm and wonder of the visible universe. These
are our schoolmasters to bring us to God in nature.
I am thankful that I was born late enough to be
taught these lessons by Wordsworth and Coleridge,
and their noble contemporaries. It has added a
great charm to my life, and I think a depth to my
religion.

The diseases of the imagination are of two kinds ·
one is of lethargy, when it is stupefied, and does not
act; the other is when it is in excess, and acts
without restraint or guidance.

All mere drudgery tends to stupefy the imagination. And all work is drudgery which is done
mechanically, with the hand and not with the mind;
when we are not trying to do our work as well as
possible, but only as well as is necessary. Such work
stupefies the ideal faculty, quenches the sense of
beauty. The day-laborer is not necessarily a drudge,
for he may try to do his work as well as he can.
When he does this he becomes an artist.

But when a man tries to shirk his work, when he does it in a slovenly way, not as well as he might, then he becomes a drudge, even though his work be that of a poet or a sculptor. He ceases to exercise his ideal faculty, and stupefies it. Then the sense of beauty dies out of his mind. When men conform to custom, though they know it is wrong custom, sacrifice conscience to convenience, principle to success, say and do, not what they believe true and right, but what they think to be popular and profitable; then, though they may be senators and statesmen, great lawyers or great preachers, they are really drudges; they are stupefying their ideal nature.

The other disease of the imagination is when it is unrestrained and unregulated. Some people live in a world of dreams, apart from life. They are cradled in illusions; they surround themselves with a world of romance; they become disgusted with actual life; they feed their minds with novels, fairy-tales, and works of fancy, and thus become unfitted for reality. They abhor everything commonplace; they indulge in reverie, and make their daily food of what should be, at best, an occasional refreshment. Now, this is a real disease of the imagination. It is fever, and tends to uselessness, unrest, and insanity.

The cure for both these diseases is the same. It is to seek beauty, not in the world of dreams, but in the actual world, and the actual life. It is to look for beauty everywhere, — in common things, common people, common work, common life. Looking thus we shall soon see that beauty is no monopoly of artists, poets, dreamers; that all life may become high art; that all we do, when done according to an ideal standard, instantly partakes of this element of beauty.   Then, too, it will be seen that all nature is saturated and overflowing with beauty; that our Italy and Switzerland are here in Massachusetts; that one look at the morning sky or the evening sunset may reveal inexhaustible delights; that

> "You cannot wave your staff in the air,
>   Or dip your paddle in the lake,
>   But it carves the bow of beauty there,
>   And the ripples in rhyme the oar forsake."

Beauty divorced from use ceases to be beautiful, as piety divorced from goodness ceases to be piety.

The greatest works of art were all made for some great human uses, — the Parthenon and Strasburg minster for worship, the Transfiguration and the Dresden Madonna to be the inspiration of the people in their churches, Shakspeare's plays to be daily bread for the people.   Art, like the Sabbath, is made for man, not man for art.

Let men be taught, then, to look for beauty in all they see, and to embody beauty in all they do, and the imagination will then be both active and healthy. Life will be neither a drudgery nor a dream, but will become full of God's life and love.

> "I slept, and dreamed that Life was Beauty,
>   I woke, and found that Life was Duty.

"Was my dream, then, a shadowy lie?
Toil on, sad heart, courageously, —
And thou shalt find thy dream shall be
A noon-day light and truth to thee."

Yes, for all duties, when thoroughly and perfectly done, according to a standard in the soul, become works of art. Beauty sought by itself vanishes in dreams; beauty sought in reality becomes the charm of our life.

The more that we see of beauty everywhere, — in nature, in life, in man and child, in work and rest, in the outward and the inward world, — the more we see of God. His divine perfection is perceived, however dimly, in all that he has made. "Now we see it darkly, as in a glass; but then face to face." That which we have learned to know and love here, by a due use and culture of the imagination, we shall see fully then, in the radiant glory of a higher world.

This is the culture of the imagination: first, to learn to see the beauty and grace which God has poured out on sky, land, and sea; on body and soul; on life and conduct; on society and art; then, to be a creator of beauty as God creates it, carrying this idea of the perfect into all that we do, learning continually to think more exactly, speak more accurately, live more truly, and finish all we undertake well. So shall we be brought into the love of that divine beauty which is above all, through all, and in us all. This is that beauty which not only dwells in the summer sun and the round ocean, but is also a beauty known to neither sea nor land, but borrowed from the prophetic soul itself, " dreaming of things to come."

I can wish nothing better for any one than to respect this great faculty ın his soul, and to train it to see and to create always that which is best. Thus a blameless pleasure will pervade our lives, — life will grow richer, not poorer, as we grow older. We shall see more and more of the divine love ın all things, and ever come nearer to God and to man.

IX.

EDUCATION OF THE CONSCIENCE.

EDUCATION OF THE CONSCIENCE.

——◦◇◦——

BY the conscience I mean the principle, or instinct, òr power within every man, which shows to him the distinction between right and wrong; makes him feel that he ought to do some things, ought not to do others; and gives him a sense of satisfaction when he does what he believes to be right, of dissatisfaction when he does what he believes to be wrong. Regarded as an intellectual power, it is the sight of duty as an idea; viewed as a motive, it is that which prompts to moral conduct; considered as sentiment, it is the feeling of merit or demerit, of remorse or self-approbation.

There are those, we know, who maintain that there is no such faculty in man as this, asserting that, in the last analysis, these convictions may be reduced to the sense of what is profitable, useful, and pleasant. The reasons for this opinion, as given by Archdeacon Paley, are such as these.

" Historians and travellers tell us that there is scarcely a vice which has not in some age or country been approved by public opinion, scarcely a virtue which has not been condemned; that in one country it is thought right for children to support their aged parents, in another to despatch them out of the way. In one age suicide is heroism, in another felony; theft was rewarded in Sparta as meritorious; duelling is praised or condemned, according to the sex, age, or station of the speaker." Hence it is inferred there is no moral sense in man.

.This objection to a moral sense would be conclusive if we maintain that conscience teaches us what is right or wrong. But this we do not say. We say it gives us the idea of right and wrong; causes us to approve what we believe right, disapprove what we believe to be wrong. What is right and wrong has to be learned, as we learn other truths, by the exercise of the reason and by experience.

The idea of right is not the same as that of the profitable or pleasant. They cannot be made to seem the same. The idea of right and wrong is primary, — it is not to be explained into any other notion. It resists all further analysis. When you reach that, you arrive at a fundamental idea, a primary fact. In reality, you may be said to be looking at God himself on one side of his being. It would be bad if we could explain it away, for then we should see so much less of God.

But it cannot be explained away. All the world

over, in all lands, in all times, wherever man is to be found, is found this conception of duty. There is no race, no individual so low, but that something seems to him to be right, something wrong. There is no language among the thousand varieties of human speech which has not the words "ought," "ought not;" "right," "wrong;" "duty," "obligation." And not a day passes but men use these words. Some things seem to all men to be just, other things unjust. Some people are said to deserve reward, others to merit punishment. When you say, "That man is a villain, he ought to be punished," you do not mean the same thing as when you say, "That man has made a mistake which is doing us harm." You do not have the same feeling toward one who injures you accidentally and one who injures you deliberately.

Is there any one who does not know the difference between regret and remorse? I am sorry for misfortune, but I feel guilty for sin. It may be a small sin which I have committed. It may be a slight deviation from the truth, a slight dereliction from duty. No matter. I often feel as deeply this small wrong-doing as if it were ever so great an injury to myself or others. For there is no great, no small, in right and wrong. In that which is expedient or inexpedient the question of more or less may be of importance. In going to the railway station it may, perhaps, be better to go by one street than by another. I may save a minute or two. But if I take the worst road, or go the longest way, I only suffer temporal evil. In regard to all success and failure, all prosperity or adversity, the proverb applies, "It will make no difference a hundred years hence." But that proverb does not apply to doing right or wrong. It makes a difference, or seems to us that it will make a difference, a thousand years hence, a million years hence. It makes a difference forever. This is the only way in which we can believe in eternal punishment. It may make a difference to all eternity whether we do right or wrong to-day.

In buying something in a shop, I find I have paid by mistake a dollar too much. That is no great matter. Or, perhaps, I have lost a dollar from my pocket-book. That does not trouble me. But suppose I receive a counterfeit dollar in change. I have a feeling that I am wronged. It is not the loss, it is the injustice, which troubles me. And now suppose that having taken this counterfeit, I pass it over on some one else. I say, "I took it; now let some one else take it." Instead of destroying it, as I ought to do, I let it slip out of my hands into those of some other person. This is an action which may trouble me a million years hence, may trouble me in heaven.

If the devil should appear visibly to any of us, — if he should enter undisguised, with visible horns and tail, and offer you millions for your soul, you would refuse, and say, " Get thee behind me, Satan." But when he comes in the form of business, and says, "Do as other people do. It may not be quite right, but every one else does it. Do not be too puritanical. Be not righteous overmuch; why destroy yourself?" then, perhaps, we sell our soul to him for a very paltry sum; and, perhaps, he cheats us out of that small sum, after all.

How the one deep voice of the human conscience sounds out of the past, striking the same chord of eternal right! Read the biographies of Plutarch. What a wholesome tonic there is in the words of those heroic souls speaking in the service of immortal justice and right! Homer makes a hero say, "I consulted my own great mind." When Dion had his enemy in his power, he said, "I have conquered Heraclides in war, now I will show that I am superior to him in justice. The laws allow revenge, but must Dion sully his glory by indulging it?" So he pardoned his foe, and set him free. Cato the Younger was such a truthful man that it became a proverb, "I would not believe it, even if Cato said it." In his day, as in ours, there were rings and lobbies, and Cato proposed a law requiring every man to declare on oath whether he had been elected to his office by such means. This made him so unpopular that he was stoned as he went to the Forum, and his companions fled, but he stood so firm and calm that the tumult subsided, and he was heard in silence "A just man and tenacious of his purpose," says Horace, "fears neither the tyrant nor the mob."

The people of Athens had such respect for the integrity of Aristides that once, when Themistocles told them he had a plan which would be of great advantage to Athens, but must not be told publicly, they said, " Tell it to Aristides, and if he says we ought to do it, we will." He did so, and it proved to be a plan to seize the ships of the other Greeks, and so make themselves masters of the sea. Aristides then told the people that " nothing could be more profitable, but nothing more unjust, than the measure proposed by Themistocles." So the Athenians rejected it, without hearing what it was.

The whole of social life is rooted in conscience. Honest men are the salt of the earth. If God had not given to us this sense of justice, society would be impossible. If all men thought only of what was profitable and pleasant, no man's life would be safe. What is it holds society together? Is it your laws, your courts, your police, your prisons, your gallows, your militia? No!

It is only for the outlaws, the dangerous classes, those who have thrown off the restraints of conscience, that we build prisons and establish courts. The law is for the lawless. But the great mass of men do right because they have a conscience. " Conscience makes cowards of us all," says Shakspeare; it makes men afraid to do the evil they would like to do. In our fancy, in our imagination, we may conceive of ourselves as having the ring of Gyges, the purse of Fortunatus. But if we had these marvellous powers we should not use them. Our conscience would prevent us. Men often imagine themselves better than they are ; but they also imagine themselves worse than they are. Dickens's character who was in the habit of uttering terrific threats against those who injured him, saying that they ought to be flayed alive, and that he should like to see them hung ; and who yet was, in reality, a very kind-hearted man, who would not hurt a fly, — this character is a very natural one. Conscience is *a power* within us, not merely a conviction or a purpose. The sense of duty becomes at last incarnate in our nature, and turns into .character. It often holds us to the right against our will, when we would be glad to go wrong. So it is that educated, trained, enlightened conscience is the cornerstone of society.

But it must be educated and trained ; for a diseased conscience, a torpid conscience, a falsely instructed conscience, an ignorant conscience, an irritable conscience, a weak conscience, a conscience defiled by evil, a conscience seared or impure, may be worse for the time than no conscience at all. Conscience is a power which can be misdirected, and will then do more harm than good. The cruelty of savages is not equal to the cruelty of saints who think it their duty to torment their fellow-creatures. Let a father only think it his duty to treat his children with severity, let a teacher believe that he ought to be stern and hard, and natural sympathy and love are frozen at their roots. From a sense of duty the Phœnicians burned their children alive; from a sense of duty tens of thousands of martyrs have been tortured at the stake; from a sense of duty husbands have been selfish, wives obstinate, friends unfriendly. Those whose hearts yearned to love each other have been cold as ice, because they thought they ought to be so. From a sense of duty men have inflicted on themselves tortures without end; have denied themselves common joys; have tormented themselves with imaginary sins; have thought it right to believe God a tyrant, and man a depraved being, to be always looking at hell, not at heaven.

Cotton Mather, who wrote a book on " doing good," so earnest, persuasive, tender, that Dr. Franklin attributed to it whatever useful acts he himself had done in the world, — this same Cotton Mather, misled by an ignorant conscience, stood by rejoicing when seventeen persons were hung at Salem for witchcraft. So hard may a good man's heart become when his conscience is darkened by superstition.

In all parts of life conscience is the most important of elements. The civilization is cheap and weak which has not the backbone of conscience in it. You cannot have a coat well made, a horse properly shod, a house decently built, a good cup of tea or coffee, unless there is conscience in those who serve you. Money will not buy good articles; it will only buy what seems good. Your clothes come to pieces;

they were not conscientiously made. Your house takes fire and burns down; for the carpenter put a beam into the chimney, because you could not know it. Your tea, sugar, flour, spices, tobacco, everything you use, is adulterated. You think you are buying coffee; you get chicory, beans, burnt sugar, and dried bread. Flour is mixed with your mustard, leaves of herbs with your tobacco. Everything is adulterated where there is no conscience.

One would think that nothing would be so sought after in business as an honest man. If my clerk cheats me, if my cashier robs the till, if a bank-teller falsifies his accounts to get money with which to speculate, I may be ruined before I know it. Nevertheless, no one goes about like Diogenes, looking for an honest man; all are looking for smart men. An honest man, a little slow, gets a salary of one thousand dollars a year; a smart man, who will rob you on the first good occasion, you buy with five thousand.

All men have conscience; almost all men mean to do right; most men do generally act up to their own standard of right. But the standard of right with most men is simply the public opinion around. What others think is right, they think right. The social standard of duty guides the conscience of nine persons out of ten. Therefore it is of the utmost importance to educate the public conscience on all subjects of practical morality.

All means should be used to keep public opinion

right in its standard of duty. A man takes trust funds and gambles with them, or a bank cashier takes the money of the bank and speculates with it. People are first angry with him, then sorry for him, then agree to compromise, then let him off, then help him to do the same thing again. This is all very kind and benevolent. But what is the result? You are educating your young men, your clerks, your agents, to believe that there is no great harm in doing the same thing. Do it on a large scale, that is all. You are systematically corrupting the conscience of the community. You are teaching them that in this kind of stealing there is no harm. To steal by picking a man's pocket sends one to the State's prison; but to steal by robbing shareholders, plundering tax-payers by means of rings and lobbies, that is financial ability; or, at the worst, if one is found out, a financial irregularity.

If these things are done in the green tree, what will be done in the dry? We are hardly three generations removed from the Puritans, men whose lives were hard, dry, austere, who were implacable towards God's enemies as they understood them, but who lived and had their being in conscience. They would have cut off a right hand, and plucked out a right eye, rather than have done wrong. If corruption of conscience is the result of our civilization, then better that all our wealth were sunk in the Atlantic. Better that every railroad were torn up, every steamer sunk, every manufactory burned to the ground, and we again be dressed in homespun, and living in log-cabins. We should then, at least, have God, truth, nature, love, justice for our friends and companions, if we did not have fine dresses and champagne suppers.

The public conscience is being fast corrupted. When corporations are in turn plundered and become plunderers, and there is no redress; when lawyers in the front rank of their profession sell their talents and influence to protect public robbers; when those who steal thousands from widows and orphans are allowed to walk the streets unharmed; when smartness and not honesty is in demand, — then society is in danger of dissolution. The salt has lost its savor; what is it good for? What is the use of the church, the school, the college, the press, if they cannot instruct the community in common honesty?

This is what the salt is for. We talk about the importance of reading the Bible in the schools, and think it will be a dreadful thing to let the Catholics exclude it from them. But if, instead of a few minutes given to reading the letter of the Bible, all our school-teachers should daily give their scholars practical lessons in honesty and generosity; if they should thrill those young hearts with noble stories of virtue, — no Catholic would object to that, I think, and those seeds would bear fruit for the healing and safety of the nation.

And if the pulpit, instead of its controversial theology or its sentimental devotion, its talk about "the church" or its abuse of heresy, should every week set up a standard of right; should call all men to "do justly and love mercy and walk humbly with God;" if it should make goodness attractive, and show that wickedness is always misery and ruin, — then the whole church would work together to build up a righteous community, a kingdom of heaven.

Beside the school, the college, the pulpit, the public mind is educated by the press. Whatever else a man does or leaves undone every day, he always reads the newspaper. Now, there are three kinds of newspapers.

First, there is the satanic newspaper, which deliberately caters to the lowest tastes; which constantly sneers at justice and humanity; which educates the community to self-conceit. Let people be accustomed every day to have it assumed that all conscientiousness is hypocrisy, all religion a sham, all interest in other men a weakness, and at last they take that tone, and lose their sense of the nobleness of virtue.

Then there is another class of newspapers, rare enough, few enough, and yet we have some such, who stand up for national justice and honor. They battle through long years against atrocious wrong, resting on no less a deep foundation than conscience. They appeal to that, and not in vain. They may be inconsistent, and often wrong, as we think; they may be prejudiced; but they do an immense service.

They are not afraid to expose iniquity in low places and in high. They throw light into the villany which likes darkness and concealment. The journals which do this are great moral guides, and de serve well of their country.

And then there is a third class, of which it may be said that they are neither cold nor hot, but lukewarm. They are never heartily in favor of right, nor openly on the side of wrong. If any effort is made to improve the community, they approve of the object, but predict its failure. They overflow in eulogy of the good men who are dead and gone, but never have the courage to speak one strong word in behalf of the good men who are fighting against evil to-day. They generally think such persons are injudicious, unpractical, and in bad taste. These journals may be said to represent the cowardice of the community. While the first class of journals educate the public mind to evil, and the second lift the national conscience to truth and right, this last sort teach the community indifference. Better that they were cold or hot than to be thus lukewarm.

What is needed is the education of the conscience. The chief diseases of the conscience are stupor and ignorance. The conscience may be inactive, or it may be badly instructed. The sins of the time, the crimes against society, the swindling transactions, the defalcations, the betrayals of trust, the repudiation of public obligations, are not usually deliberate violations of what is seen to be right, but rather come from consciences stupefied, sophisticated, and uninstructed.[1]

The education of the conscience is of three kinds. It needs to be awakened, to be enlightened, and to be trained. It is awakened by being taught the obligations we owe to God and man; that man is under law; that no one has any right to do as he pleases, but that all are responsible to God and to the truth for every action of their lives. It is roused by the doctrine of the judgment to come, by being

---

[1] Take, for example, the proposition made a few years since to pay the national debt in silver, when silver was below par, — a plan at one time very popular, and which would have inflicted so much injury on the honor and welfare of the nation, and which would have been a blow to national credit, and the source of disaster. We mistake if we suppose that the people of the West and South were deliberately doing what they knew to be wrong in supporting it. They were misled by artful demagogues. They were taught to believe that, as the letter of the law allowed payment of the early bonds in coin of either kind, there would be no injustice in paying them in a depreciated currency. They were persuaded that the demonetization of silver was a cunning trick of rich bondholders, done in order to oppress the poor, and that the people had been defrauded thus of the money which would give new activity to business and furnish employment to thousands. But when they were taught that this was all false, and that the plan was in the interest of speculators; when they saw that it would be defrauding every man who had any money due him of ten cents on a dollar; that it would be cheating the foreign creditors who lent us their money in our war when we needed it to save the nation ; that it would be cheating the widows and orphans whose small means were intrusted to the honor of the country ; that it would be cheating every farmer out of a tenth part of the

taught that all our lives are to be ultimately known and seen in the light of eternal truth, and that every man is to give an account of himself to God. It is the duty of the Church to arouse the conscience by these solemn truths, and to show to all men that for every idle word they are to give an account in the day of the revelation of God's truth; that there is nothing covered that shall not be revealed, nor any thing hid which shall not be known.

Then the conscience, having been awakened, needs

---

price of his wheat, every day-laborer of the tenth part of his day's wages; and all to put more money into the pockets of the rich owners of the silver mines, — then the conscience of the land refused to accept such a proposition. These truths were taught boldly, plainly, unequivocally, in tones which reached every log-cabin beyond the mountains. The people were taught that the collapse of business was the natural result of over-trading, over-investments in costly speculations, and pushing the credit system to an extreme point. They were taught that what we needed for the revival of business was not more money, but more confidence; that there was money enough, but that those who had it would not risk it. They were made to see that confidence comes not by repudiation of debts, not by expansion and depreciation of the currency, not by trying to cheat creditors, but by exactly the opposite course, and that all these measures would only increase the evils under which we suffered. They saw at last that the remedy for the state of commercial distrust was that each man should learn economy, give up extravagance, quit speculation, do a safe business, pay his debts promptly, and that the government should lead the way by resuming specie payments; that is, by beginning to pay its honest debts in honest money. As soon as the conscience of the nation was enlightened on such points as these, such a piece of dishonesty as the Bland bill became impossible.

14

to be enlightened; it needs to be taught the difference between right and wrong in all things. For this purpose we must have some standard, rule, code of ethics.

Many of the worst actions done in the world have been done by honest people, who conscientiously believed that they were doing right. Most persecutors, from the time of Paul down through the Inquisitors, who burned thousands in Spain for some supposed heresy, to the Alvas and Philips, Louis XIV., Bloody Mary and her more bloody father, — these have believed themselves doing God service. The instruction of the conscience is therefore of the utmost importance. But where is the code? what is the standard?

Most Christians will tell us that the Gospel of Jesus gives us a code of ethics which is sufficient for all purposes. But there is no such systematic code in the New Testament. We are there taught principles of right rather than rules. These great principles are no doubt sufficient to raise the world to a far higher condition of morals than it has yet attained. Such is the golden rule of doing to others as we would wish them to do to us; or, putting ourselves in their place. Such are the large directions like these: "Overcome evil with good;" "Speak the truth in love;" " Love God with all your heart, and love your neighbor as yourself;" " Let your yea be yea, and your nay nay;" " Love your enemies, bless those that persecute you;" " Forgive, that ye may be forgiven;" "He that humbleth himself shall be exalted;" "It is more blessed to give than to receive."

The Apostle Paul gives it as his opinion that all duties to others are comprehended in the saying, "Thou shalt love thy neighbor as thyself;" because a man who loves his neighbor as himself will not cheat him, or injure him in any other way. Still, considered in the light of an exhaustive criticism, this is not enough. For a conscientious inquisitor would honestly say, "If I were a heretic as he is, I should think that I ought to be burned alive." We need, then, a rule to show him that neither he nor his neighbor should be punished for his opinion. This other rule is no doubt to be found in such sayings as "Judge not, that ye be not judged;" "Who art thou that judgest another man's servant?" But, after all, Christianity is a spirit rather than a code. It is an inspiration from which codes and rules may come, but it does not give them.

These rules come, as we have said, from experience. No doubt there are some great ideas of right common to the whole human race, to which the soul of man in all lands and times gives its assent. These ideas may be reduced to two, — truth and love.

These two, truth and love, are the antagonist but not contradictory principles from which all ethics must be developed. They are the two poles of the moral universe, which are harmonized in God into a sublime unity, and which approach a similar unity in all good men. They are equally venerable, equally beautiful. All goodness partakes of both elements; and in all true excellence mercy and truth meet together, righteousness and peace kiss each other.

The doctrine which makes utility the criterion of ethics is inadequate, because it is always in danger of sacrificing principle to expediency; that is, of postponing truth to love. If we make "the greatest good of the greatest number" an absolute rule of ethics, we risk sacrificing those noble instincts which have made heroes, saints, and martyrs in all time. When we are obliged to ask always and only, "What good will this action do to mankind?" we may easily fail of seeing the good of the very best actions. The heart, in such cases, is often wiser than the head. So it was in the case of that noble man, John Stuart Mill, when he uttered the sentiment, the most admired, perhaps, in all his writings. Denying with great energy the doctrine that the standard of right and wrong can be different in man and God, he added that "if he must go to hell for such a denial, to hell he would go." Now Mr. Mill was a firm believer in the doctrine that the true standard in morals is the greatest good of the greatest number. Miss Frances Power Cobbe thereupon acutely remarked, that if it was right for Mr. Mill to go to hell for this conviction, it must be right for all others to do so too, and that thus all mankind ought to be willing to go to hell "for the greatest good of the greatest number."

Every case of conscience which arises must be decided by itself, according to this law of supreme and equal reverence for truth on the one side and for love on the other. Truth must not be sacrificed to love, nor love to truth. It is only because of our ignorance or our weakness that this ever seems necessary. In the highest state of the soul it is not necessary.

All real difficulties as to what is right will turn out, in the last analysis, to come from the supposed conflict of these two principles. Is it right for a physician to lie to his patient about his disease, when telling the truth might injure him? May I lie to another for his good, or to a highway robber to save his victim, or to a murderer to prevent a crime? On the other hand, must I sacrifice love to truth by telling the truth which will injure my friend; by standing by my principles and convictions when they will injure those I love? Must I be scrupulously honest when no one requires it of me, and when a great apparent injury will result from it? He who sacrifices all expediency to a theory or a belief is in danger of becoming a fanatic. He who gives up his principles whenever some risk or some evil seems likely to follow their application will soon do evil that good may come.

No absolute rule can be laid down for all such cases. There are dangers on either hand. We need principles of right-doing to guide us, to which we must cling for safety, even at the risk of seeming scrupulous and puritanical. Conscience in little things is our only safeguard against temptation. If we adopt the theory of ethics which makes right another name for utility, and makes utility the criterion of right, we are liable to imagine the thing we wish to be useful. How many men in places of trust — trustees, cashiers of banks, treasurers of corporations, town treasurers — have been tempted in this way, and brought disgrace on themselves and their families? They said, "We can use these funds to advantage for ourselves, and no harm to others. We are sure to succeed in this speculation. We shall gain, and no one lose." The only safeguard for men in such positions is an inflexible principle. "Do right, though the heavens fall." "Touch not, taste not, handle not." "Resist the beginnings." Such is the language of wisdom in all time. This is the panoply — the armor *cap-a-pie* — which alone makes one safe.

Truth embodies itself in these stern and sure laws, these inflexible rules of justice, honor, fidelity to trusts, loyalty to engagements, adherence to promises, abhorrence of the slightest dishonesty. To such a spirit the rights of all are sacred, of friends and enemies alike.

Join with that the spirit of love, which seeks the good of all, which desires to help all, — not for their gratitude, not for reputation or for praise, but because it is more blessed to give than to receive. Thus truth is for the sake of love, and love for the sake of truth. We do good to others for our own sake, in order to be true to ourselves. We are faithful to truth and right, because we know that this only will help and save the human race.

The spirit of righteousness is more than the letter; and if we live in that spirit, we shall also walk in it.

After the awakening and instruction of the conscience, comes its training or discipline. And this is each man's own work. This he must teach himself by practice. Even the Apostle says, "Herein, do I exercise myself, to keep a conscience always void of offence toward God and man." This exercise requires self-study, self-knowledge. We have all of us our besetting sins, our special moral danger, and our special moral strength. We should find out what our peculiar need is, and arrange our life and our circumstances accordingly. A bad habit, which cannot be conquered directly, may be overcome by arranging circumstances to help us. If a man is indolent, he should put himself where he will be obliged to work. If he is irritable, he should avoid the occasions which will excite his temper. If he is tempted to insincerity and falsehood, he should surround himself with all possible influences and helps to keep him to the strictest verity. And in all this he needs the help of religion, of daily prayer, and of living always in the great Taskmaster's eye.

Beside the public conscience, of which we all

partake, every man needs, for his own self-respect, to have a conscience of his own.   He needs to have some principles of right by which to live, and then to live accordingly.   " Have salt in yourselves," says Jesus.   Your conscience can no more be kept healthy without exercise than your body ; and the best exercise for the conscience is in holding fast its integrity in small things.   Here lies the chief temptation to wrong.   To tell a small untruth, to utter a little word of unkindness, to cheat in some very unimportant matter, —these are the real temptations of life which beset us.

Let a man be thoroughly conscientious, and he becomes the salt of society, the light of the world. He is the little candle which throws its steady beams very far into the night.   Society leans on such men.   The Church leans on them.   The State leans on them.   All depends on character.   One man who has a character of his own, poised on principle, is stronger than all other men who copy each other. " When the righteous die," says the Talmud, " it is the earth which loses.   The lost jewel will be always a jewel, wherever it goes ; but those who have lost it, they may weep."   " He who has more knowledge than good works is like a tree with many branches and few roots, which the first wind throws on its face ; while he who does more than he says is like a tree with strong roots and few branches, which all the winds cannot uproot."   Confucius says, " To live according to justice is like the pole-star, which stands firm while the whole heaven moves around it."

"What is a man profited, if he gain the whole world and lose his own soul?" says Jesus. The Buddhist also says that "all the jewels and gold one can collect he drops from his hand when he dies, but every good action he has done is rooted into his soul, and can never leave him."

"Happy is he who walks attended," says Milton, "by that strong-siding champion, Conscience."

X.

EDUCATION OF THE AFFECTIONS AND SOCIAL POWERS.

EDUCATION OF THE AFFECTIONS AND SOCIAL POWERS.

———◦◦———

THE community of the early Christians, as described in the Book of Acts, was, I suppose, the best society the world has ever seen, the highest social condition yet attained by human beings. That was the divine compensation which they had for their poverty, persecution, danger.

There was among them a thorough union of heart and soul, entire sympathy among themselves, absence of selfish aims, each happy to give and willing to receive ; having one faith, one hope, one love. Their hearts were penetrated to the centre with the divine truth of the new gospel, and it developed their whole life, making some apostles, some prophets, some teachers ; bringing out all the gifts and graces that were in them. They lived together, they belonged together. They were all brothers and sisters, fathers and children. They were so perfectly *at one*, that Paul could find no better similitude for this union than that of the different limbs and organs of the human body working together toward one end; all "fitly joined together, and compacted by that which every joint supplieth." A man then no more thought of saying, "This is my place," "This is my right," than the hand thinks of saying to the foot, "This blood belongs to me, not to you," or of saying to the other hand, "I have a right to do this, you have not."

This, I think, was, on the whole, the highest condition of human society ever yet attained. It had all the elements of the best society in it. (1.) A common cause, in which all were interested, harmonizing their varieties, subduing their differences, directing their faculties to one end. (2.) An enthusiasm of love, which conquered for a time the selfish elements, and made them of one heart and soul. (3.) A new and profound experience of truth, developing the best faculties of their nature. Thus they had a common truth, common work, and a common love; and if that does not make the best society, what does?

It did not last; it could not. If it had lasted, heaven would have already come on the earth. For a few days this divine life of love lasted. "The sun stood still over Gibeon, and the moon in the valley of Ajalon," and then the old difficulties came back. Hypocrisy came into the church with Ananias and Sapphira; sectarianism, with those who said, "I am of Paul," and "I am of Apollos." Old Adam was too strong for young Melancthon. But this gleam of glory remained, this enchanting vision of a pure, unselfish brotherhood, to prove the possibility of such a condition; a prophecy, that some day it would be reached again, not by a few, but by all.

Man was made for society. But, then, to be capable of society, he must first be an individual. The conditions of a musical chord are these: that there shall be two notes, which are, first, different from each other; and, secondly, in harmony with each other. So, for a perfect society, you must have first perfectly distinct individuals. Individual life and character must be developed before they can be harmonized.

Man was made for society; and an unsocial state is an unnatural state. Long ago, Dr. James Walker uttered a sentence which I have never forgotten, "There never was a greater misnomer than to call a savage a child of Nature." Nature did not make men to be noble savages, running wild in the woods, but to co-operate in society. It will do very well to spend a month or two in the Adirondacks or in the parks of Colorado in the summer, away from all social life; but it is good because these few weeks of loneliness prepare the sauce of hunger for the social feast which is to follow.

The social instinct, in its lowest form, which is merely the wish to be with other people, is shared also by animals. Most animals are gregarious; they run in herds, fly in flocks, swim in shoals. A dog is happy if you let him come into the house, and sleep on the carpet where the family are assembled; all he asks is to be with you.

When we speak of the affections or social qualities, we include a great range of human feeling, extending upward from a blind canine attachment to
the loftiest piety and most unbounded charity. The
following varieties of the social element of human
affection may be specified : —

1. *Blind attachment*, or mere adhesiveness, — the
disposition to cling to some person as a support, like
the vine to the oak, irrespective of any quality but
strength. This is born of weakness and the need of
dependence.

2. *Love of Society.* — We are all made social beings,
needing the stimulus of companions and associates.
This is the principle out of which civilization comes.
The life of neighborhoods, towns, and cities depends
on the fact that it is not good for man to be alone.

3. *Sympathy.* — This makes us feel with those
about us ; causes us to enter into their state of mind,
and to rejoice with those who rejoice, or weep with
those who weep. It is a quality which binds us to
those near to us, producing kindliness, good-nature,
pleasant manners, and good-will. But it does not
do much for those at a distance, and may lead us to
neglect them, by being so much absorbed with those
close at hand.

4. *Friendship.* — Here comes in the principle of
selection and choice. Friendship begins very early,
but in its lower stage shares the defects which
belong to *sympathy.* Little children and young
people have their friends, to whom they are ardently

attached for the time, whom they must see every day, or be unhappy. But a short separation is often death to these juvenile attachments, which have no root in their objects, but are born from the instinctive need of loving some one. In its higher forms, friendship is one of the noblest attainments of men, as we see in such instances as that of Shakspeare and his unknown friend; of Gustavus Adolphus and his chancellor Oxenstern; of Tennyson and Hallam; of Charles Lamb and his companions; of Goethe and Schiller; Cowper and Mrs. Unwin; and the immortal group which clustered around Dr. Johnson.

5. *Home Affections.* — These are the first and the last of human attachments; they begin with the first opening of the soul, and they abide when all other feelings have faded away. Families are the unity of which society is composed, as tissue is made of cells, and matter of molecules. The attractions of parent and child, man and wife, brother and sister, are fundamental and primary. They are the deep roots from which social life is developed. According as the family is, so is the State.

6. *Benevolence.* — This differs from sympathy by being not a mere feeling, but a principle of action, and which applies equally to those near and distant, to those whom we like or those whom we dislike. It is, therefore, higher and larger than mere good-nature, and fills many gaps otherwise left empty. We may connect with it pity, which is aroused by

15

the sorrows of others, even of those whom we do not know, but only hear of.

7. *Generosity or Sentiment.* — Here comes a class of sentiments in which thought and feeling unite, such as patriotism, or the love of country; loyalty to one's chief, one's order, one's associates; the sense of honor; the love of truth; heroic devotion to a cause or a principle. These sentiments may easily run into sentimentalism, but they are to be distinguished from it. They enter into all elevated social culture, and constitute a large part of the beauty and charm of human character.

8. Finally, as the perfect development and outcome of all affection, we rise into universal love or charity, which includes love to God and love to man, and is opposed to all selfishness. This is the pure atmosphere in which alone the human soul breathes its highest life. This vitalizes and purifies all other love, and takes away evil passion, low desire, and self-will from the heart.

The affections are in all languages compared with heat. Everywhere men speak of warm feelings, hot desires, the fires of love and hate, burning passions. These metaphors suggest the fact, that as heat is the great motor in the physical world, so desire and love are the great motors in the human world. As under the influence of summer heat plants unfold, so the soul of man develops in society. A solitary man cannot grow. The story of Robinson Crusoe is an ingenious fable, which could scarcely be realized;

for a man wholly alone would lose his ambition, and gradually only do what was necessary for mere existence. Out of the reach of humanity, never hearing the sweet music of human words, he would spend his time in longing for the divine gifts of society and earthly love, and look with horror on the most beautiful objects in nature around him. Indifference, inaction, stupor, come with solitude. We were obliged to give up the system of solitary confinement in our prisons because it speedily led to insanity and death. In the same way, the solitude of the early Christian hermits, who lived alone in caves and under trees, led to a kind of frenzy, and they were therefore collected into communities as early as the fourth century. Man cannot live on bread only, or on thought only, or on prayer only; he also needs human society.

Therefore as man is thus evidently a social animal, human life has been so arranged as to develop the social nature. Infancy and childhood are made dependent on parents; and life is a perpetual inter course of man with man. The family is the smallest social circle; families arranged together make neighborhoods; neighborhoods combined make townships and communities; communities united make nations.

The mere presence of human beings gives a certain satisfaction. I love to go, sometimes, to New York, simply to walk in Broadway, to feel myself in the mighty current of human life which roars

unceasingly along that thoroughfare. On entering
London, landing at Tower-stairs, in the midst of fog
and dirt, a sudden exhilaration once seized me, which
I could not explain till I found, on analyzing it,
that it was the sense of this immense ocean of human
life around me. Nature with no trace of human presence is sublime, but cold. But any remains of
human art — a fragment of a ruined building, the
arch of a bridge over a stream — at once warms up
the scene with associations of man's thought and
action. Standing on the shore, in the presence of
the majestic ocean, if you find a child's playthings
lying on the sand, a glow of tenderness is added to
your sense of the sublime. This human sympathy
is the electric chain with which we are all darkly
bound. Even misanthropy is only philanthropy
turned sour. A cold-blooded or hard-hearted man
does not become a misanthrope.

But this social instinct is not society, — it is only
its foundation. Society means a great deal more
than that. A great city is organized on the basis of
competition rather than of co-operation. It shows
us a mighty struggle for existence, in which the
strong conquer, and the weak are crushed. It is a
battle-field where courage, manliness, perseverance,
quickness of faculty, mental energy, are developed,
but where there is not necessarily any common life.
Separation, exclusion, every man for himself, is the
predominant character, as yet, of city life. There is
no city thus far in which the people have much in

common. We in Boston have some things in common, however. The Common itself, the Public Garden, the Public Library, the music, fireworks, exhibitions for the people on holidays, the public baths in summer, — all these are steps in the right direction. But a country town, where all know all, and participate in each other's feelings and wants, is, at present, a higher condition of social life than a city can be. I once saw a drop of water magnified a million times in the oxy-hydrogen microscope, and it appeared full of fierce creatures jerking violently about, butting against each other in every way, seeking to bite and devour each other. It seemed to me no bad representation of a great city.

True society begins in the home. When two young people love each other, and marry, they restore the picture of the apostolic church. They are of one heart and one soul; neither do they say that anything they possess is their own, but they have all things in common. Their mutual trust in each other, their entire confidence in each other, draws out all that is best in both. Love is the angel who rolls away the stone from the grave in which we bury our better nature, and it comes forth. Love makes all things new; makes a new heaven and a new earth; makes all cares light, all pain easy. It is the one enchantment of human life which realizes Fortunio's purse and Aladdin's palace, and turns the " Arabian Nights " into mere prose in compari son. Think how this old story of love is repeated forever in all the novels and romances and poems, and how we never tire of reading about it; and how, if there is to be a wedding in a church, all the neighbors go, just to have one look at two persons who are *supposed*, at least, to be in love, and so supremely happy.

But this, also, is not perfect society. It is too narrow, too exclusive. It shows the power of devotion, trust, self-surrender, that there is in the human heart; and it is also a prophecy of something larger that is to come. But it is at least a home, and before real society can come, true homes must come. As in a sheltered nook in the midst of the great sea of ice which rolls down from the summit of Mont Blanc is found a little green spot, full of tender flowers; so, in the shelter of home, in the warm atmosphere of household love, spring up the pure affections of parent and child; father, mother, son, daughter; of brothers and sisters. Whatever makes this insecure, and divorce frequent, makes of marriage, not a union for life, but an experiment which may be tried as often as we choose, and abandoned when we like. And this cuts up by the roots all the dear affections of home; leaves children orphaned, destroys fatherly and motherly love, and is a virtual dissolution of society. I know the great difficulties of this question, and how much wisdom is required to solve them. But whatever weakens the permanence of marriage tends to dissolve society; for permanent homes are to the social state what the little cells are to the body. They are the commencement of organic life, the centres from which all organization proceeds.

But domestic life, even the best, does not make society. Homes and happy marriages are the foundations of society, but they are no more sufficient for it than the cellular tissue by itself is sufficient to make a body. Besides this, we need the blood perpetually pouring through every part, and the nervous fluid perpetually animating every part. Something is needed to unite these separate homes into a community. What is the blood and what the nervous fluid which shall combine them into an organic whole?

The next step from the home in the social scale is the neighborhood. By neighbors we mean, not those who are near us in local position, but those who are near us in social affinity. Our real neighbors are not those who live in the next house or street, but those who are on the other side of the city, the country, the world, provided they are those who love us, and whom we love, — our friends, those who agree with us in a common purpose, who sympathize with us in our convictions, who are borne along by our side in the same current of spiritual life.

Our real society is made up of our friends. As friendship declines, society disappears. I hear great complaint of the decay of society. It is said that there is no society now, only large parties. Young people meet together in expensive entertainments; but where is that society which we all need, which consists of the coming together, in natural and easy relations, of old and young, men and women, persons of different tastes and various pursuits, coming together to give and to take; where thought, wit, fancy, feeling, rule the hour; where all is easy, unartificial, and yet refined and pure?

Unity is necessary to constitute society. A ball is not society; a club of men or women is not society; parties, in which the same people meet over and over again, are poor society. That is the penalty of exclusiveness; it excludes the new life it needs. Exclusive circles are very stupid and tiresome ones. It takes all sorts of people to make good society, no less than to make a world. "Our set" is always the word for a meeting where one is sure to be very much bored.

The great queens of society — for society, like a beehive, is always governed by a woman — knew this well. Nothing less aristocratic, less exclusive, than the salons of Mme. Récamier and the other French leaders of society in the last century. The secret is to bring together people who take an interest in each other, people who are interesting to each other. But no one is really interesting except the man who is *alive,* whose soul is on fire with thought, purpose, love. If you can find such persons as this, you may dispense with your ice cream and oysters, your footmen and music. I recollect such a series of receptions, given years ago in this city by a lady. Her means were small, her rooms poor; she offered no entertainment but a glass of water; but she knew so many interesting people, that you were sure to find in her rooms the most charming society imaginable.

Generosity and tact are also necessary to make good society. One of the greatest social powers is that of drawing out other people. Some women have this power in a high degree. By some strange tact they perceive what is the best thing in us, and by some subtle attraction they put us on our best behavior. We do not see how it is done. We merely find ourselves very comfortable, very contented, and talking our very best. The art of drawing out others is much higher than any power of display. They say of one of the queens of French society that, after she became old and poor, and had gone into a convent, she was still visited by all the brightest and best people of Paris. I do not think it was out of gratitude, friendship, or kindness that they went. No; but because she still had the faculty of drawing them out, and making them contented with themselves. This is generosity and insight joined in one; this is the charm which age cannot wither nor custom stale.

We see, then, how much of love, sympathy, generosity, self-forgetfulness, go to a right social development. Put together a company of egotistical and self-conceited people, and, no matter how brilliant they are, no matter how much they know, they have a wretched time. But the moment the early Christians came together, they were of one heart and one soul. They had all things in common. They knew how to give and take. *They* did not meet to show off their own abilities.

Carlyle says of Richter, the German poet, that the aristocracy of the little town of Hof excluded him from its circles. He did not belong to their set "So," adds the biographer, "as he could not be admitted to the West End of Hof, he was obliged to take up his quarters at the west end of the universe, where, indeed, he had a splendid reception."

The Christian Church has always furnished good society to its members. To be sure, in a morbid state of mind, it has sometimes denounced society altogether, and recommended its children to turn monks and nuns, and live alone, and has called this religion. Sometimes it has denounced innocent amusements, and made all social life to resolve itself into prayer-meetings and the singing of hymns. But, on the other hand, to how many lonely persons, to how many poor and forlorn souls, to how many weighed down by sorrow, has it not brought sympathy, friendship, and a helping hand! In many places, all the society there is, is that which is made by the churches. Men and women go in as strangers, and find themselves presently brothers and sisters. They find a kindly atmosphere, good work to do, friendly faces to cheer them, and the all-pervading sense of the highest truths; for there is in every church a basis of serious conviction and serious purpose, and without this society becomes very trivial and empty. Do you not notice the difference in this respect in different places? I go to some homes, and immediately I find people ready to speak of something important, — their minds are interested in some question of morals, intellect, politics, religion, manners, art, or literature. Then the conversation becomes at once interesting. But when people meet with empty minds, people who live only for amusement, not for anything serious, how commonplace and how superficial is the talk! Even when there is talent, culture, and knowledge, if there is not earnestness, it does not go to the roots of things, — it is unsatisfactory.

We need all kinds of society, — literary, artistic, political, neighborly; but withal we need church life and the church home.

Both thought and work tend to throw men on themselves, and to develop individual life; therefore the social element needs a more direct culture as man advances. Civilization develops thought and power, more than heart. Highly cultivated people are often cold, intellectual people reserved, men of energy hard. But sympathy and sentiment ought to be expressed as well as felt, and so every one enjoys the impulsive warmth of the Latin races more than our cool Saxon ways. No matter how much a Northern man feels, he is ashamed to show it; but an Italian will shed tears openly, and think it no discredit. Why not? The old Greeks were not afraid to shed tears, and if Achilles and Agamemnon wept, why may not we? Why not cry, if you feel like crying, just as well as to laugh when you like laughing? A man is no less manly for showing his feelings, if they are right ones.

I read a certain newspaper every week, and it is a very good newspaper, too, but it has one foolish notion. It is afraid of sentiment. It seems to think there is nothing so bad as sentiment. But sentiment is nothing but thought blended with feeling; thought made affectionate, sympathetic, moral. Since God gave us sentiment as well as thought, since he saw fit to make us with hearts as well as heads, why need we be afraid of sentiment? The heart is often wiser than the head, and the worst heresies have come from speculation, not from love. Let us not be ashamed of our affections, for these are the best gifts of heaven. Without them our life, as Cicero has said, is not really living. But what moments will compare with those in which persons become really intimate with each other; when the barriers of reserve are removed; when the deepest thoughts are kindled by the magnetic touch of a common thought; when all that is highest within the soul is made to flow freely like brooks in June, leaping down the side of the mountain! Only in such hours does man become really himself, seeing and feeling what he really is. Such communion lifts him above his average days of mere routine into a better sphere.

All the forms of affection, except the highest, are liable to go astray, to run into excess, to fall into abuse. Friendship may be too engrossing; sympathy may make us unjust to the absent for the sake of those present; benevolence and pity, unless guided by judgment, may aggravate the evils they seek to relieve; loyalty often leads to partisanship and bitter sectarianism; sentiment may pass into sentimentalism; unintelligent reverence produces the dreadful woes and wrongs of superstition. An ignorant piety torments men with fears, or hardens the heart to those who are thought to be infidels. Therefore all these affections need to be guided and regulated. This is their education.

Thus guided or illuminated, they become an immense power, — a great force. Light guides, but love moves. Love is the motor which carries mankind onward. The education of the social nature consists in changing selfish affections into generous affections, blind feelings into intelligent attachments, and the passive emotions of sympathy into the active love of benevolence.

The first step of this progress is from mere sympathy to thoughtfulness. It consists in not merely feeling for others, but thinking for them.

An emotion of sympathy, unless it passes into thoughtful goodness, profits little. What men need is not merely the goodness which feels for them, but the goodness which will think for them, — which puts itself in their place, considers their wants, anticipates their necessity, and provides for it. What a blessing is a considerate person, and how inconsiderate much goodness is! On occasions of great calamities, we think for others as well as feel for them. We send money, clothing, tools, furniture, food, — just what they want, to those whose homes are desolated by fire or famine or storms. But how inconsiderate is our average charity, which lavishes money on the poor, but will not think for them! The aid given every year in this city, much of which only creates paupers, if wisely directed, would put an end to pauperism, and greatly relieve poverty. Thought added to love makes real benevolence, and educates the character of the donor. If God loves a cheerful giver, I am sure he also loves a thoughtful giver. How grateful we all are to those who show that they have put thought into their love for us, anticipating our need, penetrating our obscure misery, and leading us up into light and peace, which otherwise our darkened and troubled soul could never find!

To educate the heart, one must be willing to go out of himself and to come into living contact with others. It is not enough to think for others, or feel for others, we must feel with them and think with them. If we would drive selfishness out of our heart, we must enter into communion with our fellow-men.

" Not what we give, but what we share,
For the gift without the giver is bare."

You cannot make a fire with a single stick, nor
can you warm your heart by solitary efforts or solitary prayers. This is the mistake of the religious
people who are always analyzing their own motives
to see if there is any real love in their hearts. Such
a process would drive all love out of the heart of
an angel. It is the mistake also of those who cultivate their tastes until they become indifferent to
man, while they admire culture, caring not for the
diamond, but only for its polish. I have known
literary men, scientific men, and artists, who had
cut themselves off from all social sympathy with
their kind, as really as the old anchorites who lived
in the caves of the Thebaid. They were hermits in
Boston or New York. I am inclined to think that
the Church may again become the centre of a new
society, which shall unite rich and poor, the wise
and the uninstructed ; which shall furnish means
of culture, works of art, pleasant society, innocent
amusement, mutual help. From whence else is a
renewed society to come ? No other root goes so
deep as religion into the human soul ; may not the
tree which rises from it again bear the blossoms and
fruit of a better civilization ? The Christian Church
has always been the home of literature and art. It
preserved in its libraries the knowledge of antiquity.
It created schools of architecture, sculpture, poetry,
music, painting. I think it will again flower out

into beauty, and bear the fruits of a better civilization ; for the root is still by the waters of life, and
fresh shoots are always coming from this ancient
trunk.

The essence of Christianity, according to the New
Testament, is love. This is the centre and axis of
the Christian life, the one thing needful. Jesus
declares that the first commandment is to love God ;
the second, essentially like it, is to love man ; and
that on these two, as pivots, hang all the law and
the prophets. John declares that he who loveth,
dwells in God and God in him ; and that love to
God and to our neighbor go necessarily together.
Paul declares that a faith which can work the
mightiest miracle is good for nothing apart from
love. The power of faith in Christ is, that it
creates this love in the soul, that it inspires at once
a divine and human affection. It brings God so
near, shows him so closely to us as a father, that we
are made able to trust ourselves wholly to him, and
to be happy in the sense of his presence. Then this
sense of the infinite tenderness descends into every
part of our life, and makes all things new. It creates
a new heaven and a new earth. Sanctified by this
sunny atmosphere of a simple piety and a simple
charity, heaven is here, the beginning of the heaven
which is to come.

Heaven in Scripture is represented as a society.
And when I think of it, I not only think of it as a
condition where we shall know and do more, but

where we shall be in fuller and larger sympathy with others. There the poor hearts frozen up and undeveloped in this life shall expand in a warm, sunny atmosphere of love! There those who have been misunderstood and misrepresented in this world shall find themselves well-known by God and the angels of God! There those who have never been able to express themselves, who have been deprived of the gift of utterance, shall know how to talk without words; like the stars, "which have neither speech nor language, yet their voice is heard!" There we shall enter into a communion so intimate, that all which the best hours of this life have given shall seem as nothing to that perfect blending of thought and love.

XI.

THE ORGAN OF REVERENCE, AND ITS CULTIVATION.

XI.

THE ORGAN OF REVERENCE, AND ITS CULTIVATION.

———◦∞◦———

PHRENOLOGISTS say that on the very summit of the brain is an organ, which they call the organ of veneration, which impels men to look up and adore higher beings; which prompts to the worship of God; which inspires reverence for parents, superiors, and elders; and which is, in their opinion, the religious organ. Whether such an organ exists, or whether it does not exist, there is no doubt that there is such a tendency in the human soul, — a tendency to look up with reverence to things higher, nobler, and better than we are ourselves.

The nature of man, full of antagonisms, has, with its self-esteem, its self-reliance, its self-will, also an opposite disposition: one which leads one to esteem others more than one's self; to pay homage to a superior virtue and a profounder knowledge. If it is pleasant to think well of one's self, it is more delightful to think better of another. The very same person who at one time seems to esteem himself, in his egotism, better than all the rest of the world, has also his moments of enthusiastic reverence for noble and generous souls, and forgets himself altogether in a joyful hero-worship.

The tendency to reverence is, therefore, natural to man. It is one of the most universal of all human tendencies; it runs upward into the purest piety; it sinks downward into the darkest superstition. It is a sail, filled with the winds of heaven, to carry us forward to a better land and time; or it is an anchor holding by the black soil of past abuses and corruptions, and so keeping the human mind back from all improvement. Let us, therefore, consider it in these three forms: its natural action, or normal state; its unnatural action, or abnormal state; its spiritual action, or higher state.

How lovely is reverence in children and young people, and how disagreeable the opposite! To look up, submissively trusting in the superior wisdom and goodness of those older than himself, elevates the child. Every one is raised by submission to higher worth. A man in the water, who cannot swim, if he tries to lift himself up out of the water, will be drowned; but if he will sink low down into it, he will float. In this world, those who are willing to sink will float; and the saying of Jesus comes true in many ways, " He that exalteth himself shall be abased, but he that humbleth himself shall be exalted." The modesty born of reverence seems natural to youth. I know that in this I am contradicting a great master of human nature, the German writer, Goethe. In one of his books he represents his hero visiting an educational institution. Seeing the boys standing erect, in various attitudes, he asks the meaning of these positions. The teacher replies, that "Nature has given many endowments to children, which the teacher has only to develop; but one thing the child does not bring into the world with him, and yet it is on this one thing that all depends for making man wholly a man. This one thing," he continues, "is reverence." He then goes on to speak of the three kinds of reverence, which must be joined into one to produce the highest quality. The first of these three reverenees is reverence for what is above us, especially for God, who images himself in parents and superiors. The second is respect for our equals; the third, or the Christian reverence, is respect and honor for our inferiors. "These," he continues, "are not based on fear, as some think; for fear and reverence are wholly different. Fear drives us away from its object, but reverence attracts us toward it. To fear," he adds, "is easy, but painful; to reverence is difficult, but satisfactory. Man does not willingly submit to reverence: it is a higher sense, which is communicated to his nature, and only in some peculiarly favored individuals does it unfold itself spontaneously."

With all deference to this great thinker, I must prefer the phrenological observers, and assume, with them, that reverence is natural to mankind. It is the crown of the moral nature. It is, perhaps, the last faculty to be fully developed in man; but it appears in innocent childhood, in the modesty of youth, and gives to both no small part of their charm. It attracts the young to the old, the ignorant to the wise, the timid to the brave, even the sinful to the pure and noble. So it tends to elevate by bringing us under the influence of those nobler and better than ourselves. The man who chooses to be with his inferiors is degraded; to love to be with our superiors elevates us. A great poet has said : —

> "Philip has that
> *Of inborn meanness in him* that he loves not
> The company of equals or superiors ;
> Never at ease except he struts the best
> And crows the loudest of the company."

There is another quality in reverence which is very noticeable. It gives a sense of what is harmonious, fit, and suitable. It perceives everywhere what is becoming. It opposes whatever is abrupt and discordant. An egotistical person, who respects no one but himself, is a jar and discord. He pushes forward his own will, notion, and purpose, in season and out of season. But he who has reverence follows the higher law which gives order to all things, and feels the beauty of that universal harmony which descends from God. He obeys the spirit of God in promoting order and beauty in all things.

Therefore it is that Shakspeare calls reverence "the angel of the world."

> " Reverence,
> That angel of the world, doth make distinction
> Of place 'twixt high and low."

The phrenologists, we have seen, make it the religious organ. I think it one organ of religion, but not the only source of religion. It leads to worship, devotion, and the exercise of piety. But piety and devotion constitute only one part of religion. Those who have a great deal of this lovely natural tendency within them enjoy prayer, enjoy worship, enjoy religious books, religious hymns, and religious meetings. But this is only one part of religion. The sentiment of piety is sweet and holy, but religion is also action and thought. It rests on a deep conviction of the reality of God's being, of duty, of immortality. It is also doing good works. We must not suppose that one cannot be religious who has not, by nature, a love for worship, for religion comes to us in many ways.

A person to whom it is not natural to look up in adoration, or to pray the prayer of sentiment, and has no tendency to natural piety, may yet be really a Christian. He may come to God through conviction and conscience; he may pray to God because he sees that prayer helps him, gives him strength to do his duty, to resist temptation. His prayers will not be long; but, then, Jesus did not ask us to make long prayers, but to make real prayers. Five words from a deep conviction are better than fifty said by rote, or coming merely from a religious sentimentalism. If you have a good deal of natural piety, be thankful; but if you have it not, be not discouraged. There are other ways of finding God.

But this faculty of reverence has also its nnnatural, abnormal tendencies. Its unnatural action is superstition. The only thing which deserves reverence is spirit; God as spirit, and God's spirit descending into man and nature as truth and love, as justice and heroism. But as God's spirit and man's spirit are seen and known through some outward form, we often confound these, and reverence the form instead of the spirit, the body instead of the soul. This is idolatry. Because God comes to us in nature, in the sun and stars, in the storm and calm, in the events of life, ethnic nations have worshipped the sun, the fire, the sky, the thunder, the ocean. So, in Christianity, men have had a superstitious reverence for forms; they have regarded them not as means, but as ends. They reverence the externals of religion, instead of its inner life.

Thus men worship the bones of martyrs, sacred pictures, sacred places. Thus, in Naples, they worship St. Januarius; in Bologna, St. Petronius. Thus, in Jerusalem, they worship the sacred fire, and trample each other to death in trying to procure it. Thus, Protestants worship blindly the Sabbath, the Bible, the sacraments, as though these were holy in themselves, instead of being good only as they can make men good.

So sensible a writer as Miss Yonge intimates that it is just possible that an unbaptized child may be damned because that rite. has been neglected. But Robertson says that such a view of baptism makes of it a charm to save the child from God, instead of a sacrament to bring it to God.

Such is the power of association, that whatever is associated with our highest hours and best feelings becomes itself an object of admiration and veneration. We read in the Bible that the brazen serpent, which Moses had lifted up in the wilderness, had been preserved to the time of Hezekiah; that is, about seven centuries. What a sacred relic it was, and how worthy of preservation! If modern Christians had only such a relic as this, — so authentic and holy, — how would they prize it! But Hezekiah found that it had become an object of worship, therefore he broke it in pieces, and called it "Nehushtan," which means "a piece of brass." This must have greatly shocked the feelings of the Israelites. This was, indeed, a sacred relic, and seemed worthy of veneration. Think of his destroying it and calling it a piece of brass!

So the Jews felt when Jesus said, "The Sabbath is made for man, not man for the Sabbath." So many persons felt when a modern writer suggested that there might be piano-fortes, or their analogons, in heaven. But these things must be said in order to bring us out of a merely sentimental habit of religious formalism to the worship of spirit and reality. When people adore a stone or a piece of brass, and call it God; when they worship a piece of bread, and call it God; when they sanctify ancient forms, liturgies, costume, candles, crosses, and think them sacred, — some one must break these idols in pieces, and say, "They are Nehushtan, — a piece of brass."

The habits of our ancestors led them to regard with reverence the house of worship. The building where the church assembled came itself to be called the church, just as the body in which the man dwells is regarded as the man. This reverence for the house of worship is passing away, and we now often miss the devout stillness and quiet which used to mark a congregation assembled to worship. Travellers say that you may go into a Turkish mosque full of people, and so intense is the stillness, that, if you were to close your eyes, you might suppose yourself alone. I confess I prefer that extreme to the other. I do not like to see people whispering, assuming careless attitudes, or reading during a religious service. I do not like a noisy introduction to public worship. This is not from my regard to a sacredness inherent in the place, but from a sense of fitness. You would not go laughing into a house of mourning, much as you may believe that death comes from God as a blessing. You would not dance at a funeral, nor pray in a ball-room. There

•

is a fitness in things, and one is disturbed by any such incongruity in the house of worship.

Let a church be like a home, but like one where the Great Father comes to meet his children, and where awe and veneration mingle with love, to make joy more sweet and more profound. The associations of a place influence the mind. These associations are helps to us. Why do you love to go to the place in the woods where you last saw your friend, and talked with him? Because the associations which surround you there bring back your friend to you, and you seem to be once more together. So when people enter the church, where their hearts have been lifted to God, and filled with a new purpose of obedience, where the hymns and prayers have taken them up to a higher plane of thought, they are, by the very associations of the place, led into a devout frame, and it is not good to have these associations disturbed.

The highest action of this sentiment of reverence is to feel the spirit of God in all things; to feel God in nature, history, providence, our own lives, and in all the good and great souls who have lived. It is to be filled with awe, wonder, and love, in view of the greatness and goodness everywhere. It is to cherish a habit of looking upward, and seeing what is noble and good in all things.

This elevates the character, gives dignity and joy to life, and produces that charming serenity, that gracious beauty, which softens all hearts. In Jesus

Christ we see this spirit in its highest form. He was a reformer; he denounced the superstitions of his day. He was called a Sabbath-breaker, because he healed the sick on the Sabbath, and walked with his disciples in the fields; he denounced the men thought most holy, the Scribes and Pharisees; but he was full of this deep reverence for God, as his Father, and the Father of all. He saw a divine goodness in all men and in all things. So he had respect, not only for the great men and the prophets, but for the poor, the low, the despised. He introduced into the world that new form of reverence, — reverence for things below us; reverence for little children, for the ignorant, the poor, the suffering; yes, reverence for the soul of man even when most degraded by sin. This is the foundation of true democracy; the only basis for any real equality. Christianity makes human equality real; not by destroying the differences among men, but by teaching the good to seek and save the evil; the wise to instruct the ignorant; the rich to care for the poor; the strong to uphold the weak. This reverence for all men, because all are God's children, is the highest attainment of man. To look up and adore is easy; but to look down and respect what is below us is far more difficult. But this spirit Christ has imparted to the world.

"He who loveth not his brother whom he hath seen, how can he love God whom he hath not seen?" says the Apostle. "He who reverences not the goodness he has seen, how can he reverence that which he has not seen?" He who despises man will despise God. Irreverence toward God often comes from disrespect toward man.

The young people of our time are said to be wanting in reverence. They are often generous and sympathizing; they are true and honorable. This class of virtues they believe in. But they do not believe in those born of reverence. They have somewhat lost the old respect for woman. They consider it in good taste to be rude to ladies, and to treat them as comrades; and ladies submit to be so treated. They do not rise up to honor the hoary head. They keep their seats in the arm-chair when their father or mother comes in. In my youth, the form which self-conceit took was admiration for one's self as a person of genius or talent before any evidence of that fact appeared. Now, the conceit which boys have of themselves is that they are singularly manly, heroic, and powerful. Then, they adored talent; now they respect force. This is encouraged by the boys' newspapers and story-books, which teach that if a boy will defy all laws, be disrespectful to his parents, and run away from home, he will certainly become an eminent person and meet with much success. So we see little boys affecting manliness by smoking cigars in the streets, by brutal manners, by airs of independence, and by general disrespect to their elders and superiors. For this reason they should be taught the beauty there is in good manners, and that without modesty there is no real manliness.

"I was born in an unlucky time," said a lady. "When I was young, I was obliged to respect and obey my parents, and now I am obliged to respect and obey my children." An irreverent age is wanting in the highest sentiment of man. To "look up" is the noblest of all powers. The small egotism which loves to look down on others wilts the soul.

During the Middle Ages the influence of the Church was so great that it produced an excess of reverence. You see this in the pictures before Raphael. Compare, for example, a "Crucifixion" by these early masters with one by Rubens. In the last, all is natural and free : each man is acting as he would in actual life. The Magdalen, dissolved in tears, embraces the feet of her friend, her fulness of life contrasting with the leaden death of Christ. The disciples, in every attitude of disappointment and despair, stand around. The Roman soldier, in the most business-like way, is striking his spear into the side of Jesus. The centurion, on his horse, is studying with deep interest the face of Jesus. But a mediæval artist, or a pre-Raphaelite imitator, would make all their faces full of the same awe-struck reverence. The cruel soldier would be striking his spear as though he were saying a prayer. The centurion would hang down his head like a bulrush. So mediæval piety turned all human life into awe, wonder, and fear. Everything connected with religion was venerable. It was sacrilege not to reverence churches, masses, saints, relics, as much as God himself.

From all this there has come a reaction. Few things now seem sacred. The awe and mystery has been brushed away from human life. Reason, science, criticism, have carried their torches, their calcium lamps, their argand burners, into every recess of the soul. So reverence has died out of the heart.

No, it has not! Nothing which God puts into man can ever pass away. What he gives, he gives forever. I see and admit the apparent irreverence of our day. I lament that young men and women are not more modest, and that no sense of sacred associations seems left to them. They have nothing holy, — no holy Bible, no holy Sabbath, nothing sacred, even in the Gospels, or the Christ. The time has come in which men peep and scrutinize over the grave of their mother. We wish now to know everything. But I think that knowledge will awaken reverence once more. The greatest and wisest of men have always bowed down in awe before the mysteries of creation. The lamp of science reveals the immense and inscrutable wonders which surround what we know. Egotism, conceit, and vanity come when we know a little; when we know more, awe and reverence return. Therefore I believe that knowledge and science is creating another reverence, surely higher and better than that for forms and ceremonies, — a reverence for all reality.

17

To educate the sense of reverence we must once more recognize its beauty and nobility. We must see that, without it, the best charm of life is gone. He who cannot look up to something better than himself acquires that cynical and contemptuous spirit which is so odious and so repulsive. The sense of reverence needs to be educated, and this is the truth in the remark of Goethe. It is cultivated by looking up and not down ; by choosing for our associates the best and wisest men and women ; by seeking for companions the intelligent, the generous, and the good. It is cultivated by looking for the good in men and things, rather than evil; by seeking truth rather than error ; by reading noble books in which this spirit prevails ; by choosing the company in which serious and noble things are treated seriously. In such society the best part of our nature grows, while, among the flippant and the frivolous, we also become small and empty. It is good to believe in heroes and heroism, in saints and martyrs. It is good to read and study the lives of the generous and disinterested, the pure in heart, those who suffer for righteousness' sake. Avoid the atmosphere which is full of sneers at generosity, which doubts sentiment, which distrusts conscience, which calls all religion hypocrisy. Those who try to exalt themselves by criticising and finding fault with that which others reverence, become very small and very mean. Fault-finding is about the poorest, as well as the easiest, work one can do. Look for truth, for goodness, for honesty, and you will find these. It may seem very smart and very witty to speak irreverently of parents, elders, the past, of religion, the church, the Bible ; but you have to pay a heavy price for that wit. Your mind grows flippant and poor. That which comes out of your mouth defiles you. This is the harm of profanity. It does not injure God to take his name in vain, but it injures you. Every time you utter an oath you are laying another stone on the wall between yourself and heavenly things. You are degrading your nature, darkening your mind, making faith in things unseen more difficult. But all serious and earnest conversation on high themes lifts us up nearer to that of which we think and speak.

He who closes the door in his heart against the noble, the great, the wonderful, the venerable, has shut himself out from the best joy of life. There is nothing better can enter into the human soul than reverence for high things. This sentiment lifts us above ourselves, brings us into the heavenly world, and admits us to the society of angels and archangels, dominions and powers, seraphim and cherubim.

He who believes in goodness has the essence of all faith. He is a man " of cheerful yesterdays and confident to-morrows."

This faith in goodness, this reverence for the divine in nature and man, is what we need. Whoever can give us this is our best benefactor. Whoever takes it away is our chief enemy. The road which goes upward toward God, beauty, truth, heaven, **is** the path of faith and worship. That which goes downward is the way of self-conceit, of contempt, of cynicism, of scorn. Let our prayer be that **we** unlearn contempt and learn to adore. Let us pray to the Most High God, to him who wrapped the cloud of infancy around us and communed with us in the undisturbed simplicity of childhood; to him who from the anarchy of dreams, with punctual care and touch as gentle as the coming of dawn, restores us every day to light and reason. Call on him in your weakness and say : —

> " Soul of our souls, and safeguard of the world,
>   Sustain, thou only canst, the sick of heart.
>   Restore their languid spirits, and recall
>   Their lost affections unto thee and thine."

XII.

EDUCATION BY MEANS OF MONEY.

XII.

EDUCATION BY MEANS OF MONEY.

———◦◊◦———

THE desire for wealth is nearly universal, and has been so from the earliest times. Money represents everything which may be purchased. To be rich means to be able to have a comfortable house in a healthy situation, with plenty of sunshine and air; to have good books to read, fine pictures to look at; to go to the mountains or to the sea in summer; to travel in Europe; to have time and leisure for study; good society, pleasant acquaintances, recreation of all sorts, — horses, sail-boats, and the like. It represents, also, the power of helping the poor, giving to hospitals and other charities, building model lodging-houses, saving the Old South Church, paying the debt of the Young Men's Christian Union, establishing reform schools, founding professorships in colleges or industrial schools where boys and girls can be taught how to make their living. He who possesses money has potentially in his possession everything which may be bought with money. We know that knowledge is power; money also is power. It is influence, it is distinction, and it seems to have in itself all earthly possibilities.

But not quite all; not the best things. Some things escape its power. All that is *purchasable* it possesses, actually or potentially; but some things are not purchasable. You cannot buy health, genius, knowledge, character, nobleness of soul, friendship or love, with money. And when you desire, most of all, any of the unpurchasable articles, money loses its power. A steamer in the mid-Atlantic encountered a storm, and was so shattered that all who could, took to the boats. One man, left on deck, offered tens of thousands of dollars in gold for a place in the boat, and, being refused, dashed the money down, where it was kicked aside as worthless by those who were trying to find some way of safety. Any higher love drives the love of money out of the heart. The love of art, the enthusiasm for knowledge, an interest in science, or religious devotion, expels the greed of gain. Agassiz refused the largest pecuniary offers for his services, saying he "could not afford the time to make money." Turner, though loving wealth, loved his art more, and often refused the highest prices for his pictures, because he could not bear to part with them. Much as we may desire the power which belongs to wealth, there is that which none of us would sell at any price. Maturin wrote a story, called "Melmoth," based on this idea. Melmoth had sold himself to the devil for unlimited wealth and power, and also on the condition that, if he could find any one to take his place, he could himself escape at last. So he seeks shipwrecked and starving mariners, those who are about to be burnt alive by the Inquisition, and offers them life, safety, riches, all earthly joy, if they will sell their soul. All refuse; no one is found, in all the wide earth, plunged in any such depth of anguish or despair as to be willing to exchange places with him. And I am inclined to think that this represents truly what would probably be the result. We do sell our souls, blindly and ignorantly, every day, for a much smaller price; but we would not do this deliberately for any kind of compensation.

The Bible is often quoted as though it said that "Money is the root of all evil." What it really says is, that "The love of money is the root of all evil." Money, in itself, is neither good nor bad; it is good or bad according as it is sought for in right or wrong ways; as it is used wisely or unwisely; lavished foolishly, or hoarded meanly; squandered where it does harm, or bestowed where it does good. It is nothing in itself, but the best thing or the worst thing, according as it is treated.

In the curious story, by Chamisso, called "Peter Schlemihl," there is a rich man, who has by his side, always, a demon in waiting, who takes from his pocket anything his master wishes. The master wishes for a telescope to examine a distant ship; the demon supplies him with one. He says, "It is very hot; I wish we had a tent." A tent instantly emerges from the capacious pocket of the convenient servant. Finally, the master wishes for carriages and horses to convey the whole party to the city, and the demon takes from his pocket as many as are necessary. It is evident that, with such an attendant, one would have no use for money, for he could have everything at once, without the trouble of buying it.

Money, taken in the largest sense, as the representative of all kinds of property, is one of the greatest means of human education. Accumulated capital means progress; constitutes the difference between the savage and the partly civilized conditions. Property, to exist, must be protected by the community from violence. Thus *law* becomes superior to *force*. In order that *any one* should hold his property securely, *all* must be defended. The weakest child, the feeblest woman or old man, holds his property as safely to-day, in Christian countries, as, in the Middle Ages, the baron, living in his castle of stone, and behind iron gates, held his. Thus the accumulation of property or capital has been gradually extending the reign of law, and beating back the reign of force. This, already, is a great education to a community; for it causes all men to feel the presence of law, as an invisible but ever-active power, ready to defend right and punish wrong.

Moreover, the presence of capital, or accumulated property, in a community, means more of the necessaries and comforts of life, — not for the rich only, but for all persons. Capital which is hoarded does not accumulate; to increase, it must be used. It cannot be used without furnishing employment and wages to large numbers of persons. Their labor creates more capital, which must also be used in producing the comforts and luxuries which all desire. Capital, associated with labor, spins and weaves cotton; makes carpets, glass, bricks; erects houses; brings water into a city; prints newspapers and books; paints pictures; builds railroads. These, which were once the luxuries of a few, gradually became the comforts, and at last the necessaries, of all. The laboring man in Boston, when he rises, dresses himself in cloth made in the factories of England or Massachusetts, from wool raised in Australia, and cotton grown in Alabama. As he sits down to breakfast, he finds that cattle have been brought from Texas, and flour from Minnesota, that he might have his steak and his bread; and ships have crossed the ocean to bring him his pepper and his salt. The table on which he eats is made of wood cut in the West Indies. The tumbler from which he drinks is the result of the science and skill which has at last made glass both beautiful and cheap. His house is more comfortable than was the palace of King Alfred or William the Conqueror. He rides to his work in a railway car which is vastly superior to the carriages in which duchesses rode fifty years ago. He stops, on his return, at the

Public Library, and has a selection of reading which would have been impossible to the greatest students fifty years ago; or he reads a newspaper in which has been brought to him whatever has happened since yesterday in any part of the civilized world. All this is the result of the love of accumulation planted by the Creator in the human soul, and the large accumulations of capital in all Christian lands.

Therefore, when labor quarrels with capital, or capital neglects the interests of labor, it is like the hand thinking it does not need the eye, the ear, or the brain. Modern society is mutually dependent, part on part; each on all, and all on each; many members and one body. If the people in America and Europe have escaped the pestilence and famine which used to desolate vast regions, and which now lay waste other countries, it is because capital is planted side by side, in peaceful union, with labor.

Moreover, in this condition, to which capital is essential, the accumulation of property is an education to the community. The love of money is often the root of evil, but it is also a motive to prudence, economy, industry, and skill. It develops the powers of observation, thought, care, patience, perseverance, exactitude. The work done each day in Boston, under the mighty stimulus of this motive, gives an education to the people far greater than all the schools and colleges can supply in the same time.

It will not do, then, to condemn sweepingly the love of money or the desire to be rich; for these are among the most powerful motives to activity, energy, and improvement. To make money is a legitimate object. The question is, *How* is it to be made? What methods are proper? What means are wise?

In making money, that which is derived from productive industry educates the worker and helps him; that which is derived from unproductive industry degrades and injures him.

Productive industry is that which adds to the real wealth of the community; unproductive industry is that which adds no value to anything.

The wealth of a community consists, not merely in outward possessions, but in all which gives value to life. Good pictures, fine poems, good lyceum lectures, scientific discoveries, health, safety, good manners, good morals, good behavior, make life more valuable. Consequently, we may place among productive laborers the poet, the painter, the judges and lawyers, the physician, the orators, the professors, the clergyman. These are all working-men, adding as much to the wealth of society as the farmer, the manufacturer, or the merchant.

But if a man spends his labor in doing what adds no value to life, or diminishes its value, he is unproductive. The gambler, who merely tries to get another man's money; the man who adulterates food, or makes poor articles which seem like good ones; the quack doctor who persuades people to take medicines which do them no good; those who manufacture and sell poisonous liquors to destroy the peace of families and the health of the community; those who write books which corrupt the mind and heart, — are plainly unproductive laborers. But I also call the man an unproductive laborer who, as a lawyer or politician, tries to make the worse appear the better reason; who seeks to gain wealth, reputation, fame, by any means, right or wrong. I call the man in trade an unproductive laborer who seeks to grow rich suddenly by speculation; instead of by faithful, legitimate business. I call the preacher an unproductive laborer who, instead of helping men to lead good lives, teaches them only outside forms, sectarian self-satisfaction, narrow dogmas, or sensational emotions. Such men, if they sincerely believe they are doing right, may be·saved themselves, so as by fire; but the wood, hay, and stubble which they have industriously put together will be burned.

Doing such work may make a man cunning and adroit, but will not make him wise. Trying to dodge the laws of the universe will certainly result in failure. Those who work in accordance with truth and justice grow nobler and stronger every day; those who seek to thrive merely by falsehood and cunning, taper down at last to nothing.

Smartness may endure for a night; but truth cometh in the morning.

There is an education, also, in using money, as well as in making it. To select, among the different articles which one wishes, that which on the whole is the best; to choose what to have and what to renounce,—teach prudence, economy, and broad views of life. Therefore it is well to give children and young people an allowance, that they may learn by experience how to make the best use of their money. Every man and woman needs a certain uncontrolled use of money, else they can never learn how to use it. I have known men who would give their wives and children whatever was wanted to buy any particular thing, but never trusted them to exercise their own discretion by having a regular sum to dispense. It was a mistake, a great mistake. For I have noticed that when these children grew up, and came at last into possession of their property, they became easy victims to adroit and unscrupulous knaves. Besides, it is so painful for a woman or a young person to have to ask always for the money they want, that it leads to subterfuges. Every one should have for educational purposes the uncontrolled use of a certain amount of money, unless they have shown themselves to be unfit for this privilege. The only way in which we can learn the use of money is by having it to use.

But the use of money may teach us higher things than prudence, economy, and judgment. We may also be educated in this way to generosity and benevolence.

Benevolence and generosity are not impulses, but habits; that is, by practice, the impulse may become a habit. Impulsive benevolence may do more harm than good. To give is an art requiring study and practice. God loves cheerful givers, but he also loves judicious givers, — givers who are willing to give time and thought as well as money. Giving money may be like pouring water on the sand, or like planting a seed in good ground. You may help a man so as to teach him to lean on you, so as to take away his self-reliance and self-respect; or you may help him so as to enable him to help himself, and to go forward in a career of activity and usefulness.

The fundamental principle which lies behind all these questions is laid down in the parable of the Talents and of the Pounds. Every man is a steward, bound to use all his powers and faculties, including his wealth, according to the will of God. We are to give an account to God for all we have, all we do, all we are. We shall hear the words, "Give an account of thy stewardship, for thou shalt no longer be steward." Not, perhaps, to any visible judge, or before any outward tribunal; but, sooner or later, we shall see where we have wasted our time, squandered our faculties, or made pitiful returns for the vast bounty of the Almighty.

The principle taught in the parable of the Pounds and of the Talents applies to every possession, faculty, influence, opportunity, knowledge, that we have. We are answerable to God for them all; we are to be judged for the use we make of them; we are to be held to a strict accountability for each, and are to receive an exact retribution for the use or the neglect of them all. Now, money is one of these talents for the use of which we are to account. If for every idle word which men shall speak they must give an account in the day of judgment, so for every idle dollar they may spend they must also give an account. If one who is made trustee of the property of the widow and orphan must take good care of it, so that the best use shall be made of it, he must take the same care of what he calls his own.

It is needless to say that this idea of stewardship, in regard to our property, is as yet very little received, and that if it were received, it would change the whole aspect of society. It would check the inordinate desire for accumulation; for if we understood that we were not accumulating for ourselves, but only taking a new responsibility, a new care, a new duty, we should hesitate. It is not difficult to see how a small income shall be spent, but not so easy to satisfy one's conscience in spending a large one. Cecil says that he once heard that a worthy young man of his acquaintance had refused an opportunity of engaging in a business which would very much increase his income. He remonstrated with him about it; but the young man replied, " I have often heard you say that with the increase of property our responsibility increases, and I do not like to take on myself this additional trust." Most men feel the responsibility for their wealth when it comes. Before they have it, they imagine that if they are rich they can do as they please with their means ; but when it arrives, they find themselves held by numerous obligations .which they never foresaw. They cannot do as they will, even with their own.

Let us admit once for all that we are stewards and not owners of property ; that it does not belong to us, but to God ; that we have no right to spend a dollar without consideration, — and a large part of writing and preaching against the love of money might be dispensed with. We do not wish to have the care of money which is not ours. We do not envy the treasurer or cashier, though millions pass through his hands, as we envy the millionaire. Inordinate love of money would be put an end to by this principle. Good men would still desire wealth, but it would be for the sake of usefulness, and the desire would be moderate and reasonable.

As with the accumulation, so with the distribution of wealth. Accept the doctrine of stewardship, and half the difficulty is removed. What would God have me do ? is a question which would throw great light on many points. Here, for example, is a Christian church, containing one hundred families, the incomes of which, supposing it to be a wealthy church, may average five thousand dollars a year, or more. To be within the limit, we will call it five thousand dollars. Let all these families accept the doctrine of stewardship. Here is half a million dollars a year, for the use of which they are to account to God. Suppose they meet together to consider their duties in relation to it. Mr. A. rises and says, " I think that, as God's stewards, we ought to spend our incomes generously, on ourselves and our families. We ought to live well, and in as good style as our neighbors. We should make a good appearance. We should have as good furniture, clothing, equipages, as those with whom we associate, and give as good entertainments as they do. If we happen to have anything left, we ought to devote it to religious and benevolent objects. My maxim is, that he who does not provide for his own family has denied the faith, and is worse than an infidel."

If Mr. A. succeeds in convincing the rest that this is their duty as stewards, the result would be this: On an average, they might give, out of an income of five thousand dollars, fifty dollars or a hundred dollars a year in charity. That is, out of an aggregate income of half a million, four hundred and ninety thousand might be spent on their own comforts and luxuries, and some ten thousand dollars a year for benevolent and religious objects. And I suppose that this is just about the proportion in many of our churches.

This is probably the actual distribution, but I do

not think that it would be easy to satisfy ourselves, on deliberate examination, that it was the right proportion.

Probably other speakers might think differently. Mr. B., for example, might think it a Christian duty to save a part of one's income. ⁻He would speak thus: "I think Mr. A.'s view wrong. It tends to extravagance. If we spend all our income, we shall be likely to spend more. If we try to dress as well as our neighbors, to have as good furniture and houses, to give as good entertainments, some of us will be pretty sure to run in debt. Besides, are we any happier for living so? Does the fine furniture give us pleasure enough to make up for the uneasy feeling that we are living beyond our means, or in danger of doing so. The only safe way is to lay up one-half or one-quarter of our income every year. Times may change. It is best to be on the safe side. Economy is a good old-fashioned New England virtue, which ought to be maintained."

As against Mr. A., there is good sense in this view. And I have no doubt that very many act upon it, and will continue to do so.

But what would be the result if it was adopted as a principle of action by our religious society? The result would be, as regards charity, the same as before, or nearly the same.

But let us listen to a third speaker, Mr. C.: " It is no doubt right that we should provide suitably for our families. Let them have what is comfortable and what is tasteful. But these are not the expensive things. Expense comes from the love of display and from unnecessary luxuries. Can we not live comfortably on half our income, or three-fourths? What shall we do with the rest? Shall we lay it up, as our friend B. suggests? But to what end? To make ourselves safe against the future? But is there no God in the future to take care of us as he has taken care of us in the past? As stewards, we can trust our Master to see to our wants and those of our families, if we make a right use of what we hold in trust for him and his children. Let us, then, determine to use for others a certain definite portion of our incomes every year, — half of our income, if it is large; or a quarter, or a tenth. But let us not leave it to accident. Let each man decide how much to apply every year to benevolent purposes. As we grow richer, let the proportion increase. If the man who has only one thousand dollars a year gives fifty to charity, or-one-twentieth, then let the man who has ten thousand give a fifth, and the man who has twenty thousand give a half, or a third, or a fourth. Then we shall have the pleasure of taking the initiative in giving; in not waiting till we are asked, but looking around for objects of benevolence. Then, if we have done any good in the world, made any one's path easier, lightened any heavy burden, sheltered the defenceless, or comforted the forlorn, we shall see and understand this by the inward satisfaction which all right-doing brings with it. Wise, conscientious, generous use of our means is repaid here and hereafter. 'Give, and it shall be given you; full measure, pressed down and running over it shall be returned again.'"

Is not this last the true principle for the use of our means?

The principle is the important thing; where this is, the right method will follow. Only we must remember that giving is both an act and a habit; an accomplishment which is to be learned, and a custom to be practised. The mistake made by many persons is to suppose that they can devote all their thought and energy for years to accumulation, and afterward learn how to use aright what has been thus gathered. It takes as much time and thought to learn how to spend money as to learn how to make money. So that, sometimes, a man who has shown great talent and energy in collecting a fortune, stands helpless before it, not knowing what to do with it after it is acquired; whereas, if he had begun in youth to practise the right way of using property as well as acquiring it, he would have the double satisfaction of receiving and giving. For certainly there is no way in which wealth can bring so much satisfaction to its possessor as when it is wisely and generously applied to all good objects. When Mr. Peabody, of London, had the happy thought of devoting a part of his large wealth during his lifetime to public objects, he showed no great generosity, for it did not cost him a single sacrifice. The poor woman in the Gospel who gave the two mites, which was her whole income, gave more than his two millions. But he showed great good sense; for this expenditure brought him a return of universal respect and good-will. Wherever he went, he was the conspicuous object of admiration and honor. He gave, and it was given him; full measure, pressed down and running over.

In Europe, it is often regarded as a religious duty to give to the beggars in the streets. Cousequently, beggars increase and abound. We are learning better methods here. We now try to prevent pauperism, and to anticipate want. Instead of giving money in the street, we establish societies which visit those who are in want at their own houses; which provide work for those out of work; which provide hospitals for the sick, homes for the aged; industrial schools for young men and women; model lodging-houses, where comfort and health can be secured at reasonable rates; homes where inebriates can be saved; reform schools, farm schools, help for discharged prisoners, bright and cheerful holly-tree inns instead of drinking saloons; free music, free libraries, free baths in summer. This is all a movement in the right direction, for it is the practical form of the doctrine of the atonement, the reconciliation of love and truth; it is thought put into our love; it is mercy and truth met together; it is the happy conjunction of good nature and good sense.

But, after all, we are only at the beginning of this application of Christianity to life. Our society is still in a very disorganized state. The vast destruction of property and disorganization of labor caused by the war, followed by the rage for speculation which always accompanies war, resulted in a great depression of business and want of confidence which held back capital from engaging in new enterprises.[1] And so we have, not wide-spread famine, as in China ; not starvation in the street, not extensive pestilence, not organized bands of robbers,—for we have risen above the social level where such evils are sure to appear. But some serious symptoms show themselves which demand a union of all good and wise men to meet the dangers of the hour. The "sturdy beggars" who infested England two or three centuries ago reappear in our midst under the name of "tramps." We do not hang them, fifty at a time, as was done in the reign of Elizabeth. Demagogues declaim against property, and teach people that those who lend them money are enemies and tyrants ; to be resisted, even to the repudiation of their debts. Wild theories of currency inflation, of communism, of a war of labor against capital, show a blind fermentation in the public mind which demands the wisest, kindest, and firmest treatment.

These are the evils of a transition state ; of a period when we have left the Garden of Eden

---

[1] This lecture was delivered in 1878, during the great business depression, which had not then ceased.

behind us, and have not yet reached the Kingdom of Heaven. Such evils are the divinely appointed whips and spurs to make us go forward to something better, and not rest indolently contented, in the negative comforts and half-virtues of quiet times. Let us believe in providence as regards the future, and do our work now, as those who are to give an account for every opportunity, talent, and privilege. In this country we are all members of each other; no man can live to himself or die to himself. If one suffers, all suffer. We are all, therefore, obliged to take an interest in the condition of those around us. For our own sakes, and for the sake of our children, if not for the sake of God and humanity, we must do our part in these hours of social struggle, lend our arm to sustain the weak and raise the fallen, and our sufficient reward will be to find that always and everywhere " it is more blessed to give than to receive."

XIII.

THE EDUCATION OF THE TEMPER.

XIII.

THE EDUCATION OF THE TEMPER.

I THOUGHT, one day, that I should like to write a sermon on *Temper*. But, on looking into the Concordance, I discovered that the word was not to be found in the Bible, — not in the form of the noun. "Temper," the noun, is not there; but the verb "to temper" is. Then I turned to the oldest English Dictionary I have, Bailey's, a little over one hundred years old, and I found the noun defined thus: *Temper* (from *temperies*, Latin), "Humor, natural disposition, constitution;" also, "moderation." "Temperament" is defined as "a proper and proportional mixture of the elements, but more especially the humors of the human body; the natural habitude and constitution of the animal humors." Pushing my researches further, I looked into a Latin Dictionary printed in 1509, a curious old Polyglot in eight languages (which once belonged to Mather Byles, and has his name on the fly-leaf), and there I found the Latin word defined to mean "the temper of the air, the healthful mixture of heat and cold, of dry and moist, in the atmosphere."

Once, years ago, travelling on a Mississippi steamer, I took up a tract, issued by the American Tract Society, which was lying on the table, and read the title. It surprised and attracted me, for it was this · "Temper is Everything." The contents corresponded to the title. It declared the essence of Christianity to be, not belief, nor emotion, nor ceremonies, nor an outward routine of decent conduct, but good temper. The writer of the tract, while writing it, seemed to have forgotten all about his Orthodoxy, and the publishers to have forgotten all about their sectarianism. It was a simple Christian tract, such as Fénelon or Channing might have written, and the Apostle Paul approved.

Temper is everything. But what is good temper, and how is it to be obtained and cherished ?

Good nature, good temper, and good humor are three qualities often confounded, but which it is desirable to distinguish. Good nature is, as the word implies, something born in us; no irritability in the blood, but, instead, a sort of natural sunshine, a born contentedness, a sympathetic feeling toward all about us. Good humor comes from pleasant surroundings, a happy environment, agreeable circumstances. A good-humored man is only good-humored while everything goes right; when things go wrong, his good humor departs, and bad humor arrives. But good temper results from culture and development of the higher faculties. It comes from self-control, observation, experience, good sense, knowledge of one's self and of others. It is, in fact, the harmony of soul belonging to a well-balanced character. It is the outward sign of peace within. While a man is at war with himself and with God; while he is rebelling against his circumstances and against divine providence; while his lower nature rules the higher, or is at war with it, so as to produce a condition of unstable equilibrium, — he cannot be good-tempered. War with himself, inward unrest, will show itself in outward discontent. But when one is inwardly at peace; when he has conquered the evil within him, and subdued his passions and appetites till they obey the voice of reason; when he has formed a habit of doing right always and everywhere; when selfishness has given way to generosity, and perfect love has cast out fear, — then all this shows itself in that equipoise of soul which we call good temper or equanimity.

While, therefore, good nature depends on the physical organization, and cannot be cultivated by effort; while good humor depends on circumstances, and is no part of the man himself, — good temper is something which we can all acquire, if we choose. We cannot make ourselves good-natured or good-humored; but we can make ourselves good-tempered. Good temper, therefore, belongs properly to the doctrine of self-culture.

This word "temper" seems at first to have in-

tended the healthful blending of opposite character
in the atmosphere; then, the harmonious balance
of opposite qualities in the human body; lastly, the
balance of various qualities and tendencies in the
human mind and heart.

The temper, therefore, of the soul is something
more than a mood.   Good temper, as we have seen,
is different from good nature.   Good nature results
from a healthy organization, a sunny constitution, a
cheerful, kindly, sympathizing disposition, which
causes one to look at the good side of the world, the
bright side of characters; to see good, and not evil,
everywhere; and so to feel and speak and act in a
kindly way on most occasions.   It is a great gift
and one to be thankful for.

God sends, here and there, these good natures
into the world to make sunshine for us.   They are
uncritical, they do not find fault, they disturb no
one's conscience, and it is rest and quiet to be with
them.   But they are made so; those who are different cannot make themselves good-natured.   Those
of us who are moody sometimes, and irritable sometimes, and indignant often, and sharp and severe in
our censures of evil; who discriminate, liking some
people and disliking other people; we, whom nobody ever calls good-natured, cannot make ourselves
so; nor, indeed, is it desirable that we should.   We
are not sunshine; but, perhaps, shade is necessary
as well as sunshine in this world.   Some people are
intended for other purposes; are made to be minis-

ters of truth, to be soldiers of the right, actively useful, or prophets crying in the wilderness. Every
man has his proper gift from the Lord, some after
this fashion and others after that; and while the
proper gift of some persons is to be good-natured,
others are not made for that, but for something
different.

But though we cannot all have good nature, we
can all have good temper; and that is something
higher. It is the blended and balanced action of all
the faculties and powers. The atmosphere is well-
tempered when it is neither too hot nor too cold,
neither too dry nor too moist; having neither too
much electricity nor too little; when the warm currents temper the cold, and the dry currents absorb
the moisture. In such days we see the feathery
white clouds lying against the deep blue sky, but
not darkening the sun nor chilling the air. Re-
freshing breezes play around the face, but do not
chill the heated body; they only cool it. In such
days it is a luxury to live. We can do anything
well. All our faculties are active. The reason is
that the atmosphere is good-tempered.

The body is in a good state when it is well-tempered; when the nervous system and the blood and
the nutritive system all work in their due harmony
and proportion; when these three great constituents
of the body are all well balanced against each other.
The body is not well-tempered in a student who
takes no exercise, and where everything goes to feed

the brain; nor in a pugilist in training, where everything goes to feed the muscles; nor in an epicure, who devotes his whole attention to eating. But, when physical and muscular exercise alternate with study, when all the organs and physical powers are in happy balance and proportion, then we can say that the body is well-tempered, or in good temper. But body and soul are distempered when out of tune, unmodulated, unbalanced.

But good temper, in the highest sense of the word, belongs to the soul. It is a sign of the harmonious and well-balanced working of the different moral powers. If I am bad-tempered, it proves something to be morbid and unbalanced in my soul. If one's character is irritable and peevish, and not merely moody, this is a symptom of irregular action of the moral nature.

This is the point I wish to urge. Good temper and bad temper are symptoms of good and bad moral health. Good temper is not a thing to be aimed at directly: it is a result. Bad temper, in like manner, is a result. It is symptomatic of some irregular, abnormal action of the soul. You cannot cure it directly by an effort to be good-tempered. You can, no doubt, by an effort, repress its manifestations. You can control yourself, so as not to say or do bad-tempered things. But the bad temper itself is to be cured, as a musician cures a discord in his instrument, by tuning all the strings. The musical discord is a symptom that some strings are out of order. Bad temper is a symptom of some moral strings being " jangled, out of tune, and harsh." First of all, then, you must tune your instrument.

For there is no such delicate and wonderful musical instrument as the soul of man. The great organs of the world are only types of it. The soul sits within, touching all its own secret and wonderful keys, drawing out all its own strange, mysterious music. The soul of man has a thousand powers balancing each other, and when tempered to each other they make the sweetest harmony. But when one is not modulated by the rest, it soon grows sharp and harsh, and then what we call bad temper, or distemper, is apt to come as a sign of this unproportioned activity.

Thus, for example, we see the perceptive powers, which are devoted to facts, balanced by the reflective, which are devoted to laws. The man who lives only in outward facts ; who knows only forms, numbers, dates, outward things, — grows hard-tempered. Outward facts, by themselves, gradually harden the nature. The man who devotes himself to reflection alone, the student of metaphysics, morals, and science, who spends his time in abstract reasoning, grows cold-tempered. His sympathies are chilled ; he is taken away from the neighborhood of men into the thin upper air of meditation, which is lonely and cold. Imagination, taste, and the sense of beauty, when cultivated alone, do, as we know well, produce irritability of temper. Artists, poets, and musicians are apt to be irritable. Men of business, absorbed in their object, which calls out daring, energy, resolution, and force acquire often a wilfulness of temper. They are apt to become despotic and domineering. It is not safe to allow any tendency to go to excess. God has balanced every faculty by some other, and means they shall all be used. He also gives opportunity and inducement to use them all. He has given us an outward world to exercise our senses,— gorgeous, and varied with a boundless variety. Does he not desire, then, that we should become acquainted with minerals and vegetables, with trees and animals, with flowers and rocks, with sky and sea ? He has given us an inward world of abstract ideas, teaching us to compare and deduce, to ascend to universal laws, analyze complex phenomena, and so enter into the mysterious workshops of his creation. He has given us fear and hope, timidity and courage, imagination and reason, sympathy and self-reliance, love of home and love of change, desire for new things, satisfaction in old things, reverence for the past, interest in the future ; conscience, which chains us to a law of absolute right; affection, which attaches itself to individual persons ; hope, that reaches forward ; memory, that reaches backward ; the combative element, which loves to fight against opposing forces ; the desire for peace, which seeks universal harmony and brotherhood. He has given us all ; and good temper in the soul is the sign of their harmonious activity; bad temper, of their one-sided and immoderate activities.

But what shall temper them? What moderate them? What produce this divine harmony? Who shall teach us how to sit and play on this wonderful instrument, so as to draw out its ineffable music?

First, we may say that God, in the arrangements of our life, helps us to temper our souls.

The old naturalists supposed four temperaments in the body, derived from its four fluids, according to the four qualities, hot, cold, moist, and dry. When there was an excess of blood, there was the sanguine temperament; of phlegm, the phlegmatic; of yellow bile, the choleric; of black bile, the melancholy. Our word "melancholy" means literally "black bile," for so do the wrecks of old theories float down the current of time in the form of words. This theory of temperaments has long ago been wrecked on some rock-bound shore of hard experience. But it remains essentially true that, in body and soul, we are differently tempered, and envisage life according to our temper of body or mind. Our wisdom is to temper our own special tendencies, and moderate them.

Observe the pains taken with the temperature of the globe. See how earth has its shores cooled and bathed by the sea and air; its surface so graded that the rains shall neither rest on it too long nor run off from it too speedily; the strata are so tipped that the water gushes out, here and there, in cool springs; the mountains and hills are so arranged that the rivers meander to and fro over the surface of each continent, fertilizing and connecting all parts; mountains rise in the heated tropics, carrying the land up into cooler regions, catching the sea-breeze, and compelling it to deposit its burden of water in daily and nightly showers. Great masses of ice at the poles set in motion currents in the ocean and atmosphere, which roll toward the equator, and bring perpetual reinforcements of cool water and cool air. Clouds sail to and fro, — the great ships of heaven, — going about their Master's business, carrying water from one part of the continent to the other; carrying, also, a freight of electric fire from where it is in excess to where it is needed. So they do the work of a mercantile navy; and sometimes, too, they meet in battle, like ships of war, and we have a terrific naval engagement, with awful discharges of lightning with rolling thunder, yet not to destroy life, but to save it. Such pains is taken to keep the earth in good temper, with equal balance of hot and cold, moist and dry. So, too, when the aurora borealis appears in the heavens, it is not merely to delight us with its beauty. Use always lies under the beauty, as the skeleton beneath the outward human form Those steady discharges of auroral light to the zenith along innumerable conducting lines come, it is thought, to equalize the electric conditions of the air. As the engine blows off its excess of steam, so the earth is blowing off its excess of electricity, and tempering its climate for human use.

If God takes such pains to temper the climate of the earth on which our bodies live, does he not also temper the climate for the soul? Let us trust in his providence; let us believe that the events of life, its trials and disasters, its varied experiences, come, not blindly nor by accident, but are sent to give the right temper to our moral and spiritual nature, to fit us for the work we have to do in time and eternity.

The word "temper" is applied to the manufacture of steel. To temper steel exactly is the difficult point, and even the cutlers themselves do not know how they do it; they see something in the look of the steel which shows them that it is of the right temper. The utmost care, the most delicate and constant attention, is necessary in that ancient and wonderful process by which iron imbibes carbon and turns to steel. The smallest crack in the side of the furnace vitiates the result. Day after day the terrible fire rages in the heart of the shut trough, and there the work goes on. So the steel gets its proper temper, whether it is to be a razor, a coach-spring, or a file.

And will not God take as much care to temper us as the steel manufacturer in Damascus or Sheffield takes of his knives and sabres? We, also, are often put into a raging furnace, and there, amid the stern experiences of life, we lie in the fire to be tempered, and go under the hammer to become compact for the work we are to do in the universe. One is to be made into a delicate instrument, like a razor; another into a hard one, like a file; and each needs to be brought to a different temper. So, too, was our nation tempered in the fire and furnace of war, and since then in the financial disasters of peace. We have gone under the heavy hammer blows of disaster and ruin. We needed to be tempered. We had been going into excesses of self-love, into aberrations of egotism, which were destroying our national life. We had been intemperate in our self-love. We had forgotten to worship God with reverence, to love man with tenderness. We needed to be tempered again, and our great war and the subsequent evils may help us into a better temper.

As we distinguished good temper from good nature, so we must distinguish ill nature and ill humor from bad temper. A person may be, by nature, irritable, and unable always to repress the outbreak of this irritability; but may wish to do so, try to do so, often succeed in doing so, and grieve when unable to do so. And a person out of humor because things have gone wrong may become good-humored again when things go right. But a bad-tempered man is apt to put the blame on others, not on himself. He thinks himself the victim, others the aggressors. He therefore never tries to correct himself, does not wish to, does not think he ought to do it.

He must be converted, wholly changed, born again, before he can be cured.

Fortunately, however, most of us are only bad-tempered to a certain extent, and may be gradually educated into something better.

The two roots of bad temper, out of which it grows, are want of conscience and want of love. When a man is not living, and does not mean to live, according to his own convictions of right, he is at war with himself. He has no inward peace. All is discord within. There is no proper balance among his powers, nor can there be till the law of right is supreme.

A bad-tempered person is always suspecting grievances,—imagining himself ill-used, discontented with his position, dissatisfied with his circumstances. He is in a condition of perpetual discontent and warfare. All contact irritates him, and he makes himself and others miserable. It is so disagreeable to be with him, that men avoid him, and leave him alone with his dissatisfactions. It is so unpleasant to oppose him, that, rather than contradict him, they remain silent; and so he loses the benefit which comes to us from a healthy resistance. When he speaks, people give way, or run away. He never blames himself, always some one else, for anything wrong; so he loses the peace born of confession and repentance. However disagreeable he is to others, he is much more so to himself, for a thoroughly bad-tempered man is a thoroughly miserable man. He

carries the fires of hell in his own soul, and surely.
we should rather be sorry for him than be angry
with him. Who can help pitying such a man as
Dean Swift, pursued and tormented forever by the
furies of blind rage, hate, and discontent, the great
est genius and the most miserable man ˙of his day ?
Who can help pitying Byron, whose magnificent
genius only illustrated the selfish bitterness of his
career ? Such a man, being at war with himself, is
out of temper with every one else. And the other
root of bad temper is selfishness. When a man
makes himself the only end ; lives for selfish pleasure, selfish gain, selfish power, fame, — then every
other man is his rival, and every success but his
own irritates him. He becomes full of envy, hatred,
malice, and all uncharitableness. If an artist, or
writer, or preacher, or politician, he is jealous of the
success of others. Instead of being inspired with a
generous emulation by the sight of another's excellence, he is filled with mean envy. Like Malvolio
in the play, he is sick of self-love, and feels every
resistance or misfortune as if it were a cannon-
bullet, while a generous and guiltless disposition
will regard it only as a bird-bolt.

The cure for bad temper is, therefore, first, to
learn to obey one's conscience, and acquire a habit
of doing what is right ; and, secondly, to learn to
forget one's self, and acquire a habit of living for
others. Then there enters the soul that good temper which is higher than good nature, more lasting

and more profound than good humor; the good temper which grows deeper and purer and sweeter with advancing years, which no wrong can embitter, no misfortune chill, which sits in the sunlight, and enjoys clear day when darkness falls around. Such an one is " his own music, his own health." He has a summer day all the way to heaven. His well-tuned humors are in a perpetual harmony. He is the man described by Crashaw : —

> " Whose latest, and most leaden hours,
> Fall with soft wings, stuck with fresh flowers ;
> And, when life's sweet journey ends,
> Soul and body part like friends;
> No quarrels, murmurs, no delay,
> A kiss, a sigh, and so away ! "

Conscience and love, when they govern the character, and are accepted as its rulers, produce this heavenly peace in the soul. All the powers fall into their places, and become harmonious under their sway. And these, again, are elevated to their supreme place, when we come to know and to love God.

Love, sitting in the heart, touches all the keys and brings out all the music. If we desire to do what will please God, and what will help man, we presently find ourselves taken out of our narrow habits of thought and action ; we find new elements of our nature called into activity ; we are no longer running along a narrow track of selfish habit ; we are necessarily brought, in the providence of God, into new relations, have new and difficult duties ; but the result appears in a healthy state of mind and heart, and that perfume and aroma which we call good temper.

Therefore, the first condition of all true life is this supreme love to God and goodness. If, each day, we seek first of all to be in a spirit of good-will, to be open to sympathy with those around us, to do what work God sends us from love for him, to do whatever our hand finds to do for others out of love for our neighbor, — then we shall have that "perfume tempered together, pure and holy," which shall make the day sweet and the night serene, the peace passing understanding which Christ's love gives, and the world cannot take away.

Have we not sometimes seen persons on whom this ineffable Dove of Peace seemed always to brood, — some persons whom nothing could disturb, no accident, no disappointment, no disaster ; who never seemed vexed, never discomposed, never sore, never out of temper; who were impregnable to all assaults of evil; who were like the rock in the sea, over which the great billows break and roar, but which stands unmoved, and emerges at last calm and firm as ever ?

What produced this divine serenity, subject to no moods, clouded by no depression, this perpetual Sunday of the heart ? It was not merely good-nature, not the accident of a happy organization. It was deeper than that. It was the perfect poise resulting from a Christian experience. It was the habit of looking to God in love and to man in love.

Wordsworth, in one of his poems, describes Matthew, the village schoolmaster, as "a soul of God's best earthly mould;" a soul which felt so profoundly that it seemed to think profoundly; a soul in which old affections were so deeply rooted that they made him unequal to any verbal expression, but gave an aroma to every utterance, so that words from his lips turned to poetry. Tears of light, dews of gladness, came into the old man's eyes in thinking of former friends and early days; mirth above, with sadness beneath; eyes dim with childish tears at the thought of what age had taken away and left behind; the wish to be more beloved; but all these forgotten presently in the joy of the moment. Thus Wordsworth describes his schoolmaster, Matthew, finding in a commonplace person the elements of poetry, because of his well-tempered soul.

This is what the Apostle Paul means by his description of charity. That wonderful description is not rhapsody or declamation; nor is it the account of an ideal, super-angelic state, impossible for us here, to be reached in some heavenly world. This divine power of love is possible for us all. Only let the love for God and man enter the soul, and then you have in you the elements here described. You will find it not difficult to "suffer long and be kind." It will seem a very simple thing not to envy, not to boast, not to behave unseemly, not to be always seeking your own. Whereas, before, you were easily provoked, now you smile at provocation, and are unruffled by injury. You become able to "bear all things" without growing angry; to "believe all things," no matter how bad and false they may be, have in them a possibility of some future good; to hope for all good, in the midst of evil, and to "endure all things" to the end, patient, because sure that the Lord reigns. This does not require that our love shall be perfect, unalloyed, or undisturbed. It does not mean that we shall be angels, but that we shall begin, under this mighty stimulus, to grow up into all things good and right.

Good temper does not come from repression, but expression; not from emptiness, but from fulness. It is not merely abstinence, though we must often abstain; nor renunciation, though renunciation is a necessary exercise; nor self-denial, though the practice of self-denial is essential to all manliness. But true temperance is higher than abstinence: it is harmonious development, well-balanced growth.

And the necessary basis of it all is faith in a living God. We cannot grow from bad temper to good temper while we only believe in force or law, in the properties of matter, or in a God far off, above the sky, a King and Judge, but no Father. To have a sweet temper, we must have faith in a divine providence. That alone lifts us above anxiety and care; that alone plants our feet on a rock, and brings content, satisfaction, and peace into the soul.

Good temper may be the last attainment of the soul. It is often the result of a long experience, and yet we have it at any moment when we are unselfish, when we are thinking of others. This gives us self-possession, inward peace, power to do any work well, satisfaction with ourselves, and a radiance of light and love which enables us to help others.

XIV

CULTURE BY READING AND BOOKS.

20

XIV

CULTURE BY READING AND BOOKS.

————◆◆◆————

THE subject of this chapter is "Reading as a Means of Culture."

The "Publisher's Circular" gives the statistics of the books issued each year from the press in England. The annual number of titles, one year with another, is about five thousand. About two-thirds of these are new books; the others are reprints. Last year there were 737 theological books, 529 educational works, 522 juvenile books, and 854 works of fiction. I have not at hand the statistics of books for the United States, but it must compare favorably with that of England, as a larger proportion of our population are able to read than in that country. The number of copies of newspapers printed and circulated every year in the United States is enormous, — I was about to say frightful. The annual circulation is fifteen hundred millions of copies, which would give about forty copies every year to every man, woman, and child in the United States.

These statistics show how much time is occupied
by the people in reading. And it is a valuable
education, so far as it goes. Poor as much is th
is printed, it is better than the common talk. T.
average newspaper is higher than the average con
versation. The newspaper does not swear, does not
use coarse and gross language ; it is often weak, but
does not talk pure nonsense. It is trying to say
something, and it has to seem to be aiming at something honest, true, and generous. The newspapers
give a vast amount of information in regard to the
affairs of mankind. The nation which reads newspapers is able to sympathize with the people of
other countries ; men's hearts are enlarged, and they
are helped to love their fellow-men. Without newspapers, we should never have felt sympathy with
Greece in her revolution, with Poland in its misfor-
tunes, with Italy in its independence and unity,
with France in her great disasters and subsequent
recovery. Without the newspapers, we should not
have sent food to starving Ireland in its years of
famine, for we should, as a people, have known
nothing about it. The newspapers create a common
feeling and a common opinion through the whole
land, and a sympathy with the people of other
lands. So they help the cause of humanity and of
social progress.

But with all this good done by reading newspapers, there is one particular evil. It produces
that state of mind which the Book of Acts ascribed

to the Athenians: "The Athenians and strangers at Athens passed all their time," so we are told in the acts, "in seeing and hearing some new thing." But this desire to know something new did not enable them to receive Christianity, though Christianity was then the newest thing in the world, and something which would make the whole world new. What they wanted was not the *new*, but the *novel*. They wished for novel sensations, perpetual change. This love for intellectual excitement weakened the grasp of their mind so much that at last they lost the power of perceiving truth. They could not tell the difference between a new gospel and a new quackery. And so it happened that in Athens almost alone, of all places where Paul preached, — in Athens, the eye of Greece, the literary emporium of the earth, — in Athens there were no converts to Christianity, and no Christian church. We nowhere read or hear of the church at Athens, and we have in the New Testament no epistle to the Athenians.

Because, therefore, the people of Athens were so fond of *new things*, they could not see nor know *the new thing* when it was before their eyes. What Paul said to them was a slight excitement, gave them a half-hour's entertainment, about as much as would have been occasioned by a new statue by Praxiteles, or a new oration by Lysias, or the arrival of ambassadors from the great king, or a fleet of triremes sailing up the Gulf of Salamis, or the celebration of the mysteries at Eleusis. "There is a

Jew come to the city preaching a new doctrine;
will you go and hear him, O Cleon ? He speaks to
the people on the Areopagus." " Certainly, provided
he gets through in season for the tragedy of ' Œdipus
Tyrannus,' which is to be acted to-day in the Theatre
of Bacchus." And so they hear Paul, and then
listen to the rhythmic strain of Sophocles; and by
the time they have reached the catastrophe, the
woes of Œdipus have made them quite forget the
story of Christ's death and resurrection.

So Paul departed from among them. There was
no depth in that soil.

The newspaper creates and feeds the appetite for
news. When we read it, it is not to find what is
true, what is important, what we must consider and
reflect upon, what we must carry away and remember, but what is new. When any very curious or
important event occurs, the newspaper, in narrating
it, often gives, as its only comment and reflection,
this phrase, " What next ? " That is often the
motto of the newspaper and the newspaper reader,
" What next ? " The only reflection and moral
derived from learning a great fact is simply this,
" Now let us hear of another." The whole world
rushes to the newspaper every morning to find out
what has happened since yesterday; and the moment
it finds what has happened, it cares no more about
it. We think no more of yesterday's newspaper
than of yesterday's dinner. We forget both as soon
as possible. This is a mental dissipation which

takes away mental earnestness, and destroys all hearty interest in truth. It also weakens the memory. The memory, like all other powers, is strengthened by exercise. We cultivate our memory by remembering. But if we read, not intending to remember what we read, but expecting to forget it, then we cultivate the habit of forgetting. I think that the effect of reading newspapers, in the way we read them, must be to weaken steadily and permanently, the memory of the nation. Every generation will be born with a worse memory than that which preceded it. The proper way to cure this evil would be to select every day from the newspaper certain important facts to be carried in the mind, considered and thought about. These would be fixed in the memory. They should be made the subject of conversation with friends or in the family, and this would improve the memory, instead of destroying it.

In short, in reading, and in all that we read, our mind should be active, and not passive. Milton says :—

" Who reads
Incessantly, and to his reading brings not
A spirit and genius equal or superior,
Uncertain and unsettled still remains,
Deep versed in books and shallow in himself."

And Lord Bacon tells us that " reading makes a full man, conference (or conversation) a ready man, and writing an exact man ;" and that we should read, not to contradict and confute, nor to believe and take for granted, nor to find talk and discourse, but to weigh and consider. Montaigne, who had a passion for books, who never travelled without them, and called them the best viaticum for this journey of life, said that the principal use of reading, to him, was, that it roused his reason. It employed his judgment, not his memory. "Read much, not many things," is good advice. There was an old saying, "He is a man of *one book.*" If one reads but one book, he may read that one book so well as to be a very hard man to encounter. But he is a happy person who enjoys his books, and to whom the day does not seem long enough for reading. For books are friends who never quarrel, never complain, are never false; who come from far ages and old lands to talk with us when we wish to hear them, and are silent when we are weary. Good books take us away from our small troubles and petty vexations into a serene atmosphere of thought, nobleness, truth. They are solace in sorrow, and companions in joy.

Knowledge of books, and a habit of careful reading, is a most important means of intellectual development. It gives mental breadth, poise, and authority. The man of great practical abilities, but unacquainted with the history or theory of a subject, is liable to make serious mistakes. He cannot be trusted. If he is conscious himself of his ignorance, he is timid; if not conscious, he is rash. It would be impossible for our members of Congress to commit so many blunders if they should pass an examination in political economy before taking their seats. To read two or three good books on any subject is equivalent to hearing it discussed by an assembly of wise, able, and impartial experts, who tell you all that can be known about it. You see the whole field, understand all that can be said on one side or the other, know what has been the result in practice of either course. The experience of the whole world, and of all past history, comes to your aid.

The moral influence also of good books is very great. They purify the taste, elevate the character, make low pleasures unattractive, and carry the soul up into a region of noble aims and generous purposes. All first-class books are eminently moral; and all immoral books are, so far, poor books. Homer, Shakspeare, Plato, Dante, are pure in their spirit, and elevate the character. No one can make a thorough study of such books as these without being a better man. Milton says, and says truly, that " our sage and serious poet, Spenser, is, I dare be known to think, a better teacher of temperance than Scotus or Aquinas." Who can read the biography of Dr. Franklin without learning to admire such a life of perpetual study, unfailing industry, large patriotism, temperance, good-humor, and general good-will ? When we read the story of Washington we become sure that disinterested public service is a real thing. The charming allegory of the " Pilgrim's Progress " teaches, in pictures too vivid to be ever forgotten, of the temptations and dangers we must encounter in any serious effort to save our soul.

Religious books are usually considered dull and uninteresting; but that they need not be so appears from the example of this book of Bunyan's, and from the popularity of religious books far inferior in their quality. In fact, religious books stand at the summit of literature. First come the Bibles of the race, — the books of books, — and, before all others, the Christian and Hebrew Bible, which constitutes the chief reading of millions of the most civilized races of men. Then come the Bibles of the Hindoos, the Persians, the Chinese, the Buddhists, also circulated by millions of copies during numerous centuries. Next come religious books of the second class, as the works of Homer, Hesiod, Eschylus, Pindar; the great poems of Dante and Milton ; and, after these, the lives of saints, the liturgies and hymns of the. ages, the manuals of devotion, " The Imitation of Christ," " Taylor's Holy Living," the works of Aquinas, Luther, Calvin, Wesley, Swedenborg, Channing. The vast circulation of such works testifies that there is nothing so interesting to the human heart as religion.

But " let him that readeth understand." It used to be thought a great credit to a boy to " love his book," to be fond of reading. But all depends on what we read and how we read. One may have a morbid love of reading. The habit of reading may become an evil. I have known persons who had acquired such a love for novel-reading that it was a real disease. They swallowed novel after novel as a rum-drinker swallows his glass of spirits. They lived on that excitement. They were passive recipients of these stories, and the more they read the weaker grew their minds. The result of this sort of reading is mental imbecility. Better, instead of it, to walk in the fields, to dig potatoes, or to talk with the first man you meet.

I do not mean to say that novel-reading is necessarily bad. It was formerly thought wrong to read novels at all; or, at least, wrong to read anything but the regular moral romance : the writings of Miss Edgeworth, Miss Burney, and the like. But novels in which the moral is too prominent are usually not so influential as those in which it comes, as in life, out of the incidents themselves. "The Vicar of Wakefield" has not any moral which compels your attention. "Don Quixote" has no obtrusive moral. But who can read the first and not sympathize with the good man, who, with all his ignorance of the world and its ways, commands our respect by his honorable purposes and his loyalty to truth and right. So, while we read "Don Quixote," we smile at the folly of the good knight with the surface of our mind, and love and honor him in the depths of our heart, for the magnanimity and nobleness of his character. We smile at him, but respect him. Such books make us feel how much better is inward purity and uprightness than any mere knowledge of the world or outward success. That is their moral, and it is a great one. But it is nowhere stated in so many words.

The great merit of Walter Scott's novels is their generous and pure sentiment. There is a strain of generosity, manliness, truth, which runs through them all. They nowhere take for granted meanness; they always take for granted justice and honor. Now this is the real, though subtle, influence which comes from novels, poems, plays. This indirect influence, this taking for granted, is the most influential of all. Some books take for granted that man is selfish and mean. Others take for granted that he is noble and true. Some assume that all men are led by selfishness, and all women by vanity. Such books are deeply immoral, no matter what good maxims are tacked to them. For our standard of right and wrong is usually that of the public opinion just around us, and the books we read create a part of that public opinion. Such works as those of Dickens have gone into public opinion, and have been the guides of the public conscience. They have made us all feel the duty of caring for such poor orphans as Smike; they have made us love the lowly; they have infused an aroma of generous feeling into the public mind. Catholics have their confessors, and those priests whom they call their directors, to whom they go to tell them what they ought to do. Such writers as

Scott and Dickens are the directors of the public conscience. Well when they direct it aright.

Novels are good or bad, like other books. To ask whether we ought to read novels is like asking whether we ought to go into society. Choose your associates; choose your books. Do not read anything and everything because it is printed. Meanness, cynicism, cruelty, falsehood, get themselves printed. Protestant countries have no index of prohibited books, no restraint on unlimited printing. It is all the more necessary that each one should examine for himself the character of what he reads, and find what effect it has on him.

Let him that readeth understand. " Weigh and consider."

I return to the maxim to which I referred above, *non multa, sed multum.* Read much, but do not read many things. Select the great teachers of the race, the great masters, and read them. Read Bacon, Milton, Shakspeare, Dante, Homer, Herodotus, Thucydides, Schiller, Goethe, Lessing. Do not read about these authors in magazines, but read the authors themselves. He who has once carefully read Bacon's " Advancement of Learning," or Milton's " Areopagitica," or the " Phœdo " of Plato, has taken a step forward in thought and life. We read many criticisms on books; it were better to read the books themselves. Who, in visiting Niagara, instead of looking at the majestic cataract itself, would wish to see it reflected in a mirror in

a camera obscura ?   Drink at the fountain, not from
the stream.   Read Pope, rather than Dr. Johnson's
account of him.   Read Milton before you read Macaulay's article on Milton.   Read Goethe, and then
Carlyle's essay on Goethe.   Literature tends too
much to diluted and second-hand reading.   Instead
of great books, we read the reviews of books, then
articles on the reviews, then criticisms on those
articles, then essays on those criticisms.

   It is an epoch in one's life to read a great book
for the first time.   It is like going to Mont Blanc
or to Niagara without the journey or the expense.
When I was a boy I lived in the country, and had
constructed for myself a reading-room amid the mas-
sive limbs of an old chestnut-tree.   There I retired,
and spent long mornings in reading the plays of
Shakspeare, the " Paradise Lost," the songs of Burns,
the poems of Wordsworth or of Walter Scott.   I
immersed myself in them.   The hours passed by,
the sun sank lower toward his setting, the shadows
moved on ; entranced in my book, I read and noticed nothing.   To read a good book thus is an
event in one's life.

   I once spent a long day in reading the Book of
Job in the translation of Noyes.   I had never read
it before from the beginning to the end.   It was a
day much to be remembered.   I beg of you to take
such books as these when you have time enough,
and read them through ; else you cannot know how
great they are.   Such books are not meant to be

read as serials, or to be issued in monthly numbers.
To read Milton's "Paradise Lost," take a long summer's day. Go into the country, and sit in the woods
alone. Read on and on, and give the whole day to
it. Only so can you realize the majesty of that
muse, —

> "Sailing with supreme dominion
> Through the azure depths of air,"

— the genius which paints in turn the sublime hor-
rors of hell, the tender beauty of paradise, —

> "The spirits and Intelligences fair
> And angels waiting on the Almighty's chair."

In reading a book, you will notice that besides
the thoughts, besides the visible moral, it has a soul,
a leaven of character. The words of a book may be
very moral, but the tone immoral. The words may
be religious, but the tone sceptical. For the religion
may be a mere smooth, cold crust over a deep running tendency to doubt ; the morality may be ex-
hortation to correct conduct coming out of a spirit
which does not believe in right or wrong. That
book, to me, is not moral which is stuffed with
moral maxims, or in which good people end by
getting rich and prosperous ; but that which makes
goodness seem both beautiful and possible ; which
makes it seem worth while to live, that we may live
generously and nobly. That book to me is religious,
not which exhorts us solemnly to become pious under penalty of going to hell if we are not, but in

which love to God and man seem natural, easy, and beautiful.

A book may be religious without being Christian. The religious feeling which pours itself out in expressions of awe, reverence, fear, remorse, trust, is nearly the same in all lands, all times, and all religions. Something of it is to be found in Buddhism, in Mohammedanism, among the Hindoos and the Chinese. But Christianity adds the element of faith in God as a living friend, close to us, who cares for us all, loves all his children, and whose true service is not solemn ceremonies or tremendous sacraments, but doing good to the poor, the lonely, the downtrodden, the oppressed. The spirit of Christianity is the spirit of Jesus. When a book has not the spirit of Christ, it is none of his, though it may be full of religious notions, and may be popular enough to reach a hundred editions. The book which has in it the spirit of Christ is an apostle of Christianity, though it be a novel by Dickens, or a poem by Tennyson.

Biography, history, and travels give us more information than any other kind of works. They should be read together. One illustrates the other. And I think these are the books to read in classes. The best way of learning history is to have a class, in which a certain period of history shall be the subject of the lesson, and each member of the class read in a different book about that period. Then, when they come together, each has something to tell to the others, and something to learn from them. And, in like manner, it is well to form classes to read other works and pursue other studies, for so the stimulus of society and co-operation aids the solitary study which accompanies it.

I will close these remarks with a few rules to assist in reading to advantage.

1. One rule is, to read what interests you. Interesting books are those which do us good. Unless a book interests us, we cannot fix our attention to it. Unless we attend to it, we do not understand it, or take it in. Then, we are wasting our time on a merely mechanical process, and are deceiving ourselves with a show devoid of substance.

The best books are the most interesting. Those which are clearest, most intelligible, best expressed, the logic of which is the most convincing; which are deepest, broadest, loftiest. Therefore, read the books on subjects which interest you, by the best writers on those subjects.

The two finest prose essays in the English language are Lord Bacon's "Essay on the Advancement of Learning," and Milton's tract on "The Freedom of the Press." And these are also interesting to that degree that, having once read them, you will never forget them.

The most interesting books, as regards their subjects, are well-written biographies and well-written books of travels. The one shows us human nature, the other the world and life. Therefore the undying charm of such works as "Plutarch's Lives," Xenophon's "Memorabilia of Socrates," Johnson's "Lives of the Poets," the biographical essays by Macaulay and Carlyle, and the like.

This rule of reading what is interesting is so important, that it is a good appendix to the rule to stop reading when we find we cannot fix our attention and are reading mechanically. For to read without attention is to form a habit of inattention. To read without interest, will tend to a loss of interest in all reading. To go through the mechanical form of reading when our mind is not in it, weakens the mental powers, and does not strengthen them.

Therefore, select the best and most interesting books to read.

2. The check on this rule, which will prevent its abuse, is another; namely, "Read actively, not passively."

A person may be deeply interested in a sensational story, but it is often a purely passive interest. He does not think about what he is reading. The result is a momentary excitement, and after it is over he has received injury rather than good from it. He is less fit to think or to act than he was before.

We should always, in reading, exercise memory, judgment, and the faculties of comparison and reason. We should repeat in our own words the substance of what we read, take notes of it, converse about it, fix it in our memory, discuss it with others,

and compare it with other books on the same subjects. This takes time; but it is far better to read
a few books carefully and thoroughly, than many
books superficially. Good books should be read
again and again, and thought about, talked about,
considered and re-considered. So, at last, what we
read becomes our own.

3. Therefore, there should be a third rule; namely,
to read with some system and method. Arrange
circumstances so as to keep yourself up to your
work. One method is for two persons to read the
same book, and to meet together to talk about it.
I read a large part of Goethe and Schiller and some
other writers in this way, in company with Margaret Fuller, spending two or three evenings every
week at her house, talking with her about what we
had been reading. An extension of this method is
to form a class to read on certain subjects; for example, a new book, a period of history, a country
and people, a system of philosophy, a science, and
then to meet and discuss together this common sub-
jcet. Such a class might be formed in connection
with every book-club. Where this cannot be done,
a person might, at least, have a note-book, and
write down the heads of what he reads, and his own
thoughts about it. To these notes he would afterward refer with pleasure and advantage.

If a person, in the course of some years, should
read in this way such writers as Shakspeare, Milton,
Bacon, Locke, Gibbon, Wordsworth, and our best

American writers, he would, by this method alone, acquire a good education and a large intellectual de velopment. Any one important book read in this way would enlarge amazingly the sphere of one's knowledge. I knew a gentleman who read thus "Carlyle's History of the French Revolution;" looking up every event, person, and place referred to, and taking notes of all, and thus he became thoroughly versed in the whole history of modern Europe.

Let us be thankful for books. I sympathize with Charles Lamb, who said that he wished to ask a "grace before reading" more than a "grace before dinner." What a consolation to the self-denying life of that good son and good brother were his books!

Let us thank God for books. When I consider what some books have done for the world, and what they are doing, how they keep up our hope, awaken new courage and faith, soothe pain, give an ideal life to those whose homes are cold and hard, bind together distant ages and foreign lands, create new worlds of beauty, bring down truth from heaven, — I give eternal blessings for this gift, and pray that we may all use it aright, and abuse it never.

Thank God for books, —

> " Those stately arks, that from the deep
> Garner the life for worlds to be ;
> And, with their glorious burden, sweep
> Adown dark Time's untravelled sea."

XV

THE EDUCATION OF COURAGE.

XV.

THE EDUCATION OF COURAGE.

———•◦•———

COURAGE is the most universally admired of human qualities. Only be brave, or seem so, and men will respect you, women admire you, and children worship you. Hence there are so many sham forms of courage, so many imitations. Manliness is so good a thing, that all that simulates it has a certain prestige. Courage is a fundamental faculty, on which the whole of human attainment rests, as on a solid basis. To defy danger, encounter difficulties, despise hardships, risk evil in the pursuit of what is good, true, and noble, — this is a motor which carries the world onward. If we would be of any use, we must not be afraid of responsibilities; we must be ready to run a risk of failure, to expose ourselves to be misunderstood; to encounter opposition, censure, dislike. All true life is a warfare. He who would be true to himself and his own convictions, who has a desire to obey his conscience, and be a law to himself, will immediately find himself in the heat and thick of battle. Drift with the current, think as others think, let your thoughts keep the main track, say what all men are saying, and no warfare is necessary. But stir an inch from the beaten road, attempt any improvement in anything, a thousand prejudices are aroused, and all vested interests become alarmed. Therefore, while we admire courage, we shrink a little from the courageous man. We know it is a great quality, and that it is required for all good conduct. We admire it, but fear it.

But how enchanting are all tales of prowess, all stories of adventure, of heroic achievement, of dangers dared! - Courage is the theme of Homer, Virgil, Spenser, Walter Scott; and, to come down lower, you will find the little boys reading stories of noble pirates and chivalric robbers, and feeding their poor little minds with this amazing trash, which is just now poured from the press in the form of boys' newspapers. For courage is so attractive, that when you cannot get the real article, even the counterfeit is accepted. Rudeness, vulgarity, brutal language are cultivated by boys in order to give themselves the air of manliness. For this end they learn to smoke tobacco, to drink intoxicating liquor, to use profane language. These evil habits are cultivated in order to acquire the semblance of manliness. As you pass through the street to-morrow, out of every ten men you see, one or two will be poisoning the air with the fumes of tobacco, and distributing these noxious vapors into the faces of those they meet. Of these thousands of smokers, hardly one formed the habit without pain and difficulty. It was excessively disagreeable at first; but then it seemed manly, and, therefore, desirable. There is, of course, nothing specially courageous or manly in exciting or stupefying the nervous system with this narcotic; but to boys and youths it seems so, and therefore they begin the habit, which afterwards becomes a comfort sometimes, or a necessity.

If courage is thus universally admired, and if, indeed, it is so important an element in all human virtue, why has it been regarded rather as a Pagan than as a Christian virtue?

Certainly, courage is, and always has been, as necessary to the Christian as to any one else. If you define a Christian as one who is trying to be good and to do good, then, certainly, he needs courage for both these tasks. There will be fightings without, and fears within, to encounter every day. He may not be provided with bowie-knife or revolver. He may not wrestle with flesh and blood. But he will be pretty sure to come into conflict with the rulers of the darkness of this world; that is, those who depend on popular ignorance for their success. He will have to fight with "spiritual wickedness in high places;" that is, with enthroned falsehoods, erroneous public opinion; dangerous influences in society, in church and state. The ingenuous youth who admires pirates and prize-fighters may see nothing of manliness in this, but in reality it requires no little courage to fight the good

fight of faith. Horatius Cocles defending the bridge
was not more heroic than Martin Luther on his way
to Worms. The brave men who die in battle seldom need as much courage as that bank cashier
who recently, in Maine, endured a slow martyrdom,
rather than reveal the secret of the safe and betray
his trust. Marshal Ney, "the bravest of the brave,"
was no braver than many a fireman who penetrates
through smoke and flame into the burning building
to save property and life, and dies, perhaps, in the
fulfilling of that duty. Honored be all courage
shown for noble ends, and in the discharge of patri-
otic duty! Honored forever be the courage of the
three hundred at Thermopylæ, of the six hundred
who rode into the jaws of death at Balaclava; of the
heroes who fell at Fort Wagner, at Gettysburg, and
all those whose precious memory makes our land
more rich and sacred! But honor also to the same
great element of courage, whatever weapon it uses,
or to whatever humble scene its task may call it!
It is needed all day long in common life, that we
may not shrink timidly from difficulties, but encounter them; that we may not postpone our duties,
nor make excuses for our neglect, nor evade telling
the truth when it is disagreeable to others, or involves mortification to ourselves; that we may be
loyal to our friends, to our cause, and to our convictions, when the opinion around us is hostile to them.
We are seldom called to encounter great dangers;
but, if we have the courage of our opinions, we are

always in danger of being ridiculed or scolded, or having disagreeable encounters with overbearing people, or positive people, or dogmatists.

One of the evils of cowardice is that it tends to falsehood. Fear is the mother of lies. Slaves, living in terror, defend themselves by lying. A tyrannical schoolmaster educates his scholars to concealment, dissimulation, subterfuge. A religion of terror creates hypocrites. Under despotic governments, which reign by producing fear, the soil is undermined by conspiracy, stratagems, and secret treason. Only courage is truthful; cowardice is always false. Therefore, free governments are good, for in them all evils come quickly to the surface and can be cured. Therefore, the parents who win the confidence of their children by treating them as friends, are safe from the dissimulation which is born in households where sternness and severity govern. Liberal Chris tianity has its defects and its faults ; but, at least, it educates men to courage, and the offspring of cour age, honesty, and truth.

That conscience is a source of courage appears from many instances. It is evident that, in the story of the Good Samaritan, the good man was willing to stop and run the risk of the return of the robbers by delaying his journey, because it was a matter of conscience with him to give effective help to the sufferer. An impulse of kindness would merely have led him to give some temporary aid, and then to hurry away to send relief. Sir Samuel

Romilly, one of the great reformers of the English law, rode out of his garden gate one morning, on horseback, on his way to London ; and his favorite dog rushed out after him, and by his actions Sir Samuel Romilly soon became convinced that the dog was mad, or going mad. He rode by his side, near the dog, thinking how he should prevent mischief. He would not ride on, and call others to his aid, lest they should be bitten. It would not do to let the dog get on the main road to London, crowded with people. So, when he reached the gate of a friend's garden, he rode up to the dog, threw himself upon him, caught him by the neck, raised him in the air so as to prevent him from getting away, held him in the air with one arm while he opened the gate, went in, called for a chain, fastened one end to a tree and the other to the dog's neck, and then threw him toward the tree, and so prevented him from doing harm. Now, this was courage born of conscience. Conscience would not allow this good and brave man to call for help. The dog was his own ; he himself must run the risk.

We shall never cultivate our courage if we suppose it is only needed on the rare occasions in which we may be called to risk our life, or encounter great peril. The only way to educate this power for great occasions is to practise courage in all the small events of life. We shall train ourselves to bravery only by having the courage to tell the truth, to do what is just, to adhere to our convictions in the midst of the strain and stress of business, the turmoil of the world, and the performance of every-day duties. And certainly Christian faith will help us to do this.

The mediæval idea of Christ was of one who came to suffer and die, not resisting or opposing evil. The mediæval idea of Christianity was of passive submission to all evil and wrong. The mediæval saint was not one who fought bravely the battle of life, but one who retired from the world to live in a monastery a life of self-denial and prayer. That mediæval notion of Christianity has come down to our time, and it is often assumed that Jesus taught and practised only the passive virtues of meekness, long-suffering, patience, submission to wrong, and non-resistance. No doubt he told his disciples not to resist outward evil with outward evil ; not to retaliate wrong with wrong; not to fight for truth with the sword. And, no doubt, it was very necessarv at a time when the Messiah was expected to be an outward deliverer, a warlike king, to show in the most convincing way that he was not the prince of war, but the prince of peace. And if, now, we are to overcome evil with good, we must not begin by attacking it with evil. "Love your enemies, bless them who curse you, do good to those who despitefully use you and persecute you," is as much the Christian duty now as then. We must not resist wrong with wrong, but we *must* resist it with right.

And certainly the real Jesus, the Jesus of his-

tory, was anything but a mediæval saint, with head
bowed down like a bulrush.   He was not at all like
a sheep dumb before its shearers.   His short career
was passed amid a storm of opposition, which he
faced with a manly courage of the highest order.
He exposed the hypocrisy of the Pharisees, and encountered all their rage alone.   Alone, for he had
no one to understand him, no one on whom he could
lean.   Yet he went straight forward on his appointed
course, without hesitation, opposed by all parties, —
Scribes and Pharisees, whose power was threatened
by his influence ; Sadducees, whose worldliness was
rebuked by his lofty morality ; Herod and his followers, to whom the name of any Messiah was a
danger; the mass of Jewish zealots, who hated Rome,
because he preached forgiveness to enemies and a
peaceful kingdom.   Amid all this tumultuous tem-
pest of ill-will, he went straight forward, foreseeing
his death at hand, but determined to do his work,
and declaring with his last breath that he was indeed a king, since he had come to bear witness to
God's truth.   There certainly has never been greater
courage than this.   And the reason that we do not
notice it is that in the wonderful harmony of that
divine character no one trait is ever prominent, but
always one is balanced by its opposite, — courage by
prudence, humility by self-reliance, tenderness by
firmness, love to God by love to man.[1]

[1] Since this lecture was delivered, an excellent book developing
the same idea has been written by Thomas Hughes, called " The
Manliness of Jesus."

Nor has there ever walked on this planet a braver man than Paul. He, also, passed his life amid opposition both from foes and friends. The other apostles could not understand the breadth of his view, and had no sympathy with his liberal Christianity; so that he, also, was almost alone, hardly ever understood. How touching is his account of his career: "In journeyings often; in perils of waters, in perils of robbers, in perils by mine own countrymen, in perils by the heathen, in perils in the city, in perils in the wilderness, in perils in the sea, in perils among false brethren, in weariness and painfulness, in watchings often, in hunger and thirst, in fastings often, in cold and nakedness. Besides those things that are without, that which cometh upon me daily, the care of all the churches." And yet, I suppose that the greatest courage of all was when he was obliged to oppose the Apostle Peter to his face, and accuse him of dissimulation at Antioch, and so probably to offend mortally all the followers and friends of that apostle. No wonder he said toward the end of his life, "I have fought a good fight!" Did Hannibal or Napoleon ever show more courage than he?

One reason why Christianity has not been thought favorable to courage is, as we have said, that we still believe, more or less, in the mediæval type of Christianity, which made it passive, not active; submissive, not aggressive; a life of humble endurance, not an energetic assault on evil.

And another reason is that Christianity is really opposed to a great deal which passes for courage. It opposes caution to rashness, sensibility to insensibility, modesty to boldness, and reverence to audacity.

For rashness is not courage. Rashness flings itself into danger without consideration or foresight. But courage counts the cost, and does not make any display of itself, but, when the hour comes, is prepared to meet it.

Nor is insensibility to danger the same as courage. Insensibility is a brute quality, not a manly one. It comes from ignorance, stupidity, want of imagination, or habit. There is no courage in encountering peril which we do not see, in going into danger of which we have no feeling. The surest test of courage, presence of mind, cannot coexist with brute insensibility. The sense of fear is necessary to all real courage. He who says, " I was never afraid," says at the time, " I have no real bravery." Not to be destitute of fear, but to be able to control it, to be self-possessed in the midst of danger, — this alone makes the real hero. The sense of danger is at the heart of all sublime courage, all heroic self-devotion. Montaigne tells us of a king of Navarre who, when his attendants were arming him for battle, was trembling with excitement; and they tried to compose him by saying that the danger would not be very great. But he answered: "You understand me very little ; for, could my body know the danger my courage will presently carry it into, it would sink down to the ground."

Nor is audacity courage. That boldness of manner which is affected by coarse minds, that overbearing assumption which seeks to carry all before it by an air of defiance, is seldom able to stand up before true courage. True manliness is modest, not audacious. It makes no pretence, utters no threats, but, when the time comes, it speaks and acts with power. There is a power in its eye before which audacity breaks down. They tell a story of General Jackson, who, when he was a judge, was holding a court in some small settlement. One of the desperadoes, who then were often to be found in the West, a border-ruffian and murderer, came into the court-room with brutal violence and interrupted its proceedings. The judge ordered him to be removed. But, as he was a desperate man, and armed to the teeth, the officer hesitated to arrest him. " Call a posse," said the judge, " and arrest him." But those who were called also shrank from attacking the ruffian. " Call me, then," said Jackson. " This court is adjourned for five minutes ; " and, going directly to the man, ordered him to drop his weapons, which, after a moment's doubt, he did, afterward saying, " There was something in his .eye that I could not resist." This was true courage conquering audacity.

All these other qualities which pass for courage — rashness, insensibility to danger, audacity, boldness — are natural ; but true courage is an accomplishment. It is acquired by discipline and education. It consists in self-possession, self-control, presence of mind, and devotion to what is true and good. It has its root in conscience. It is said by Shakspeare that "conscience make cowards of us all;" but when it makes us fear evil, it lifts us above all other fear. Conscience in the soul is a fortress which no power of man can conquer. It lifted poor, cowardly Peter, who had just denied his Master, to that height of heroism that he could say to the assembled court of his nation: "Whether it be right in the sight of God to hearken unto you more than unto God, judge ye. For we cannot but speak the things we have heard and seen." It has enabled women and children, in all ages, to endure a martyr's death, when one word would have saved their lives. Conscience in the soul is the root of all true courage. If a man would be brave, let him learn to obey his conscience.

The love of truth, also, is associated with courage. He who loves truth desires to utter it, whether men will hear or whether they will forbear. He has what is called the courage of his opinions. Truth, strong in itself, makes men strong. A clear conviction in the mind gives strength and courage to the weakest person. He who believes in the eternal laws of the universe; who does not believe in chance or luck, but in reason ; who therefore pursues with unfaltering step the flying footsteps of truth, — he is lifted above fear. Some men have this belief in

truth, in fact, in reality, so strong that they trust
themselves to their convictions, and are safe. They
stand firm on their instincts.

We must, however, admit that rashness often
takes the color of courage in the domain of thought.
It is now common to talk of "brave thinkers," meaning by this merely those who are ready to deny all
received truths, and accept anything which is un-
usual. Because courageous thinkers are often heretics, and are obliged to oppose the common belief,
it is assumed that any one who opposes the common
belief becomes thereby a courageous thinker. Because most men receive, without inquiry, all tradi
tional belief, many think it brave to reject all
traditional belief without inquiry. I often receive
newspapers published in the interest of freedom
of thought. The honest men who publish them
announce that the object of their periodical is to
oppose received views, whether in religion, morals,
family life, finance, labor. They simply propose
to abolish the Christian religion, do away with
wages, overturn the banking system, make it un-
lawful to take interest on money, and put an end
to marriage. Having accomplished this, they will
then look round for something else to do, and end
by requesting a subscription of twenty-five cents for
their journal. These writers seriously believe themselves to be "advanced thinkers." They mistake
rashness for courage, denial for discovery, sweeping
criticism for thorough examination.

Such errors, however, soon cure themselves. They should not make us suspicious of free inquiry, for the world cannot move forward except by the fullest and freest examination. The education of courage is to be faithful to our convictions and our duties in small things. Peter was courageous enough to draw his sword to defend his Master, but not courageous enough to encounter the ridicule of the soldiers and the handmaidens in the priest's hall. As much courage is shown by a child who tells the truth, when it is hard to do so, as by a soldier going into battle. If we would be brave on great occasions, we must begin by being courageous in small ones. If you do not fear ridicule, unpopularity, or being called singular, you will be prepared to encounter the gallows or stake, if those should be necessary. He who is faithful in little will be faithful also in much.

The conventionalities of society educate us to cowardice. To most of us it may be said, as in the play · "Thou art a blessed fellow to think as every one thinks. Not a man's thought in the world keeps the roadway better than thine." A breeze of free thought coming into a church, a drawing-room, or a political convention makes the air pure for a long time.

We all shrink, like cowards, from new duties, new responsibilities. We do not venture to go out of the beaten track of our daily life. Close to us, on each side of the road, are those whom we might help or save with one good action, one kind word. But we are afraid. We say: "I, am not prepared; I am not ready; I have not time; I am not qualified; find some better person; send some one else." Perhaps we have only one talent, and, therefore, instead of using it, we hide it, and when the Master comes we shall meet him with the old answer: " I was afraid, and went and hid thy talent in the earth. Lo! there thou hast that is thine."

Therefore, that conscience may act freely, let us add to it faith. If the Lord calls us to do any good thing, let us believe that he will give us strength with which to accomplish it. Be strong in the Lord, and in the power of his might. Wait on the Lord, and he will strengthen thine heart. This simple trust in God turns cowards into heroes; takes away all fear; gives a calm confidence, and enables one to go to the most difficult and dangerous tasks with hope and assurance. The Puritans in England, who trusted in God, beat the Cavaliers on every field. Wesley was amazed at the calmness of the Moravian women in the midst of an awful storm at sea; but they said, " Why should we fear? We trust in God." "The Lord is my salvation, whom shall I fear? the Lord is the strength of my life, of whom shall I be afraid?"

This is the way to cultivate courage: First, by standing firm on some conscientious principle, some law of duty. Next, by being faithful to truth and right on small occasions and common events. Third,

by trusting in God for help and power.   Such is
the man

"Whom neither shape of danger can dismay,
  Nor thought of tender happiness betray;
  Who, not content that former worth stand fast,
  Looks forward, persevering to the last,
  From good to better, daily self-surpassed."

XVI.

ON FINISHING EVERYTHING; OR, THE TWO EXTRA PENNIES.

XVI.

ON FINISHING EVERYTHING; OR THE TWO EXTRA PENNIES.

———◦◇◦———

I HAVE always specially admired, in the story of the Good Samaritan, the closing incident: "On the morrow, when he departed, he took out two pence, and gave it to the host, and said, Take care of him, and whatsoever thou spendest more, when I come again I will repay thee."

That last delicate touch given to the portrait of the man of Samaria marks the consummate artist. It completes the picture, and makes it perfect. It suggests, in the finest fashion, the advance from conscience to love. It shows that the motive of the good man was not merely to do his duty, though that lay at the root of his conduct; but also the desire to help the wounded man, and to help him thoroughly and effectually. Here is the superiority of love over conscience in human affairs. If I am only trying to do my duty to my neighbor, I may say, "How much must I do?" which means, "How little may I be allowed to do?" But, if I love, I say, "How much can I do? What more? What next?" "Love," says the Apostle, "beareth all things, believeth all things, hopeth all things, endureth all things." It works without any limits except the outward limits of occasion and opportunity. It is like a fire, which burns as long as there is anything to burn. When it has done *all*, it still considers itself an unprofitable servant, and says, "I have not done half I should like to do."

It is this little surplus, this unnecessary but lovely finishing touch, which makes the perfection of character. Without it, excellence may be hard, cold, and mechanical. The beauty of holiness comes with the unexpected gift which no one had any right to claim, — the two pennies extra, — which add the completing charm to the beauty of holiness.

The late Henry Ware told me that, when he went to Europe, he took many letters of introduction. But, after delivering one or two, he made no further use of them; for he found that, when he brought a letter of introduction, all that was done for him was done from a sense of duty. The man who received it looked embarrassed, and seemed to be saying to himself, "How much am I obliged to do for this gentleman? How *little* will answer?" Afterwards, instead of handing his letters, he called and introduced himself, saying, "I am an American; I have heard of you in America, and wished the pleasure of seeing you." Then the personage so addressed felt free to do as much or as little as he liked, and generally liked to do a good deal.

I, myself, had such an experience once. On the summit of the Flegère, a mountain which one ascends in order to view Mont Blanc and his surrounding glaciers and peaks, I met an English gentleman, and fell into conversation with him. He found I was interested in pictures, and made me promise to visit him, on my return to London, and see his private collection of the works of Turner and other modern artists. I did so, and he devoted whole days to showing me galleries which I could not otherwise have seen. He felt toward me exactly as the good Samaritan felt toward the Jew of Jerusalem when he took out the two pence, and said, "Take the best care of him; I will be responsible."

All excellence of character begins in conscience and the sense of duty. That is the deep root which is indispensable to its life and growth. Any benevolence which rests only on sentiment is like a tree without a root. Sooner or later it dries up and is withered. The storm will blow it down. Nevertheless, unless we have something more than a root, our tree is not a tree. It must grow up out of the root into the stalk, leaf, flower, fruit; that is, out of conscience into love.

As there is no beauty to a root, as all the beauty of a plant is in its stalk, leaf, flower, so all the beauty of a good action resides in that part of it which is spontaneous, free, and loving. What attracts us is that. I feel little gratitude, though I may feel much obligation, to a man who helps me from a sense of duty. But I am grateful, above all things else, for love. If any one is generous, is kindly, is glad to distribute, ready to communicate, he attracts all hearts to himself. Such an one makes goodness seem really good. God, it is said, loves a cheerful giver, and love is always cheerful. Man, also, loves a cheerful giver. No one likes to see good done gloomily, grudgingly, and of necessity.

Jacob Abbott, whose books show such a perfect knowledge of the nature of children, somewhere gives these four rules for parents : —

1. When you refuse, refuse finally.
2. When you consent, consent cheerfully.
3. Often commend.
4. Never scold.

Children, in fact, can be led anywhere, and made to do anything, by those whom they love. They are said to be ungrateful; and so they are for all that is done for them from duty; all the usual regular care taken of them they accept as a matter of course. But only do something unexpected for their happiness, and you win their hearts. Tell them a story, take them to see a sight, do anything for them which shows that you take an interest in them and in their pleasure, and you acquire an unbounded influence over them. I do not mean that you are not to be firm and decided. "When you refuse, refuse finally." Do not say, "Well, my dear, I think, on the whole, you had better not go out. I'll think of it, and perhaps I'll let you go by and by. I am afraid you will take cold. I had rather not have you go; but, if you insist on it, I suppose you must." Do not say that, but either say "No," and end there, or else say "Yes, if you wrap yourself up, it will be all right, and I hope you will have a pleasant time."

These are the two extra pennies which constitute a large part of the joy and good of life.

Some people fail from attempting so much, and never accomplishing anything. Finishing a thing, doing it thoroughly before we begin anything else, is very important to our own happiness and the good of others. "The *end* crowns the work," said the practical Romans. Better to finish one small enterprise than to leave many large ones half done.

Nature finishes everything, and that makes a large part of her charm. Every little flower is perfeet and complete, from root to seed. Every leaf which will open in the next spring-time will have its little ribs and edges as exactly and completely finished as if it were the only leaf God intended to make in the whole year.

Let us learn to do everything as well as we can. That turns life into art. The least thing, thoroughly well done, becomes artistic. It is a fine art to walk perfectly well, not in the heavy, mechanical way in which most of us walk. It is a fine art to speak well, to articulate distinctly, to pronounce correctly, to use the right word and not the wrong one. Anything complete, rounded, full, exact, gives pleasure; anything slovenly, slip-shod, unfinished, is discouraging.

It is said of Washington Allston that once having dressed for a party, and being on his way to it, he suddenly stopped because he remembered that there was something out of order in his dress, which no one would see. But he himself would know that the defect was there. That was enough. He went home, and gave up his visit rather than go in a slovenly costume.

This may have been an extreme instance of the artistic feeling of the perfect. That, in this artist, this sense of perfection outweighed the power of production, appears from the fact that he was never able to finish the picture which was to be his masterpiece. He left it, after many years of labor, in an incomplete state. His ideal was so high that it palsied his hand. He could never satisfy himself. This is one danger. The sense of the perfect, the complete, may prevent us from doing anything, because we cannot do as well as we can imagine and conceive. This often becomes a real drawback on goodness. Because I cannot do a work as well as it ought to be done, I do nothing. Because I cannot help the poor, the suffering, the sinful, as much as they need to be helped, I do nothing. This is an error on the other side. I once heard Dr. Tuckerman, the first minister-at-large in Boston, describing the case of a family of which the husband and father was an intemperate man. Dr. Tuckerman said that he had never been able to make him leave off drinking entirely. But he had succeeded in inducing him to stop for weeks at a time. Said he, " If I could not do more, I was glad to do that. It was a great thing for his family that he should abstain for many weeks together. A few weeks of comfort and peace were worth a great deal to them."

Nevertheless, an important part of culture is to acquire the habit of finishing every work. Work which is not finished is not work at all. The difference between active work and active idleness lies just at this point. Idleness begins many things with vast energy and enthusiasm; but becomes discouraged, soon tires, and leaves its employment half done to begin something else. Work does not stop till it has completed its task.

This want of fixed purpose you will often notice in children before they have formed the habit of labor. Watch a boy on his holiday. He has determined to make something or do something. He thinks he will dig his garden all over. He begins with great energy, but soon becomes tired of this hard work. It occurs to him that he wants to make a boat. He drops the spade, and goes to the tool-house. But after he has worked with chisel and

saw and knife for half an hour, this task also becomes uninteresting, and he decides that what he
really wishes is to read his new book. He reads for
a while, and then concludes that it is best to go
fishing. So the day is frittered away, and nothing
is accomplished. Worse, there remains in the evening a weariness born of this irresolution, and the
absence of results.

A good deal of the happiness of life comes from
the sense of accomplishment. God has mixed a
feeling of content with everything finished. Every
one enjoys an accomplishment. If you have half
learned two or three languages, you take little
pleasure in them ; but if you have learned one, so
as to read or speak it easily, this accomplishment
brings pleasure. A man who has learned to do
anything well, enjoys doing it. This is the lure
which wise Nature uses to lead us to finish our
work.

One advantage of sending children to school is
that they can be kept in their classes at one study
till they have really learned something. What a
pleasure to a child when he has learned his alphabet
or his multiplication-table ; when he has mastered
his geography, so as to really know the countries of
Europe, Asia, and America ; when he has become
familiar with the history of some nations ; when he
can read with ease a Latin book or a French one ;
when he can write a neat and legible hand ! Therefore, a wise teacher prefers to teach his classes a few

things thoroughly, rather than many things imperfectly. For everything perfectly learned is a spur to further acquisition; while all cloudiness and confusion left in the pupil's mind discourages him, and takes away the nerve for study.

Nor do I object to giving prizes for the best work done, for it leads persons to do their best, and exercises them in aiming at perfection.

It is a great thing for a young person to recognize the charm of perfect work, finish, completeness. It is a celestial inspiration which lifts the soul above worldly vanities and low ambitions, and will ennoble the whole of life. Not to do merely what others do, not to satisfy the demands of the world, but to aim at an ideal good, makes true manhood.

At this point, the highest human wisdom joins hands with the best religious teaching. All human greatness is the result of patient continuance in well-doing; of earnest, noble endeavor; of extraordinary generous seeking. And what does the New Testament continually teach, but that we should endeavor to be perfect as our Father in heaven is perfect; not to pray, nor to give alms, nor to do any good work, to be seen of men; but privately, secretly, to be seen of God. Always we are to bear about in our heart the pure ideal which we pursue, never condescending to anything below our best standard of right. The power of Christianity shows itself in taking the humblest souls, and filling

them with this purpose of infinite good. A poet
has said : —

> " A vast idea rolls
> Before me, and therefrom I glean
> My liberty."

We are set free from all lower influence when we
accept the control of this commanding beauty.

Much of the joy of life consists in doing well
everything which we do. We have no real satisfaction in our work until we have given the extra two
pence, and so completed it. If the Samaritan had
gone away without doing that, he would have been
dissatisfied with himself. He would have said, " I
have taken a good deal of trouble about that man,
but, perhaps, it will end in nothing. The innkeeper
may turn him into the street, and so all my pains
will be thrown away." But he finished his good
action, and left it perfect behind him, for an everlasting joy and blessing to mankind.

This is why the New Testament lays so much
stress on finishing every good work. It tells us not
to be weary in well-doing, for in due season we
shall reap, if we faint not. "We are the house of
Christ, if we hold fast the confidence, and the rejoicing of hope unto the end." " If any man draw
back, my soul shall have no pleasure in him."

Love to God and love to man are the only motives
which will last. We must take a real interest in
those we do anything for, in order not to get tired of

our work. Some ministers get tired of their parishes after they have been with them a year or two, and are always changing. It is often because they do not take an interest in the work and in the people for their own sake.

When a man says, " I have done my part, now let some one else come and take my place," it is evident he never really was interested in what he was doing.

Let us all enlist for the war. Let us never be contented to give up any good work until nothing remains but to take out the two pence and give to the host; and so to make arrangements that the work shall go on well after we have gone away. I do not recollect that I ever heard a mother watching by her sick child, a wife watching by her sick husband, say, " I have been here three days and nights. I think I have done about my share of watching ; let some one else come and take my place." No ! but the divine power of love supplies new strength to mind and body, enables her to go without rest, without sleep, and she never thinks for a moment of giving up her place to another as long as anything remains to be done.

Perfect honesty, in like manner, is never satisfied with doing as much as is expected, as much as is customary. After it has done that, it takes out its two pence and gives them to the host. This makes a man who has been released from a debt, and who is afterward able to pay it, pay all the

interest with it. Such completeness shows that it
is because he loves honesty, not because he wishes
to appear honest. It is the same with truth. A
perfectly truthful man, who loves truth for its own
sake, is not contented with being as truthful as
other people. He wishes to be entirely accurate, —
to have truth in the inward parts, and truth in its
perfect outward utterance. Dr. Johnson said, "If
your boy says he looked out of one window when
he looked out of another, give him a whipping."
We have outgrown whipping, but the idea is still
a true one. This is the "two pence" in truth-tell-
ing which makes it perfect and entire, wanting
nothing. It is the distinction of modern science
that it loves truth in this way. It verifies everything. I have a book, published about two hundred
years ago, which gives the scientific notions of that
day. Among other statements, it tells us how two
people may correspond at a distance : Take two
magnets and support them like compass needles, so
that they may turn freely, each around a card circle.
On the circumference of each circle write the
twenty-four letters of the alphabet. Then, if a
man has one of these magnetic needles and cards in
Rome, and another man has the corresponding one
in England, and they wish to converse, they have
only to turn one of the needles so that it will point
to a certain letter, and the other will turn immediately to the same letter. The only difficulty was
that the author had not taken the trouble of trying

the experiment, to see if it would work. The chief difference between ancient and modern science is that the last verifies everything; that is, puts truth into it. "Man," says Lord Bacon, "the minister and interpreter of nature, does and understands as much as he can observe of the order of things or of the mind, and can know and do nothing more." To love and serve the truth, and to surrender to it our own opinions, makes the man of science. To serve and love beauty, and renounce our own fame, makes the artist. To serve and love goodness, and forget our own selfish advantages, makes the Christian.

If in man justice is to be swallowed up in love, how much more in God! If our goodness consists not in doing what strict justice requires, but a great deal more, how far beyond any mere justice must the divine love go! If the charm in men and women which makes us love them is in this superfluity of good-will, this giving all they have and doing all they can, how can we love God unless we see the same element in him? We are the poor traveller, wounded by our sins, left half-dead in our helplessness and loneliness, with no power to do anything for ourselves. God is not like the priest nor like the Levite. He does not come and look on us, and then pass by. He does not say, "Do this, do that, or perish forever." He knows we can do nothing till he helps us to do it, and, therefore, like the Good Samaritan, he comes to us. He does not wait till we are able to come to him. He comes to every one of us, and pours some oil and wine into our wounds. Sometimes the oil and wine consists in human sympathy which God sends to us in our sorrow ; human love, which he sends to us in our loneliness. Sometimes it is an opportunity of doing good to some one else which relieves our heart of its own gloom. God's spirit is like the wind, which comes and goes a thousand ways, running on no narrow railway track, but in various manners softly breathing around us. It is in all that moves the heart, to awaken its better purposes, and to make things new there.

It does not run in the narrow railway track of the church only ; the means of grace are not merely Sundays and sermons, prayer-meetings and revivals :

> "Sometimes a light surprises
>   The Christian while he sings,"

and sometimes as bright and sweet a light surprises the sinner in his tears. Sometimes it is the aspect of nature, the heavenly peace of a summer's day, the innocent face and voice of a little child in his play, the beauty still more divine on the face of our dead friend in all the rapture of its repose. God can speak to the heart by anything, — by a weed, a grain of sand, a dream. He " who rebuked a prophet by the voice of an ass, and warned his apostle by the crowing of a barn-door fowl," can make the meanest thing the channel of his love.

Moreover, if God finishes everything in nature, if he is the consummate artist who makes the rhodora beautiful in the wood where no human eye can see it, and paints in exquisite tints the shell on the floor of the ocean, we may trust that he will not rest till he has made all our souls and all our lives pure, generous, noble, beautiful. We are as yet only the ugly roots of a future beautiful plant. The best man or woman is only a shoot a little way out of the ground. We are God's plants, God's flowers; be sure that he will help us to unfold into something serenely fair, nobly perfect, if not in this life, then in another. If he teaches us not to be satisfied till we have finished our work, he will not be satisfied till he has finished his. He will not be satisfied with simply binding up our wounds, by leading us to repent, with simply pouring in the oil and wine of his forgiving love. He will also set us on his own beast, and bring us to the inn, and take care of us there; and if he seems to go away and leave us, if his spirit sometimes seems to disappear again out of our hearts, he will have left the two pence with the host, and seen to it that all that we need we shall certainly have at last.

If we can believe this of God, then we can love him as we love our father and mother, as we love our friend, in whose answering love we have perfect confidence. Such a confidence in God as this is alone the source of genuine piety. Not till we cease thinking of him as justice, as power, as sovereign, as king, not till we are able to trust in him as one who means to save us perfectly, and unfold us into all the strength and beauty for which he has designed us, can we love him with all our heart, and our brother man like ourselves.

XVII.

EDUCATION OF THE WILL.

XVII.

EDUCATION OF THE WILL.

——•◦•——

BEFORE explaining *how* the will may be educated, I must first show that it is capable of
education. Many think that strength of will is a
purely constitutional matter, a question of organization, a natural endowment. Some persons, they
say, are born with strong wills, and they carry
everything before them; others, with weak wills,
and they give way before every one else. Will, so
they think, is only a matter of organization and
temperament.

This opinion is very strongly expressed by Mr.
Emerson in an essay on Power. "Success," he
says, "is a constitutional trait." "Courage is the
degree of circulation of the blood in the arteries."
"This affirmative force is in one and not in another,
as one horse has the spring in himself, and another
in the whip." "When one has a *plus* of health, all
difficulties vanish before it." "Success is, therefore, constitutional; depends on a *plus* condition of
mind and body, of power of work, on courage, and
is of main efficacy in carrying on the world."

It is very certain, I readily admit, that some men are born with great force of will, and others with weak wills. It is also very certain that you cannot, by any amount of discipline, of education, make an Andrew Jackson, a Napoleon, a Martin Luther, out of a man born with a feeble will, any more than you can make a piece of oak timber out of a pine log. Such men as I have mentioned were created with a vast amount of organic force; and that is something not to be manufactured by any school, any training, any culture.

But the point is here. If this organic strength, hidden in the convolutions of the brain, and in the force which drives the blood through the arteries, is not born of education, may there not be another kind of force of will which can be thus created? And may not this latter kind be the better kind?

We have seen, in our past lectures, that many other human powers have a physical basis in the organization, but also a moral basis in the soul. We have seen that there is a physical courage and a moral courage; a natural conscience and an educated conscience; a good nature, located in the bodily disposition; and a good temper, which comes from culture and discipline. There are instinctive perceptive powers, and educated powers of perception. There is instinctive reverence, belonging to the organization; and an educated reverence, which is developed by conviction, insight, and self-devotion to the highest good. Now, we ask, " Is strength of will also of two kinds, — one kind natural, organie, instinctive, belonging to the brain and blood; and the other the growth of purpose, culture, discipline, and a religious conscience?" I think it can be shown that there are these two kinds; that strength of will can be cultivated, and that such an educated will constitutes a greater power to endure and to do, than that which merely comes from the natural organization.

Mr. Emerson is no doubt right in declaring that there is a constitutional force of will which in sures success. But success does not come merely from constitutional forces: if it did, the savage would not retire before the civilized man. Culture adds a new force to nature. The early white settlers of Kentucky soon became more than a match for the Indians in everything wherein the Indian excelled. They learned to know the forest signs as well as the Indian, or better; they became better marksmen, quicker in their perceptions, more rapid in their actions; and in a struggle hand to hand they could master the Indian. Education in the white man had added a force to nature. Nor is it always true, that "for performance of great mark it needs bodily health;" for men like John Calvin and Robert Hall, William Pitt, Pope, and William of Orange, King of England, were all invalids, and all did great things. Of the last, Macaulay says: "From a child he had been weak and sickly. In the prime of manhood his complaints were aggravated by se-

vere disease. His slender frame was shaken by a
constant cough. Severe headache frequently tortured him. Exertion soon fatigued him. . . . Yet,
through a life which was one long disease, the force
of his mind never failed to bear up his suffering and
languid body" Dr. Johnson makes the same remark concerning Pope, that "his life was one long
disease." The incessant labors of Calvin were pursued amid continual bodily pain and ill-health. Dr.
Kane, who suffered all his life from severe maladies,
was one of the most active explorers of our day.
He climbed the Himalayas, descended into an un-
explored crater of a mighty volcano, ascended the
Nile to a great distance, traversed Greece on foot,
studied the glaciers in Switzerland, visited Dahomey
in Africa, fought like a hero in the Mexican war,
and ended his career by the immense labor and exertion of his Arctic voyages. Mr. Emerson is, therefore, not wholly correct in saying that "if Eric is in
robust health, has slept well, and is thirty years old
at his departure from Greenland, he will reach New-
foundland. But take out Eric, and put in a stronger
and bolder man, and the ships will, with just as
much ease, sail six hundred, a thousand, fifteen
hundred miles further." "Sickness is poor-spirited,
and cannot serve any one; it must husband its re-
sources to live."

Plutarch tells us that Julius Cæsar, the greatest
of soldiers, statesmen, writers, rulers, "was of a
slender make, fair, of a delicate constitution, and

subject to violent headaches and epilepsy" But this did not prevent him from becoming the master of the world.

What, then, constitutes strength of will? It is that quality of the mind which is prompt to decide, and, having decided, cannot be moved from its purpose, but holds on through evil report and good report; overcomes obstacles; shrinks from no difficulty; relies on its own judgment; does not yield to fashion, — and so presses to its mark always.

Strength of will is the power to resist, to persist, to endure, to attack, to conquer obstacles, to snatch success from the jaws of death and despair. It is the most vital element in character. It is essential to excellence; for of him who has it not it must be said, " Unstable as water, thou shalt not excel." A man of weak will is at the mercy of the last opinion; is unable to make up his mind, or, having made it up, to keep to it. He is undecided, and cannot decide. He sees the right, and drifts toward the wrong. He determines on a course of conduct, and then quits it on the first temptation. Weak as a breaking wave, a helpless idler, wax to take a stamp from anything stronger than himself, if he adopts a right course, it is only by accident; and if he is virtuous, it is only a piece of good luck.

Some races are gifted by nature with strong wills; what they will, they will powerfully; what they do, they do with determination. Our Yankees inherit this trait from their English forefathers, and the stern discipline of two centuries of hardship and struggle have strengthened it. Woe to the child who happens to be born with a weak will in New England! His is the fatal error in all eyes in our energetic community. To be inefficient or shiftless is the unpardonable sin, to the mind of a born New Englander.

But there are dangers from this quality of will. Unless guided by conscience, it becomes wilfulness. It makes despots and tyrants, and there are tyrants in all circles of society. Men and women who have will-power in excess tyrannize in their families, in society, in business. They must have their way in everything; they must always take the lead. They dogmatize, and are overbearing in conversation and among their associates. They have too much confidence in themselves and their own judgments, and so are in danger of making grave mistakes. Failure and ruin may come from too much will as well as from too little. Mere strength, unguided by wisdom, tends to destruction. But the power of self-restraint, self-denial, renunciation of private wishes before a great commanding good, — these are the secrets of the highest power. When a man is able to rise above himself, only then he becomes truly strong.

We have had an illustration of the two kinds of will in two of our presidents, — General Jackson and Abraham Lincoln. General Jackson was gifted by nature with immense force of will. It made him successful in war and public life. It was an energy which few could resist. It brought him into innumerable difficulties, and usually brought him out of them triumphantly. It was the cause of great mistakes and great successes. His independence caused him to refuse to vote to thank Washington for his services as President; made him resist his whole party in his opposition to the United States Bank, and carry his point, in spite of friends and enemies; led him publicly to defend Aaron Burr when he was on trial, though he had before offered his services to the Government to arrest him. His force of will once saved his arm, which the medical men had determined to amputate. It led him to take the responsibility without fear, whether he was right or wrong. It made him a great general, but a dangerous President. His strong will was often wilful, and guided by passion and prejudice more than by reason.

On the other hand, we have an illustration of educated will in Abraham Lincoln. How slowly, how hesitatingly he moved at the beginning of his presidency! Very different from Jackson, he devolved responsibility on others, leaving to soldiers to manage the war, and leaving to his secretaries full power in each of their departments. Though always opposed to slavery, he refused to pledge himself to take any active steps against it until the time seemed fully ripe. Slow to decide, when he had decided he was firm as a rock in mid-ocean. He weighed beforehand difficulty and opposition, but never shrank from them when they came. He carefully counted the cost before he acted; but when he decided to act, all his hesitation disappeared. Far inferior to Jackson in natural strength of will, he far surpassed him in the firm and unyielding pursuit of great ends, not his own, by conscientious means. Jackson was a mighty power, going like a cannon-ball to its end, —

> "Shattering that it may reach, and shattering what it reaches."

Lincoln's force was that of a river, sure to reach the ocean at last, because obeying the eternal laws of God, but winding around obstacles, patiently lingering along savannahs and morasses, never standing still, never forgetting its end. His was the

> "Supple-tempered will,
> Which bent, like perfect steel, to spring again and thrust."

Jackson was honest no less than Lincoln, and both were illustrations of Horace's "just man, tenacious of his purpose, who fears neither the rage of the people nor the threats of the tyrant." Jackson's career was like that of a wild storm, violent and destructive, though sublime; while that of Lincoln was as the shining auroral light of a near morning, which shines more and more unto the perfect day.

Natural force of will differs from the educated force of will in being more liable to be blinded by passion and prejudice, to be led out of its true course by caprice, and enslaved by personal ambition to selfish ends. It is self-will rather than free-will. Thus blinded by egotism, it no longer acts according to the eternal laws, and plunges into fatal mistakes and ruin.

The man in modern times who combined the strongest will with the most powerful intellect was the first Napoleon. But an uninterrupted course of success darkened the majestic mind of this great egotist, and led him at last to irretrievable destruction. But history tells us of another great French captain, who, though a woman, ignorant of war, displayed unparalleled military skill, awakened boundless enthusiasm, went straight forward from triumph to triumph, and won the greatest triumph of all in her martyr death, so becoming

"The whitest lily on the shield of France."

Her unbending force of purpose, which overcame all obstacles, was animated by pure patriotism, unselfish devotion to her country, and a simple trust in God. Therefore were revealed to her, an innocent child, secrets of power which had been hidden from the wise and prudent statesmen of France and from all its bravest soldiers.

All imperialism seems doomed to destruction. By imperialism I mean a mighty will joined to a powerful intellect, and guided by selfish ambition. Imperialism in France has gone down twice into ruin. Whoever seeks to acquire all power in his own hands for personal ends, whether he is an imperial banker or railroad king, an imperial orator, politician, statesman, editor, merchant, speculator, man of science, — seems surely destined to decline and fall. Force of will joined with intellect, but without conscience, carries such men up to a great height of popularity and power; and then, blinded by their own success, they commit errors which bring them suddenly to the ground.

Self-reliance, self-restraint, self-control, self-direction, these constitute an educated will. If the will is weak, it must be taught self-reliance; if it is wilful, it must have restraint; if it is violent, it must acquire self-control ; if it is without any true aim, it must be educated to self-direction. Freedom is self-direction. No one is really free who cannot guide himself according to his own deliberate judgment; a man who has no principles, therefore, cannot be free. Such an one is like a ship without compass or chart, sure to drift where the winds blow it or the currents drive it. The poor drunkard is the slave of the bottle. He knows that it is his ruin; but it says to him "Drink," and he must obey. But Napoleon was no less the slave to his ambition. He knew that his campaign in Russia was beset by unknown dangers; he saw the awful abyss before him; but ambition said, "Go forward and try to become king of the world!" and he was obliged to obey. He was drunk with ambition.

The two diseases of the will are indecision or weakness of will, and wilfulness or unregulated strength of will. The cure for both is self-direction according to conscience and truth.

Weakness of will, or indecision, arises from different causes. One is a disproportion between the ideal and the practical faculties. This is best shown in Shakspeare's Hamlet. He is unable to decide, because he has too many ideas together in his mind. A man who sees only one thing, easily makes up his mind. But one who, like Hamlet, sees both sides of every subject, often cannot decide to take either side. Is the ghost really his father's ghost, or is it not a false demon sent to lead him astray? He cannot decide. Does it bring airs from heaven or blasts from hell? Is its intent evil or charitable? Impossible for him to make up his mind. This is the disease of excessive mental education, when the intellect is cultivated out of proportion to the active powers. The natural cure for this is action, work, daily returning duties, which must be done, about which there can be no hesitation, no delay.

Another source of weakness of will is a defect in the power of concentration; inability to fix the mind on one subject, and to hold to it till it is done. Many persons are so made that they no sooner have begun one thing than they are beset by the insane desire of doing something else. They are allured away by every accident. The cure for this disease is to shut off all extra work, and keep to your own. Narrow the channel of your stream, and it will run with greater power. Keep to your point. Remember the saying of Christ, "One thing is needful." One thing, always, is needful; all others are secondary and auxiliary. Do the work first which is next at hand. "Do your nearest duty," say Goethe and Carlyle; but the Book of Ecclesiastes said it long before, "Whatever thy hand finds to do, do it with all thy might."

There is an anecdote related of himself by Alfieri, in his very interesting autobiography, describing the way in which he compelled himself to keep at his work. Being very fond of horses and of riding, he often left his desk and writing to take an excursion. No matter what resolution he made, the temptation of a fine day was too strong to be resisted. So he directed his servant to tie him in his chair, and to fasten him by knots he could not himself loosen, and then go out of sight and hearing for a certain number of hours. Thus Alfieri was obliged to keep at his desk. He adds that to avoid the ridicule of his being found by chance visitors thus fastened, the servant covered him with a cloak before departing. Thus the higher nature conquered the lower.

What force of will has been shown by great discoverers, — by Franklin, Parry, Kane, in their Arc tic journeys, by Livingstone and Stanley in their African explorations. Such histories show us how much man can do and bear, sustained by a firm determination. It makes us stronger ourselves to read of such strength.

Discipline, no less than concentration, is a cure for a weak will. There is great power of strength in habitual work. The day-laborer, who takes his tin pail in his hand every morning, and goes to his work, feels new power, self-respect, and hope coming into his soul. He has a mission, a duty, a place in God's universe. He stands high above the luxurious idler who, three or four hours later, turns on his bed and says, "I wonder what I shall do to-day!" The ruts of human life are full of healing for sick souls. We cannot be always taking the initiative and beginning life anew. We need to be carried forward by our daily work, as the boat is taken down by the current of the stream. Daily work is one of the blessed influences which keep the soul strong and sane.

Necessity is a great power to help us all. We are saved by work, and we are made to work by necessity. The necessary tasks of life give unknown power to the will. There was a story in our family, which I used to hear when a boy, that Governor Brooks, when an officer in the Revolution, received an order from General Washington to go somewhere, when he was lying helpless from rheumatism. He replied that he was unable to go. General Washington sent back his order, "Sir, you *must* go!" Then Colonel Brooks mounted his horse, and went, and did the required work. Here, also, the ascendency of Washington's supreme soul enabled his subordinate to make the effort. Whatever Washington commanded must be done. A weak soul weakens us, a strong soul strengthens. Plutarch tells us that the immense influence of Julius Cæsar made heroes of his subordinates. Common men, says he, became invincible when serving Cæsar. One man, in a sea-fight, had his right hand cut off, but pushed on and won the victory. A private soldier in one engagement plunged into a morass, and helped to beat off the enemy, but lost his shield. Cæsar ran to meet him with a shout of joy, but the soldier, in tears, begged pardon for the loss of his shield. I was told by Mr. Speed, Abraham Lincoln's attorney-general, that after the battle of Fredericksburg, Lincoln alone for many days furnished a supply of faith and hope to the nation. Hundreds of leading men, from all parts of the country, went sadly into his room, and came out cheerful and hopeful.

The will of Michael Angelo was strong, but if that of Pope Julius had not been stronger, we should not have had that greatest work of human art, the Prophets and Sibyls of the Sistine Chapel. Michael Angelo refused positively to paint the walls, because he did **not** understand painting in fresco. The Pope insisted, and Angelo then went to work, made his own colors, mixed them, tried them, learned how to paint, and having thus taught himself the art, pro ceeded to excel all that had ever been done in it before, and also all that has ever been done since.

But the great physicians for all weakness and all wilfulness, for all the diseases and imperfections of the will, are reason, conscience, and faith. The sight of what ought to be done, the feeling that whatever ought to be done must be done, and the trust that whatever must be done God will help us to do, — these great agencies turn our cowardice into courage, and help us to say, "When I am weak, then I am strong." To renounce one's own private will gives to the will the highest power.

Animated by great truths, weak women have not feared to die the death of martyrs. In a great cause not their own, men have gladly perished. Inspired by the commanding sense of duty, they have accomplished the impossible. And in how many scenes of common life do not these great powers strengthen the weak, restrain the strong, give self-control, self-restraint, self-direction; teach men to deny themselves, to conquer appetite, to rise above their besetting sins. Faith in God is the source of all power. Before a soul inspired by this faith, the animal strength of a Napoleon or a Jackson is only weakness. This is the force to make the human mind invulnerable and invincible. He who fears God has no other fear. Insight, conscience, and faith are the powers which rule the world. If you would educate your will to real˜ and permanent strength, it will be by their inspiration. Submis sion to duty and God gives the highest energy. He who has done the greatest work on earth, said that he came down from heaven, not to do his own will, but the will of Him who sent him. Whoever allies himself with God is armed with all the forces of the invisible world. That is why King Herod feared John, a captive in his hands, "knowing that he was a just man." Mere power shrinks and trembles in the presence of conscience. So Comus, in Milton's poem, says when the lady speaks : —

> "She fables not ; I feel that I do fear
>   Her words, set off by some superior power."

This is the divine influence which is able to create strength out of weakness, and cure all the diseases of the human will.

XVIII.

EDUCATION BY MEANS OF AMUSEMENT.

XVIII.

EDUCATION BY MEANS OF AMUSEMENT.

——◦◦◦——

THE subject of this chapter is the Education which can be given by means of Amusements; or, Recreation as a Source of Culture.

Perhaps it may surprise some persons to hear that amusements may become a means of culture. But it ought not to surprise us. The love of play and sport shows that amusement is evidently one of the original instincts of human nature, and, indeed, of the whole animal creation; and such instincts are not implanted in vain. All young creatures play. Dogs are very fond of play; kittens play by the hour; insects, birds, fishes, play in the air, in the water, among the trees. And by play they develop their faculties, quicken their senses, acquire alacrity of perception, rapidity of movement, power of attack and defence. I saw, the other day, as I passed over the Common, some fine dogs, which had been confined, I suppose, all the morning in the dog-show, brought out by their owner to take a run on the open Common. Nothing could exceed the evident delight which they took in the mere exercise of their limbs in the fresh air. They coursed up and down at full speed in every direction, darting away to the furthest part of the Common, and then back like the wind to their master, and away again. The passers-by smiled in sympathy with their joy.

Animals enjoy playing, and do a great many things merely for amusement. A kitten plays with a ball of thread, or chases its tail, from this impulse of sport; a dog will enjoy himself by the hour in running after what you throw, and bringing it to you. Even whales are often seen at play in the ocean, tumbling over in the water, and throwing their huge carcasses into the air in pure fun. There are birds which arrange bowers and gardens for their amusement. Thus all through creation runs this alternation from work to play, from play to work. Even animals which seem to be all work and no play, like bees and ants, probably have their recreations.

The instinct of play in man is stronger and deeper than in animals; for it is as universal in childhood, it develops into a greater variety of forms, it continues during life, it grows up into various fine arts, and is at the basis of many noble works. Many trades depend on it; people get their living out of it, and work to enable others to play.

The plays of children evidently grow out of a deep instinct. The ancient tombs of Egypt, which contain the fossil remains of the customs of dead races of men, have pictures of children playing top and ball, as they do in our streets and on our Common. Dolls, like the children's dolls of to-day, are found preserved in the tombs, and are to be seen in Egyptian museums. In fact, children are very conservative in their games and their toys; their amusements continue much the same for thousands of years; their almanac of sports, though unwritten, is very precise. Top time, ball time, kite time, marble time, return annually, as regularly as spring, summer, autumn, and winter.

The stories told by nurses and mothers to amuse children frequently can be traced backward to a hoar antiquity. Childhood, says a poet,

> " Has its legends, gray with age,
> Saved from the crumbling wrecks of yore,
> When Northern conquerors moored their barks
> Along the Saxon shore."

The plays of children make a very important part of their education. Their importance, however, has been overlooked. Amusements, though constituting so large a part of human life, have been thought unworthy of the notice of serious people. I have looked in vain in the American Encyclopedia for any article on toys, or games, or amusements. But wise men have not so undervalued this part of human life. Montaigne says: " It is to be noted that the play of children is not really play, but must be judged of as their most serious actions." Lord Bacon says of games of recreation : " I hold them to belong to civil life and education."

Certainly the love of play was given to children as a most important means of education. Anything which makes them run to and fro, chasing and being chased, is intensely amusing to them ; and so it develops their muscular power, alertness, quickness of eye, skill in balancing, in turning round and round, watchfulness, patience, and many other faculties. Out of the four hundred muscles of the human body, a large majority are probably exercised in these violent games, while regular work only exercises a limited number. Therefore the Lord sends the love of active plays first, in order that all the body shall be developed to some extent, and all the perceptions roused and quickened. Children have an instinctive desire to be in motion, to look at everything, touch everything, ask about everything, play with everything. This instinct ought not to be repressed, but encouraged. It is a great mistake to make children sit still long, except sometimes that they may learn to sit still. It is, no doubt, inconvenient to their elders, this perpetual prying activity, this insatiable curiosity, this asking of innumerable questions; but if they do not do all this, how shall they learn ? The Lord made them so, and he made them so for good reasons. The child does not need much for his amusement; expensive toys are usually wasted on him. Give him a bit of string to tie knots in; something to roll, to push, to set up and take down, to take apart and put together; a heap of sand, a bunch of sticks, paper to tear or to cut, water to sail his boat, sand to dig, — and he is fully satisfied. How suggestive is the story of the young prince, for whom a box of costly playthings had been brought from Paris, who soon grew tired of them, and going to the window, said, " Mamma, may I go out and play in that beautiful mud ? "

Going on further, the principle of games can be used to a much greater extent than it is in the training and instruction of the child's mind. " Why forbid us to learn by play ? " asks the wise Roman, who probably had been told by pedants then what we hear from them now, that if you make study too pleasant, it will cease to be a discipline. But why not introduce into schools games of history, of biography, of geography, of chronology, of arithmetic, to prepare for which study is necessary. Then, instead of a class coming out to recite stupidly and blunderingly its half-committed lesson, you would call the class out to play the game of question and answer; and every eye would be watchful, every ear attentive, every faculty intent, and the whole intellect roused to its highest activity.[1] What could be better discipline than this ? Is there any better

---

[1] This suggestion was already made by Locke, in his admirable Treatise on Education, in which so many modern improvements in education were anticipated.

exercise of the intellect than that which calls all its
powers into the fullest action ?

This principle has long been practised in schools,
but only accidentally, not systematically, except in
the method of Kindergartens. Why not carry it
further ? When I was a boy at school, mental
arithmetic was thus taught, and with great success.
Every boy who gave the right answer went up, all
who gave the wrong went down ; so we were all
winning and losing and winning again our positions,
from the beginning of the recitation to the end.
Capping Latin verses was also made a game, and
the boys who would have found it hard to learn
twenty lines of Virgil as a task, committed to memory hundreds of their own accord, in order to be
prepared for the contest which was to come.

Moral lessons and moral discipline, also, come
from games. The intense enjoyment of play enables
children to support pain, teaches them to obey
rules, to control themselves, to submit to discipline,
to bear fatigue without complaint, and so largely
helps in the formation of character. No doubt children quarrel and scold a good deal during their play;
but they gradually learn to control their passions,
repress their anger, be careful of their speech, knowing that otherwise their companions will refuse to
play with them. Can any one doubt that this makes
an important part of education ?

But the instinct of play and the desire for amusement is not exhausted in childhood. Grown men

and women need amusement, also, only of a higher kind. The rude games of children are replaced by those in which skill, art, taste, appear. Graceful dances, artistic and dramatic representations, athletic exercises, have existed among all races and in all times, and show how deep this instinct goes, and that instead of trying to eradicate it, we should seek to purify and elevate it. We should substitute for low pleasures those of a higher kind; coarse and brutal amusements should be supplanted by nobler ones; instead of the pleasures which degrade, we should give those which elevate.

This process has already been going on under the influence of civilization and Christianity. You will find all over Europe, wherever the Romans extended their sway, the remains of vast amphitheatres, where the whole population of a city assembled to witness the fights of gladiators with each other and with wild beasts, and where thousands of human beings were often "butchered to make a Roman holiday." All that has gone, — gone so far away that we can hardly realize that such a state of things ever existed. The ferocious bull-fights of Portugal and the boxing-matches of the English are also passing away. The theatre, though not what it ought to be, and can become, is vastly better than it was in England or France two hundred years ago. The grossness of those times would not now be tolerated on any European stage.

What is needed in order to carry on this reform

is (1st) to admit the importance of the subject, the vast influence which amusements exercise on the character for good and evil; and (2d) to find out how, instead of attempts to suppress and eradicate amusements, we can purify and ennoble them.

When thoughtful and Christian men apply their minds to this subject, they will, I think, come to these conclusions.

Amusements are good and not evil in proportion as they are (1) Inexpensive, and so within reach of all; (2) Not exclusive, but social; (3) Not leaving one exhausted and with distaste for work, but more able to return to work; (4) Not degrading the tastes, but elevating them.

All these conditions are fulfilled by the recreations which are public and free, such as public gardens, concerts, libraries, zoölogical gardens, museums of natural history and science, galleries of art. These should be provided in all our cities and large towns. And this might be carried still further by having, in the vicinity of cities, parks where various innocent amusements should be provided for the people, and in the cities themselves large, well-lighted buildings, where there should be halls for conversation, for reading, and for games, open every evening to the poorest people. This, I am satisfied, is the only way to conquer the attractions of the saloons, of drinking-places, where poison is sold which drives men mad, and leads to murder, ruin, and despair.

Total abstinence is a good thing, as a security for those who are in danger, and as the only safeguard of those who have become intemperate. Very often, the only means of reaching temperance is by abstinence. Prohibition is also a good thing, when an evil has reached the height which intemperance has obtained in all modern nations. If I could do it, I would not allow a drop of intoxicating liquor to be sold in the United States. Not that I think it wrong to drink a glass of wine or beer; but that I should think it well to give up half even of the comforts as well as the luxuries of life, in order to put an end to the frightful evils of intemperance. Unfortunately, it has not proved possible to carry out any law of prohibition. But if I cannot have universal prohibition, I would have local option; and, in addition to that, I would have temperance men devise new plans and try new methods. It is not enough to induce men to abstain; we must provide some other excitement, some other pleasure to take the place of the old one. Negative morality is not enough; self-denial is not enough; we need positive good to take the place of evil.

A working-man goes from his home early, and works all day in the wet and cold. His dinner is only cold meat and bread, or some indigestible pie or cake. He comes back tired to a dreary and dirty home. Is it strange that he should long for one hour of pleasure and comfort? He finds a saloon open, warmed and lighted. For a few cents he can get a drink which will exhilarate him and cause him to feel cheerful. He can here smoke and talk with others who have also laid aside care. Is it strange that the saloon should be patronized, — so long as the community provides no innocent recreation as cheerful and pleasant?

One of the stories told by Jesus, which exhibits in a striking way his consummate wisdom, is of the evil spirit, which, having been driven out of a man, returned again, when he found the house of the soul swept and garnished indeed, but empty. Then, he came back into the house, with seven other spirits worse than himself, because the house was empty. Negative reforms leave the house empty. They take away the old excitement, which, poor as it was, did fill and occupy the mind, and they substitute nothing else. If you would cure men of low enjoyments, you must substitute higher ones. If by replacing the maddening alcohol with light wines and beer I could drive out those dreadful poisons, I would gladly do so. For though the use of these may, when carried to excess, occasionally produce intoxication, they do not madden and deprave; they do not lead to wife-beating and wife-murder; they do not destroy the moral fibre, and bring men down to the level of the beast, and below it. Beasts are temperate; but the intemperate man goes far below their level.

No reform is of any permanent value which is merely negative. Self-denial and abstinence are only the first steps upward. Every man must have something to enjoy; some recreation for his weary hours. The true recreation is that which re-creates, which brings back a new life to mind and heart. The true refreshment is that which makes the soul fresh, strong, vigorous, prepared for new work. When amusement is made the end of life, when people live for pleasure, then they are dead while they live. But we should breathe pleasure as we do the air, to strengthen us for work, duty, progress, usefulness.

The Christian Church has in past times been too ascetic. Its morality has been of the Jewish kind, one of negatives. You must not do this, it said; you must abstain from that. This world is a vale of tears. Get out of it; keep away from it. This kind of teaching failed, and always has failed, to reach that large class who are full of life, health, energy, and who wish to exercise their powers. These have looked on the Church and Christianity as something to be respected, but to be avoided. They saw nothing attractive in them. The Church proscribed dancing and the theatre as immoral and evil. But the love of these amusements was too natural a feeling to be uprooted. Consequently part of the world danced and went to the theatre, and half-felt they were doing wrong, and the other part abstained and condemned the others. The one class despised the other as puritanical, and these condemned the others as worldlings.

But the gospel comes to make all the creation of God·*one.* It is the atonement of the pleasures of childhood and the work of manhood, of amusement and labor, of this world and the next, of present joy and future happiness. It sanctifies play, and makes work a source of joy. It smiles on the gayeties of the child, and helps the earnest purpose of the man. It says, "I pray not that thou shouldest take them out of the world, but that thou shouldest keep them from the evil." Asceticism throws away a great power given by God to help and improve us. It abandons to evil what might be a vast motor force leading to good. John Wesley saw the true principle when he adapted hymns to cheerful tunes, declaring that the devil ought not to have all the good music. The principle of amusement may be used to make all study, all culture, all improvement attractive. Thus the study of history has, in our day, by Macaulay, Motley, Carlyle, and other writers, been made as amusing as novels, — much more so, indeed, than the majority of novels. The principle of amusement has even gone into sermons and lectures; and here again we are only following Jesus, who made religious and moral instruction amusing by putting it into parables; that is, into amusing stories. Many of the proverbs of Solomon are very witty and entertaining. Therefore we ought to change the mere natural desire for pure amusement into the higher enjoyment of amusement connected with study and useful labor. A certain smile of gayety plays over the face of all well-done work. Why should we not do all our work cheerfully, instead of doing it gloomily and with a sad countenance. Therefore, when Jesus commenced his ministry, his first miracle was to make wine at the wedding, adding to the gayety and mirth of the occasion. There he showed that gayety and mirth are acceptable to God, and that there is a time to laugh as well as to weep. For doing this he was called a gluttonous man and a wine-bibber; but he was not deterred by these calumnies from what he thought right. He said, "The Son of man comes eating and drinking." If Christianity has ever been made to frown on innocent pleasure, to denounce this world as evil, to teach ascetic self-denial, and to exalt monastic virtues, this was no part of the teaching of Jesus. His view was far broader than that of his followers; his morality more rich and full; his sympathy with all human instincts and tendencies more universal. He himself lived a life of self-denial, but he asked no others to share it, except when necessary for something beyond. Other religions have taught that self-denial for *its own sake* is good; Jesus only enjoined self-denial for the sake of a higher end.

If, therefore, I am asked whether such amusements as dancing and the theatre are Christian, I reply, Certainly they are, if they are not abused or carried too far. To these and to all other amusements apply the rules I before gave: 1. Let your amusements be inexpensive, so that many may share them. 2. Let them be social and open, for whatever is open to all eyes is more likely to be innocent. 3. Let them be such as do not leave you unfit for your duties, but which refresh your weary mind and body, so that you can return to your work with renewed strength. 4. Let them not be such as degrade and corrupt, and enslave you to a habit; but such as elevate, strengthen, and purify the soul. The amusements which stand these tests are innocent, useful, and Christian. The theatre is a great means of influence, and the time has come when it should be used for good, and not for evil. But this can never be done while good people stay away from it, or only go incidentally, and leave it to be patronized by those who only desire low excitement. The managers of a theatre are obliged to meet the tastes of those who come, not of those who stay away. We may assume at once that the drama is so suited to the nature of man that it is likely to endure. As it cannot be abolished, all that remains to do is to elevate it. At present it is allowed to become anything it will. Plays are often acted, I am told, and exhibitions made, in Boston, which would not be permitted in Paris; most things are permitted, — vulgarity, profanity, licentious exhibitions, and immoral plots. This is not done because the managers prefer it, but because they must suit the tastes of their audience. Two methods may be applied to cure this evil. First, in licensing the theatre, some censorship should be exercised over its representations by the city government. No play and no exhibition should be allowed of an immoral tendeney. And, secondly, those who really wish to reform the stage should unite and agree to patronize the theatre as long as it complies with certain conditions. They might say to the managers and proprietors, " We will agree to take so many thousand tickets for the season on condition that you exclude everything vulgar and immoral." Make it profitable to have an innocent drama, and an innocent drama will come. But the chief thing to remember is this, that mankind need some sort of recreation; that if they cannot have good amusements they will have bad ones; and that therefore it is the duty of all, instead of merely condemning wrong and evil recreations, to seek to replace them by better ones. Let us try to be like God, who opens his hand and satisfies the desire of every living thing. He sends abounding pleasure to childhood and youth in the mere exercise and development of their faculties. He makes everything beautiful after its kind and in its time; he covers the prairie with flowers, the dawning sky with rosy clouds, and fills the early air of morning with the songs of birds. He nowhere leaves the bare skeleton of utility uncovered by the rounded forms of grace. He intends that life should be cheerful as well as earnest, full of joy as well as of work. He has left a large place in the world for recreation and amusement. Let us see that this is not abused, but used. When he has made all the earth to keep holiday, let not our hearts be sullen; but let us sympathize with all natural pleasure, all innocent mirth, and so keep out whatsoever is evil. "Thou, when thou fastest, be not of a sad countenance, nor disfigure thy face," but take thy self-denials gayly and cheerfully, and let the sunshine of thy gladness fall on dark things and bright alike, like the sunshine of the Almighty.

XIX.

EDUCATION OF HOPE.

XIX.

EDUCATION OF HOPE.

———•◦•———

THERE are two kinds of hope : an illusive hope — a will-o'-the-wisp, which comes from an excited imagination — and a substantial hope, born from experience, tears, and wrongs. Patience worketh experience, and experience, hope. It is the purpose of this chapter to distinguish these, and to show how a true hope may be built up in the soul.

The phrenologists tell us that there is a natural organ of hopefulness whose function is to give an expectation of good things. Some have more of it, others less ; but all have some. It is an especially human organ. Animals live in the present. No bird or beast tries to improve his condition, or to make his to-morrow better than his to-day. Man does this, and his power of doing it is the condition of his progress, both individual and social. Hope may often deceive us, but without it man could never have risen out of the savage state. Without hope, no culture, no civilization, no progress in wealth, art, science, literature. " Forgetting the things behind, reaching out to those before," — this is the secret of human progress. Fear of evil may keep men from going backward, but only hope of something better can carry them on.

This organ of hope in the brain is balanced by another, that of caution. Hope sees the good before us; caution, the dangers to be encountered on the way. Both are necessary to progress. A man who has too much caution and too little hope is easily discouraged. He is so afraid of evil that he does not try to get the good. He is the slave of anxiety and fear. He will never attempt any difficult enterprise. Such men do nothing to carry forward the world. Better have too much hope, and try, and fail, than not to try at all.

This, then, is one distinction between the true hope and the false one. The hope which deceives, is that which promises us future good with no co-operation of ours. We think to have the end without using the means. We trust in luck, in fortune, in genius; not in thought and work. What we wish and vaguely expect is to find some pot of gold in the ground, to draw the prize in the lottery, to be helped by some powerful friend. Those in whom this fictitious and illusive hopefulness is strong, love to read fairy stories, and imagine themselves the heroes; are tempted to gamble at cards or in stocks; prefer speculation to legitimate business; wish to be rich at once. All they undertake, they undertake blindly, trusting in their good-fortune, refusing to look at the conditions of success, or the difficulties in their way. So their life is apt to be one long failure.

The true hope, on the contrary, is one which is willing to think, wait, and act. It is in no hurry, does not expect instant success. This is what the Scripture means by the "patience of hope." True hope is very patient. It relies on the working of immutable laws, which are sure to bring success at last. The man who has this principle in him does not read fairy tales, but the biographies of those who have done great things. He sees how many difficulties they encountered, how many disappointments they met, how often they were baffled. He sees how they had the "patience of hope;" how they tried again and again and again; how they learned something by every failure; and how, at last, when success came, they had fairly conquered it by honest, careful, thoughtful, persevering work.

Nothing educates the practical faculty of hope more than the knowledge of what men have done by patience, wisdom, and determined purpose. We look back at the great men of history, — Columbus, Socrates, Dante, Washington, Luther, Milton, Paul, — and commonly we think only of their success; their whole career seems to us one of steady triumph. But study their lives intimately, come close to them, and then you see how they fought their way against constant opposition, slander, hatred, failure. The ideal man whom we call Socrates, the great shining light whose moral beauty illuminates Paganism, whose grandeur of soul has won the praise of the earth, — what was his real life? He lived by hope. Men whose names are now forgotten — or would be forgotten but for him — lorded it over him, and looked on him with supreme and supercilious disdain. The great Gorgias, the famous rhetorician, thought it almost a condescension to argue with him and refute him. When the celebrated sophist, Protagoras, arrives at Athens, the disciples of Socrates all leave him to go to hear this teacher, much greater, as they think, than their own master. No one, in the days of Socrates, anticipated that this plain-spoken, straightforward man, who cannot make an oration, or even a speech, who can only talk right on, is likely to be remembered. His companions and friends admired and loved him, but people generally thought him too combative, too plain-spoken. No one could tell exactly to what party he belonged: he opposed all parties in turn. He had found fault with the politicians, the orators, the tragic and comic poets, the artisans; he was by no means popular at Athens. His power was this, — that he lived in a world of ideas, he believed in great truths, he had faith in principles. He was strong in the hope which these inspired. Nothing which he saw around him could give him courage; but his hope of the triumph of truth was enough for him.

We think of Columbus as the great discoverer of America; we do not remember that his actual life was one of disappointment and failure. Even his discovery of America was a disappointment; he was looking for India, and utterly failed of this. He made maps and sold them to support his old father. Poverty, contumely, indignities of all sorts, met him wherever he turned. His expectations were considered extravagant, his schemes futile, the theologians opposed him with texts out of the Bible, he wasted seven years waiting in vain for encouragement at the court of Spain. He applied unsuccessfully to the governments of Venice, Portugal, Genoa, France, England. Practical men said, "It can't be done. He is a visionary." Doctors of divinity said, "He is a heretic; he contradicts the Bible." Isabella, being a woman, and a woman of sentiment, wished to help him; but her confessor said no. We all know how he was compelled to put down mutiny in his crew, and how, after his discovery was made, he was rewarded with chains and imprisonment; how he died in neglect, poverty, and pain, and only was rewarded by a sumptuous funeral. His great hope, his profound convictions, were his only support and strength.

Look at the starved features of the melancholy Dante, the exile, condemned to be burnt alive on false charges of peculation, based on public report. Think of the poor wanderer, unconscious of the glory that was before him, writing a pathetic letter to his beloved Florence, saying, "My people, what have I done to you?" But he, also, clung to his ideas, denounced the temporal power of the popes, put his soul into his great poem, lived in the hope of the triumph of justice and truth, and so fought his good fight. When invited to submit, and confess himself in the wrong, and so return to his dear city, he refused, saying " he would live under the sun and stars and see the truth, but not make himself infamous even to return to Florence."

All great men have lived by hope. Not what they saw, but what they believed in, made their strength. Milton was the object of bitter opposition and sharp criticism. He was odious to the Royalists, disliked by the Presbyterians, abused by the great Salmasius. and, in his old age, blind and poor, his friends in exile and ruin, fallen on evil days and tongues, he had nothing to console him, except his visions of eternal beauty, and his lofty hope of doing a great work, which the world would not willingly let die.

Paul, the apostle, whose chance letters have influenced the world more than the noble poems of Dante and Milton, or the discovery of Columbus, was a very unpopular man. He lived by hope; he had nothing else to live by. "We are saved by hope," says he; "but hope that is seen is not hope, for what a man seeth, why doth he yet hope for?" Hope, with him, is one of the principles which endure through time and eternity. Knowledge passes; opinions change; doctrines and creeds, however true, must be revised; but hope remains.

They say that Paul and Seneca may have met

in Rome. I doubt it. It is hardly possible that Seneca could have wished to see Paul. Who was Seneca ? The favorite of the Emperor, having a splendid palace in Rome, numerous villas and gardens, twelve millions of dollars in cash, the greatest reputation for philosophy, learning, and literary power of any man in the city. If Seneca had been asked, "Who is Paul ? " he would have said, "A wretched Jewish prisoner, disowned by the Jews themselves, preaching about another Jew crucified in Syria; a miserable zealot, a fanatic, believing in the resurrec tion of the dead and other like follies." Paul leads to-day the thought of mankind, as he has for centu ries; but, when alive, he was hated by the Jews with a deadly hatred. More than forty of them took a solemn oath not to eat nor drink till they had killed him. He was almost as odious to his fellow-Christians in Judea. They said, "Paul is no apostle, and cannot be, for he was not a witness to Christ's resurrection, and has never even seen him. There are only twelve apostles, and Matthias makes the twelfth ; therefore Paul is an impostor in claiming to be one." His own churches turned against him, bewitched by the arguments of his enemies. A man of many sorrows and few joys ; obscure, despised, longing to depart and be nearer to Christ, — what could the great Seneca see at all interesting in him ?

The power which moves the world is hope. An anxious, doubtful, timid man can accomplish little. Fear unnerves us ; hope inspires us.

Every man must have something to look forward
to. The condition of human happiness is to hope
for something better hereafter than we have now.
Give to Solomon all riches, all knowledge, all power,
leave him nothing to hope for, and he cries out, "All
is vanity." But let Paul be obliged to earn his
bread by making tents; let him be beaten, shipwrecked, imprisoned two years at Cæsarea, one year
at Rome, opposed by Jews, opposed by Pagans, opposed by Jewish Christians, and let him retain his
hope of the triumph of Christianity as a universal
religion, to which every knee shall bow; let him
keep his hope in Jesus as the Christ, who shall reign
till all enemies are subdued under him, — and he is
so happy that he considers himself to be sitting in
heaven with Christ even now.

Two gifts are offered to men in this world; they
very seldom can have both. One is success, with
weariness; the other failure, with hope. The last
is much the best. The man who succeeds finds
that his success does not amount to a great deal;
the man who fails, but keeps his hope, is the happy
man.

We have had in this State of Massachusetts a
man who was all his life fighting a good fight for
ideas and principles. He was always an unpopular
man with many, especially with the scribes and
pharisees of politics. The chief priests and elders
of political parties never liked him. He could not
compromise, he was not a man of expedients. He

was not a man of majorities; he was usually on the side of the weaker party. But the common people believed in him; the people of Massachusetts and of the United States trusted him as an honest statesman, a man of principle, one who could always be depended on to defend the right. He was very odious at the White House, very much disliked by the politicians who thought only of the next election. But he lived by hope, by faith in great truths; and now, when that noisy hour has passed by, and the great verdict of history is being rendered, the name of this Massachusetts statesman is rising to take its place with the greatest in our annals. The petty wrongs and insults offered to Charles Sumner are forgotten; the light of his honest and truthful record illuminates American history.

Such is the power of hope born out of faith in ideas.

Perhaps it may be said, " It is well for those who are naturally hopeful; but what for us who are not so ? How can we, who naturally look on the dark side of things, who are easily discouraged, learn to be more hopeful ?"

The organic faculty of hope differs in different men. Some have more, others less. But the higher kind of hope, the religious hope, born of conviction, all men may have. All true religion is hopeful; because the difference between religion and superstition is that to the religious man God is goodness, to the superstitious man God is terror. True religion is that which trusts in the goodness of God ; which believes good stronger than evil, truth more powerful than error, right sure to conquer wrong. It is a kingdom of heaven coming to take the place of hell on the earth. It is, indeed, faith, not sight. But this faith comes to us in all our best hours. When we are in our highest mood, we believe in the goodness of God ; in the commanding authority of duty ; in the immortality of the soul. When we are true, brave, strong, generous, pure, we believe in God. When we are cowardly, mean, selfish, then we believe in the devil.

If, then, we wish to cultivate and strengthen our hope, it must be by increasing our faith in goodness. We must have faith in the true God, and that is essentially faith in goodness. Faith in God grows as we live in it, and from it. As we believe in justice, truth, honor, and act from that belief, our faith in God and goodness continually becomes stronger.

The faith of reason gives us confidence in the divine laws as the regular method by which truth and goodness are to prevail. As the world acquires more faith in the supremacy and universality of law, it also comes to believe more in progress. Our trust in the order of the universe gives the hope of great advances and improvements in the material and moral order. No matter what difficulties intervene, we trust that order will emerge out of confusion, and prevail more and more.

Faith in God as goodness inspires faith in ourselves; and, therefore, hope that we are made for something, meant for something, and that by perseverance we can accomplish something. Thus faith in Divine Love is the root and the strength of all sure hope.

Jesus was full of this divine hope. In the midst of loneliness, opposition, and apparent failure, he looked forward to the hour when he should draw all men unto him; when he should judge the earth by his truth; come in his kingdom, and be recognized as the light of the world, and the king of truth. His was no illusive hope, fed by his wishes alone. He saw all the evil, the wars, the persecutions, which should precede his triumph. But he had no doubt of the result.

His religion has, therefore, always inspired hope, both for this life and the life to come. This hope has been a constant motor-power carrying civilization forward; creating faith in the divine laws; inspiring science, art, and literature. Modern civilization has been fed at its roots by this perpetual hope, born of the Gospel. Christian nations live in a perpetual state of expectation, always hoping for something new and good; heathen nations expect little, hope for little, and therefore accomplish little.

The Bible is a book filled with hope from end to end, and therein lies much of its power. As, in the Book of Genesis, the rainbow of hope floats over the retiring waters of the flood; so the same meteor of spectral beauty floats on over law and prophets, gospels and epistles, and glows most brightly at the close in the Book of Revelation, which shows us a new heaven and a new earth. The law looked forward to the prophets; the prophets to the days of the Messiah; and those days to his coming as the universal king and Saviour. The power of the Gospel is its spirit of hope.

And modern science is also filled with the same spirit. It is always looking forward to some new discovery of divine law. It predicts progress, it announces advance, its theme is continual development. According to science, all things are working together for good in the domain of nature; according to Christianity, all things are working together for good in the domain of spirit.

The path of progress also for each individual soul lies along this highway of hope. This is the way of salvation. Until we attain this divine hope in the supremacy and ultimate triumph of good in the universe, we are lost souls, dead souls, — dead while we seem to live. Without hope, there is no spring of vital power in the human heart which can carry it forward. A man having no faith in providence, in the love of God, in human progress, in immortality, may be, indeed, a conscientious, honest, and good man. But his goodness is without enthusiasm, with no magnetic power, with no force to create life in other souls. It is a discouraging goodness, a chilling and unattractive goodness. But with hope at the centre of the soul all things become alive. As the days of spring arouse all nature to a green and growing vitality, so when hope enters the soul it makes all things new. It insures the progress which it predicts. Rooted in faith, growing up into love; these make the three immortal graces of the Gospel, whose intertwined arms and concurrent voices shed joy and peace over our human life.

XX.

EVERY MAN HIS PROPER GIFT.

XX.

EVERY MAN HIS PROPER GIFT.

———⋅◦⋅——— ⋅

IT would be a source of great comfort to us if we could all be satisfied that each of us has his proper gift. We sometimes desire the gifts of others, and undervalue our own; hence envy, rivalry, jealousy, and all uncharitableness. It would be very good for us if we could only believe the fact, that every one has " his proper gift."

How different are human characteristics! How plain that God loves variety, and abhors uniformity; and how he must dislike that kind of unity which a narrow religion and a narrow morality are so apt to demand.

Look at a heap of sand. We cannot say that each grain has its proper gift, differing from every other. They might change places, and no harm come. Those that are at the top might just as well be at the bottom, and the heap would remain the same. But consider a watch. In a watch the case is different. There each wheel, spring, screw, pin, has its proper gift from the watchmaker, and neither can do the work of another. They cannot change places. Moreover, the smallest and most insignificant part of the watch is essential to the integrity of the whole. Omit a single wheel, and the watch refuses to move. Take out one screw, and it goes badly.

Each part of the watch is different in form and function from the rest, and thus each is adapted to work with the rest. But in a heap of sand there is neither diversity nor adaptation. The particles resemble each other, and therefore cannot cohere nor co-operate. The parts of a watch differ from each other, and therefore can cohere and can co-operate.

Is human society like the heap of sand, or is it like the watch? In its lowest condition it is like the sand; in its higher, it is like the watch. And social progress consists in passing from one of these conditions to the other.

Take a tribe of North American Indians, or a tribe of African savages. Each man's function is like that of his neighbor. There is no division or distribution of labor. Every man is a hunter, a fisherman, a fighter, just like every other man. Every woman is a cook, a nurse, and a tiller of the ground. No one has any proper gift peculiar to himself; no special function which others cannot perform as well. Therefore the parts of savage society do not cohere nor co-operate.

But consider a great civilized community or a

great city. Every man has his own trade, his own occupation; one after this manner, and another after that. There are put down in the Boston Directory some two thousand different trades carried on in this city. The simplicity of savage life has unfolded into all this complex and diversified industry.

This is a watch with two thousand different parts, each fitting into the rest. All are necessary to the full life and activity of the city. No one can do the work of another; but, by each doing his own work, the whole is carried on. Every day each of these two thousand industries goes on, and not a man in them may know exactly how, or when, or where his special work is to be wanted, or how it is to fit into the rest. But it will be wanted, and it will fit into its place.

If the industrial world is thus developed into variety and combination, into difference and adaptation; is it not so, too, in the moral, intellectual, and spiritual world? Does culture make men all morally and spiritually alike, or does it develop differences? I think it evident that, as men ascend in the scale of being, they do not become more alike, but more different, more individual, more personal.

Take the great intellects of the race, those who have unfolded the most extraordinary power of genius. Are Plato, Socrates, Aristotle, alike? Are Homer, Virgil, Dante, Spenser, Shakspeare, Milton, repetitions of each other? Are Fénelon, Channing,

27

St. Francis, Confucius, Buddha, cast in the same mould ?   Are Peter, James, John, Paul, fac-similes of each other, or of their Master ?   No.   As men unfold and develop, they unfold into originality, individuality ; each one becoming more and more himself, less and less like any one else.   And by becoming himself, by growing up into what he was meant to be, he becomes able to contribute some important element to human progress.   We do not want imitation, — not even an imitation of Christ. Having had one Homer, we do not want another ; having had one Plato, we do not want another ; and having had one Christ, we do not want another. Christ does not make his apostles feeble imitations of himself, but as they grow up into him, they grow up into themselves.

Every man has his own organic gift, his own gift of disposition, faculty, ability.

One man's gift is to tell the truth.   He is a great truth-teller.   He does not know how to say any-thing which is insincere, or even equivocal or dubious.   He comes right out with his thought. It is sometimes quite alarming to have such a man near you, for his word breaks through the thin ice of decorum and propriety on which people are walking, and they suddenly get a cold bath in the icy waters of truth.   Or, to change the figure, his word is like lightning, whose keen blue bolt shatters the tall trees from top to bottom, and sets the houses on fire, but clears up the air and makes it pure, destroying the seeds of malaria and pestilence. One may suffer, but many will be benefited. He may be very blunt and rude, but his word is wholesome, and does us all good. He was made to do this service. Let him not exaggerate his special tendencies, but let him use them.

Another man's organic gift is to be good-natured and agreeable; not to be too truthful; at all events, not to come out with the sharp battle-axe of criticism and denial on all occasions. As in the garden we have vegetables, fruits, and flowers, so in the human garden called society we have strong and useful persons, men and women of energy and praotical talent; then kind persons, those who make life sweet and dear; lastly, agreeable persons, who make it beautiful by their capacity of imparting pleasure by a mere expression, a smile, a gracious gesture. Let us be thankful for wholesome vegeta bles, for sweet fruits, for lovely flowers. I do not blame my sweet corn and tomatoes because they are not strawberries and pears; I do not quarrel with my roses and petunias because they give me nothing for my breakfast. And so, too, if an agreeable person comes to see me, I thank God for that visit. If I find a man helpful and wise, I am grateful for him; if I meet another who has sympathy and kindness, though nothing else, I am glad of that.

Some persons have the gift of seeing abstract truth and absolute right. They see what ought to be done. They see the great end, and the circuitous road disappears.   They are prophet voices in society, terrible critics and censors; they are for laying the axe at the root of the tree.   They abhor all compromises between good and evil.   They can make no allowance for temptation, for circumstance, for habit.   Radical as John the Baptist, they cry aloud in the wilderness of life, and say, "Every tree that brings not forth good fruit must be hewn down and cast into the fire."   Such men are very useful.   Their fate is hard, and their work severe. They are more feared than loved.   They are favorites with no party.   They are called impracticables by some, fanatics by others.   Yet they maintain in the world the conviction that right and wrong are two things, and not the same; that truth and falsehood are deadly foes, not companions and friends. They testify evermore to the eternal nature of moral distinctions, to the great gulf fixed between good and evil.

God gives a practical talent to other persons. That also is a good gift.   They can see at once how to remove or avoid difficulties; they can arrange anything that is to be done so that it shall be done successfully; they can organize victory in great matters or in small.   They have no love for abstractions.   They are not for cutting their way straight forward through rocks and swamps and the tangled wilderness; they prefer to bend a little, this way and that, and so get there sooner.   They know well, what the poet says, that —

" The road the human being travels,
That by which blessing comes and goes, doth follow
The river's course, the valley's peaceful windings
Curves round the cornfield and the hill of vines,
Honoring the holy bounds of property,
And thus secure, though late, reaches its end."

There is a gift of exceeding serenity with which God endows certain souls. Perhaps they never say or do anything extraordinary, but an influence like that of a calm October day attends them. A Sabbath-morning rest tranquillizes all hearts when they come. No impatience, no petulant dissatisfaction, no turbulent doubts, no stormy rebellion, can easily resist the holy calm which their presence brings. They seem to be so well poised and centred themselves; they certify to us such a profound inner harmony; they are so at one with God and with God's world, — that they inspire tranquillity. They sing to us a perpetual hymn of quiet.

There is another gift, a gift of sweetness. How, in our troubled lives, could we do without those fair, summery natures, into which, on their creation-day, God allowed nothing sour, acrid, or bitter to enter, but made them a perpetual solace and comfort by their sunshine and their cheerfulness ? These are the objects of universal love, because their sympathy is universal; they are those who cannot be provoked; who think no evil; whose tone, when they find fault with us, is sweeter than that of

most others when they praise us; who make sunshine in a shady place; and who are able to medicine to minds diseased, simply by the balm of
their sympathy. We do not, perhaps, seek them in
our strong and ambitious hour; but when life begins to grow hard with us; when disappointment,
bereavement, pain, attack us; then the soft tone of
their sympathy, the kind readiness of their friendship, their brotherly and sisterly pity, are a cheer
and a blessing. It is a great thing to have this
sweetness; that is a proper gift from the Lord.

Some men are born to be mediators; they can see
the truth on both sides; they can enter into very
different states of thought, purpose, feeling. They
introduce us to each other; they break down the
middle wall of prejudice between man and man, between sects, schools, parties, races, nations, so making peace.

Others, again, are not thus wide; not so compre-
hensive, but narrow; narrow, swift, straight. They
may be full of prejudices, and be wholly unable to
do justice to men unlike themselves. But they
have a work to do. They are like railroad-cars
which run on a narrow track, and cannot get out of
it.* They will run over everything in their way, but
they can go far and fast in one direction.

Hopefulness is a gift. It is a help to us all to
have some one who is inclined to hope; who has
faith in good as stronger than evil; who trusts in
God, and looks forward to a kingdom of heaven.

Such hope inspires us all with courage; makes us more ready to undertake any work, and encounter any danger.

But others have a gift of cautiousness, and that is equally important and valuable. They show the difficulties in the way, and so save us from a thousand errors. They sometimes check us when we wish to go forward hastily, or turn us backward when we think we might move on; but this saves us from mistakes and long wanderings, which would use up strength and heart.

God gives to one man the gift of writing books, speeches, or sermons; and he writes, prints, and preaches what may call men to repentance, and awaken the sense of responsibility, or the feeling of religious trust. But God bestows on another the gift of living sermons, and wherever the man goes his life preaches. It preaches conscientiousness. He is one who would not do another a wrong for any gain or success. It preaches generosity. He forgets himself; he delights in helping his neighbor. It preaches humility. He is willing to do any lowly act of goodness, to bear any burden. He has his proper gift, and he uses it properly. Who shall say that he has not turned as many to righteousness as any golden-mouthed Chrysostom of ancient or modern days?

One man, like Dr. Lardner, or Bishop Butler, or Archdeacon Paley, may write books on "The Evideuces of Christianity," or "The Credibility of the

Gospels," and so convert many sceptics. Another may, by his goodness, translate the Gospels into daily life, and so make them credible. His good life is the best evidence of Christianity.

Even the sceptic, the doubter, has his proper gift from the Lord. Else, why did Jesus choose Thomas as one of his apostles ? Hume, Hobbes, Tom Paine, Voltaire, all have their use. They came to point out the weak places in the popular religion, and thus lead us to mend them. Every attack on Christianity, from the time of Celsus and Porphyry to that of Strauss or Frothingham, has strengthened it, brought out new defenders, new arguments, and better ones, in its behalf. We ought not to be angry with the honest critics and doubters, but make use of them.

That variety which is good in the natural world, why should it be bad in the spiritual world ? We do not quarrel with an apple because it is not a peach, nor with a pine which gives us lumber, because it is not mahogany to give us furniture. Why, then, should Orthodox and Unitarian, Methodist and Quaker, quarrel ?

What sort of a garden would it be in which there was only one kind of flower or one kind of fruit? Rather a monotonous and stupid garden, probably. But the church has hitherto seemed to consider itself, not a garden of fruit, but an army of soldiers, who are all to be drilled in one way, to be dressed in the same uniform, to be just of the same height, and carry the same regulation weapons. For the

object, too often, is not to educate men to do good
and to bear fruit, but to fight with other sects, to
give battle for creeds, to win victories for the church.
The man who sings, "Am I a soldier of the cross ?"
often means, "Am I not a soldier of this or that de-
nomination ?"

There is also a gift of insight. I used to notice
these varieties of gifts with delight in classes for the
study of history, or of the Bible; and I have known
persons often, who, by simply fixing their thoughts
quietly on a subject, would be sure to have a sight
of some truth connected with it. Then another
would have not this, but dialectic power; power of
seeing the reason or the unreason of a thing; power
of distinguishing between things different, showing
what was proved and what was not proved by a fact
or an argument. Another would have judgment, —
judgment enriched and made clear by knowledge of
the world and of mankind; such judgment as would
seem like a fan in the hand to winnow the chaff
from the wheat. Another would bring a deep inner
experience, a whole internal life of struggle, prayer,
self-devotion, self-surrender, trial borne, duty done,
temptation resisted, God sought after and found,
Christ's salvation received and lived. Still another
would have experience of human wants and how
they were to be helped; he would know what men
suffer and what they desire. Thus, each one contrib-
nting, according to his own gift, the whole subject
would be thoroughly studied. So that I have often

felt, while listening to such a conversation, that I could understand the words of Paul, and say that to one was given by the spirit the word of wisdom, to another knowledge by the same spirit, to another faith by the same spirit, to another prophecy, to another discerning of spirits, and the like.

There is nothing which would make us more tolerant of differences, more charitable to those from whom our opinions and tastes render us averse, than these considerations.   These differences are from God ; he made us to differ, and he appointed this difference for wise ends.   I sometimes think that the wisest axiom in the world, the saying that goes further than any other toward explaining the universe, is that popular proverb, " It takes all sorts of people to make a world."   This proverb expresses the wonderful fulness and richness of the world, its thousandfold varieties, all working together in one grand harmony of adaptations.   Attractions and repulsions, loves and hates, co-operations and competitions, rivalry and opposition on the one side, partnerships and associations on the other, all result at last in an orbed and beautiful whole.   If any of us had made the world, what a very stupid one it would probably have been.   Utilitarians would have excluded poets and artists, poets would have shut out utilitarians.   Conservatives would banish reformers, and reformers would exclude conservatives. The orthodox dogmatists would have prevented all heretics from making their appearance, and *vice versa.* But God lets them all come in, and, in his hospitable world, provides room and place for all. The poor Bushman, the Hottentot, the wild Australian, the idolatrous and heathen multitudes ·who worship Boodh, or who bow to a Fetish, he lets them all in ; just as he admits spider and snake, hippopotamus and rhinoceros, tiger and monkey. So in our society he gives room for the conceited pedant, the foolish fop, the shallow prattler, the buffoon, the bully, the blackleg, the border-ruffian, the repudiator, the empty-headed communist, and the political wire-puller. It takes them all to make God's world, and all have their uses, however we might wish, in our haste, to exclude them "For God hath chosen the foolish things of the world to confound the wise, and weak things of the world to confound the mighty, and base things of the world, and things which are despised hath God chosen ; yea, and things which are not, to bring to nought the things which are."

Let us also firmly believe that each of us has his gift. Let us not imagine that we are disinherited by our heavenly Father, any one of us. Let us be ourselves, as God has made us, then we shall be something good and useful.

One star differs from another star in glory, but every star contributes to the splendor of the winter's night. The man who has one talent must not bury it in the earth ; the man who is called at the eleventh hour is equal in fidelity, if he works that one hour, to those who have labored all the day.

It is a matter of great importance to find what our proper gift is. A man who might be extremely useful in one situation goes into a place and work he has no talent for, and so loses his labor, and his life is of no profit. He has mistaken his calling, we say. That word "calling" indicates the old religious feeling about occupation; it expresses that we should do that work which we are called to do, not the work we choose ourselves. Well would it be for young men entering life to fall back on this old idea. Now, a young man selects the business which he thinks will give him the best chance of making a fortune, of getting a good position in society, of leading an easy and comfortable life. He does not ask, "To what business am I called? For what has God given me capacity? In what can I be the most useful to the world and do the most good? What occupation suits my special gift and power?" But not asking such questions, he not only throws away usefulness, but happiness with it.

Let every one be himself, and not try to be some one else. God, who looked on the world he had made, and said it was all good, made each of us to be just what our own gifts and faculties fit us to be. Be that and do that, and so be contented. Reverence, also, each other's gifts; do not quarrel with me because I am not you, and I will do the same. God made your brother as well as yourself. He made you, perhaps, to be bright; he made him slow; he made you practical; he made him speculative;

he made one strong and another weak, one tough and another tender; but the same good God made us all. Let us not torment each other because we are not all alike, but believe that God knew best what he was doing in making us so different. So will the best harmony come out of seeming discords, the best affection out of differences, the best life out of struggle, and the best work will be done when each does his own work, and lets every one else do and be what God made him for.

XXI.

LET US DO WHAT WE CAN.

XXI.

LET US DO WHAT WE CAN.

———•◇•———

THERE is a story in all the Gospels of a
woman who put precious ointment on the feet
of her Master, so that the house was filled with its
odor. Judas found fault with her, on utilitarian
grounds. He thought it would have been better
to have sold the ointment and given the proceeds to
the poor. So it would, on utilitarian principles.
According to the rules of political economy, Judas
was right. Matthew says the other disciples agreed
with him, and were indignant at "the waste." "To
what purpose is this waste?" said they. Yes, the
ointment was wasted, if everything is wasted which
does not produce a visible, outward result. If nothing is useful but what can be measured, weighed,
tabulated, counted, and put into statistical tables,
then this action was useless. But if that is good
which feeds the mind and heart, which strengthens
the soul; if affection is useful, and sentiment is
useful; if man does not live by bread only, but by
every word which proceeds out of the mouth of

God, the ointment was not wasted, but put to its highest possible use.

In front of a building on Tremont Street, in Boston, there stand some statues, carved of granite, graceful and pleasing works of art. They cost several thousand dollars. The building would have answered all its purposes as a Horticultural Hall just as well without them. The amount which they cost would have provided a comfortable home for a number of persons who are now living in cellars and exposed to disease. According to the utilitarian view of things, then, it was a waste to put the statues there. But every poor man in the city is a little better, every child who lives in a cellar is a little happier, for being in a city in which, besides cold brick walls, there is something to please the eye and fill the heart. Even the poor street-boy who blacks your shoes does not live by bread alone. And God, who squanders beauty every day on the clouds of morning and evening; who wastes it in tender grasses, mosses, and ferns in the depths of inaccessible woods; on lovely creatures who live in the depths of ocean; he, no doubt, thinks it a good thing that we also should do something for the souls of a community, no less than for its bodies.

Why not sell the Public Garden for several millions of dollars, and give the money to the poor? You could provide several dinners for every poor person in Boston out of the proceeds. But the dinners, once eaten, are gone, and those who ate

them are no better for it. But now, every poor
man and woman, after the labor of the day, can get
a breath of fresh air, scented by fragrant shrubs, in
the evening twilight; poor children can go and see
those beds of tulips, such as the gardens of no
millionaires can rival. There, in the soft atmosphere
of night, in sight of the eternal stars, young lovers,
who have no rooms where they can meet, may walk
together and sit together, and talk their foolish little
chat. The poorest man in Boston is ennobled in
his own esteem, and takes courage when he thinks
that the Common, and Public Garden, and the
Public Library belong to him and to his children.
Is it not a good thing that the poor of Boston should
have for their use the best park, the best garden,
and the best library in the State?

Jesus, therefore, did not blame Mary, but defended
her against the blame of Judas. He said, "Let her
alone. She hath wrought a good work. She hath
done what she could. She hath come beforehand
to anoint my body for the burying. Wherever this
Gospel is preached, this shall be spoken of in her
praise."

But suppose, now, that this woman, instead of
doing "what she could," had stopped to consider
what might be done, or what ought to be done, or
what she would like to do. Suppose she had said,
"What good will it do for me to go and carry my
ointment? It will seem presumptuous, silly, ridic-
ulous. They will laugh at me, perhaps blame me.

I should like to do some great thing for the Master.
I wish I could induce the Pharisees and Scribes to
accept him as the Christ. That would be worth
while, for they have influence. But it would be of
no use for me to go to him. Nobody cares for me."
If she had reasoned thus, and acted accordingly,
she would have reasoned and acted as you and I
are continually reasoning and acting; but, then, she
would not have received the censure of Judas, nor
the praise of Jesus; nor would the Scripture this
day be fulfilled in our ears, that wherever the Gospel
is preached this is spoken of in her honor.

"She hath done what she could." This is the
essential thing. We are not bound to do great
things, but only to do what we can. When conscience tells us that something ought to be done,
when our heart prompts us to do anything, then
let us go and do it. Let us not fritter away the
impulse, and freeze the motive by asking, What
good will it do? Some things are good in themselves. Some things are an end in themselves.
They are their own excuse for being. And such
are all acts of conscience, religion, love, faith, which
we are led to do, not from selfish considerations, but
from a generous impulse of the soul.

What a change would take place in all our lives
if we only made up our minds to do what we can
every day; having faith that, if we do anything
right, however small, God will help us to do more.
We do nothing because we cannot do everything.

We do not begin to do a good thing because it is not already done. We do not take the first step because we have not already reached the goal. Sometimes indolence prevents us from doing what we can. In all revolving machinery there is one point where the motor force does not operate. To get over that point of inertia is the difficulty. So with us; frequently all motives fail to move us to begin to do the right action. If we get over that point of inertia, all goes well enough.

Then, again, selfishness often keeps us from doing what we can. We are afraid that if we do anything, we may have to do more. We are not happy while we live only for ourselves, but then we cannot make up our minds to live for others. So we wear life away, and accomplish nothing for others or ourselves, because we cannot, just for once, forget ourselves entirely in some generous action, some great cause not our own, some conviction of duty. I see many people to whom God has given all means, all opportunities, who could every day be a blessing to some one with hardly any more effort than is required to put out their hand; who, instead, have built themselves into a sort of fortress; have intrenched themselves with all possible defences against any chance of coming into contact with those whom they could aid. I pity them; they do not know what they are losing.

Sometimes, also, conscience keeps us from doing what we can. There is so much that we ought to do, such a burden of responsibility on our conscience, that we are paralyzed by it. We are discouraged by the amount of obligation. We are also discouraged by the amount of our past neglect. We have left undone so much that we ought to have done, that it seems hopeless to try now to do anything. We are like a man who has gone so deeply in debt that he sees no chance of ever paying the whole, and so he does not try to pay anything.

The imagination sometimes prevents us from doing what we can. The ideal so far surpasses the possible that we are discouraged. Everything we do looks so mean by the side of our idea of what might be done. With the summit in our eye, we walk on the plain, and do not attempt to climb.

Moreover, a false theology sometimes, by its exorbitant demands, prevents us from doing what we can. It tells us that our best works are sinful; that all common goodness is only filthy rags in the sight of God; that unless we are in the true church, and hold the right creed, and have gone through the right experience, all our virtue is good for nothing. This is discouraging; and, just so far as it is believed, it prevents people from doing what they can. It tells them they can do nothing till God comes and gives them a new heart. It teaches " inability " to such an extent that people regard it as a religious act to do nothing. They say they honor God by ceasing from their own works.

But, now, the peculiar and essential doctrine of

Christianity — the gospel in the gospel — lies just here; that God promises to help us to do all so soon as we are willing to do something; that he forgives us our debt as soon as we are ready to forgive our debtors; that we may leave the past to him and the future to him, if we will only do now whatever our hand finds to do. Christ comes as a present Saviour to give us our daily bread, to help us now, and to make now the day of salvation. Saving faith is being willing to trust our salvation to God, and not to be anxious about it at all, just as a child is not troubled about to-morrow's dinner, or its winter's clothes, but leaves all that to its father and mother.

Those who try to believe too much often end by believing too little. Those who try to feel too much at last freeze their hearts, and cannot feel at all. Never try to believe more than you can. If you can only believe a little, but believe that honestly, it will either lead to more, or else it may do you as much good as more belief. God, who has chosen the foolish things of this world to confound the wise, and feeble things to confound the mighty, and things which are not to bring to nought those which are, sometimes chooses atheists and infidels to confound by their goodness the most orthodox believers. I do not believe in holding up gamblers like John Morrissey to public admiration because he did not take bribes in Congress; but even he may rise up in the day of judgment, with the people of Sodom and Gomorrah, to condemn the professors of religion who, while teaching Bible-classes on Sunday, are robbing the corporations of which they are treasurers during all the rest of the week.

It is time that a little more stress was laid on simple honesty. It is not every man who can be a great saint, or a mighty preacher, or a founder of hospitals; but every man can be faithful in his work. If he is a mechanic, he can do his work well, and not put sham work in the place of true. If he is the president or director of a bank or of a manufacturing corporation, he can do his duty by thoroughly examining the affairs of the institution, by not allowing the cashier or treasurer to run away with the funds, and then being astonished and saying he did not know anything about it. The Apostle John could find no better thing to say to his old friend than this: " Brother, thou art faithful in all that thou doest." But we are more advanced, and want "smart" men, not faithful men; and when the smart men run away with our property we wonder why it was so. Possibly, if " they did not know everything down in Judee," they did know some things of which we might make use.

If we wish to be useful, the only way is to do what we can. Do not seek for a great thing, and do not be afraid of a great thing if it comes. If you see that something ought to be done, then probably you are the person to do it. If you are, you will be enabled to do it. The greatest deeds have not been done by the greatest people, but by the most faithful people; by those who are not in a hurry to find the great thing, and, on the other hand, not afraid of it when it is sent to them. We learn thus how God's strength is made perfect in our weakness. We take one step, and it leads to another. Luther did not commence the Reformation with any deliberate purpose of doing such a work. He simply did what he could to put a stop to the practical evils resulting from the sale of indulgences; and so he was led on till he found himself contending, single-handed, against the whole church. Then he was obliged to say: "Here I stand! I cannot do otherwise. God help me!" And then the whole Reformation followed.

We, who have not to reform the universal church, but only to reform ourselves and to reform the little circle around us, may have a work to do just as important in the sight of God as that of Luther. Who knows what great influences may go out of the small sphere in which you and I are placed? Who knows what may be done by that child over whom your life sheds light or darkness, according to your fidelity? As the great Amazon or Mississippi, which flows through half a continent, comes from the blending influences of sun and shower, of dew and snow-storm; comes from affluents fed in many a quiet valley, — so the great river of God, the kingdom of truth and love, comes from the co-operation of thousands of hearts and lives, which are ignorant of each other now, but which are working together unconsciously. They shall see each other hereafter in the judgment, and recognize each other as fellow-laborers in the great cause of the Gospel.

Suppose that we wish to be loved by our friends. That is right. We all need to be loved in order to be happy. The man who has no friends may have everything else, but he must be an unhappy person. The whole secret here, also, is in doing what you can for your friends. You cannot get affection by looking for it or seeking it. It must come of its own accord, if at all. It comes from little things, not great ones. We communicate happiness to others, not often by great acts of devotion and self-sacrifice, but by the absence of fault-finding and censure, by being ready to sympathize with their notions and feelings, instead of forcing them to sympathize with ours. If we are captious and quernlous, if we complain of this and find fault with that, we may be right in our judgments, but we repel sympathy. It is so much better, and so easy, to look at the good side of things first, and, if we must find fault, do so afterward. We cannot, to be sure, make ourselves attractive and amiable by an effort. But this is something we can do. We can think and speak of what is pleasant rather than of what is disagreeable; of sunshine more than storm; we can, in little things, try to make others happy.

Or, suppose we wish for improvement. That is a right thing to desire. Progress is essential to peace.

To go round and round in a circle without going forward is tedious. The reason why so many people are not happy, who have all the means of happiness, is that everything seems just the same to-day that it was yesterday. Life grows very tiresome where there is no progress. But there are only two kinds of progress, — one outward, the other inward. We can make progress by getting more and more of outward things, or by becoming more inwardly. As long as we can keep getting on in the world, getting up higher in society, growing richer, becoming more famous, there is a certain sort of satisfaction about it. But this does not last. The only real satisfaction there is, is to be growing up inwardly all the time, becoming more just, true, generous, simple, manly, womanly, kind, active. And this we can all do, not by an effort, not by a struggle, but by doing each day the day's work as well as we can. A man grows good and strong and wise, just as an elm-tree grows large, stately, and graceful; grows more and more luxuriant with its thousand swinging branches and myriad flickering leaves. It is by being true to himself and to his work, standing where he is, and being faithful in the least thing that comes. Then he grows, day by day, and we have the joy of seeing a generous, pure youth pass into an active, useful manhood, active manhood mature into the sweet and tender wisdom of age. Men and women, standing in their place, doing their work, trusting in God's love and help, grow deeper, soar higher, spread more widely as the years pass. They do not, perhaps, pass for saints, for they do no extraordinary things. They do not retire into convents to pass days in prayer. But every one learns to honor and love them increasingly; men come to lean on their strength, take counsel of their experience; they spread light and peace around them, day by day, and so cause the kingdom of God to come more and more, simply by doing what they can.

Whenever we do what we can, we immediately can do more. When men are ascending a mountain, each step, so insignificant in itself, carries them on and up, till new scenes open before them. They have only to keep walking on, taking one step at a time, and presently they find themselves rising above the region of forests, begin to get glimpses of blue lakes lying below them, of sister peaks rising above them, of the great snow-covered fields which soar upward, pure and cold, into the glittering air; they see the distant ocean, spotted with white sails, the forest rolling its sea of verdure far away up to the pale horizon. So, as we keep doing what we can, steadily, constantly, life opens before us, heaven opens above us, the world comes around us, rich, varied, beautiful, and we find ourselves on great eminences of thought and love, hardly knowing how we came there, for we have been only doing what we could all the time, — no more, no less.

Half the good that is done comes from being thoughtful, considerate, and accommodating. Some people are always so. In almost every village or town you find some one person who is always ready to think for others, to consider what others feel, and to accommodate his wishes and acts to their needs. Perhaps it is a good old lady, one who has long since risen above the prejudice of sect, party, caste in society, and amuses herself every day by helping those forlorn people whom we call "inefficient," in studying the difficulties of stupid people who do not know how to help themselves, in entering into the immense affairs of little boys and girls. She is the help and reliance of old and young, good and bad, saint and sinner.

One of the best things in the Gospel of Jesus is the stress it lays on small things. It ascribes more value to quality than to quantity; it teaches that God does not ask how much we do, but how we do it. The generous widow who put her two coppers into the treasury gave more than all the rest. The Publican who prayed the shortest prayer on record, a prayer in seven words, went down to his house justified more than those who had recited long liturgies. Thus the Gospel rebukes the indolence which will not begin to work, the selfishness which lives only for itself, the timidity which is afraid of God, the scruples of conscience which avoid responsibility. It says to all, Begin now, at once, to do what you can for God, for man, for truth, for right. Begin, and he will take the responsibility for the result. Begin, and do what you **can, not** thinking of the past or the future, but only of that now, which is always the day of salvation. Your past sins shall be forgiven if you begin now to do right, for that is repentance. Your future salvation you may trust to God, while you are doing what you ought now. This trust, which throws off all anxiety about past sin and future salvation, while it does what it can now, leaning on God's help, — this is the faith which saves the soul, which casts out all fear, which fills the heart with peace, which takes the sting from death, and surrounds us with the summer atmosphere of hope and love.

THE END.

Lightning Source UK Ltd.
Milton Keynes UK
UKOW06f2322290316

271155UK00007B/50/P

9 781330 341438